Shipping Conferences

A Study of their Origins, Development and Economic Practices

B. M. DEAKIN
in collaboration with T. Seward

This study is concerned first with why
and how these collective organisations
came into existence during the
last quarter of the 19th century, how
they changed and developed in the inter-
war period, how they are organised
and how they operate today.

Shipping conferences are 'price makers'
on an enormous scale and particular
attention is paid to this function. The
authors construct a price model and
apply it to a sample of fifteen thousand
observations in order to detect the principal factors which influence the price
makers. The prices formed are related
to costs and then compared with various
pricing practices and rules.

The economic and financial performance
of particular conferences are examined
for the light they shed upon such
aspects as their utilisation of capacity;
margins of profit; employment of capital,
the return upon it and the provision
for its replacement. A scale of comparison
gives an indication of the relative performance of individual conference
members.

This book will be of interest to all
concerned with maritime economics or
the working of price and output agreements.

University of Cambridge Department of Applied Economics

OCCASIONAL PAPER 37

SHIPPING CONFERENCES

A Study of their Origins, Development
and Economic Practices

Shipping Conferences

A STUDY OF THEIR ORIGINS
DEVELOPMENT AND ECONOMIC PRACTICES

B.M. DEAKIN
in collaboration with
T. SEWARD

CAMBRIDGE
AT THE UNIVERSITY PRESS 1973

Published by the Syndics of the Cambridge University Press
Bentley House, 200 Euston Road, London NW1 2DB
American Branch: 32 East 57th Street, New York, N.Y. 10022

© Department of Applied Economics, University of Cambridge 1973

Library of Congress Catalogue Card Number: 73-75852

ISBN: 0 521 8734 1 hard covers
      0 521 9742 9 paperback

Set in cold type by E.W.C. Wilkins Ltd,
and printed in Great Britain by Alden & Mowbray Ltd,
at the Alden Press, Oxford

Contents

Tables

Figures

Preface

This study arose from some earlier research on six sectors of public transport and communication in the United Kingdom which was undertaken by us at the Department of Applied Economics over the period 1965 to 1968.[1]

In its origins and over its four year span the present study owes much to the collaboration of a number of shipowning firms in the United Kingdom. Either directly or through introductions to others, the directors of these firms have enabled us to move freely in the hitherto closed circles of freight shipping conferences and to gather information and opinion over a wide field. This help was indispensable and we are very grateful to Sir Frederic Harmer and Sir John Nicholson who made it possible and who also took a close personal interest in the progress of our work and gave us valuable advice and guidance on many technical aspects of shipping. A very large number of their colleagues, associates and staff have also assisted us in many different spheres of our enquiries. Without their patient and courteous help, especially in the early stages of research, we would not have been able to carry out our study.

In the very large task of locating and gathering data we are much indebted to Mr. R.J.O. Bridgeman, Mr. J.P.J. Corbett, Mr. J.M. Pakes and Mr. K. Wright. We express our warmest thanks to them and to many others in the P and O and Ocean Steam Ship Companies and other shipping organisations who gave so freely of their time to discuss with us particular aspects of ship operation under conference conditions.

Outside the shipping industry we have benefitted from discussion and correspondence with Professor E. Bennathan and Mr. R.O. Goss, both of whom have worked for many years in the general field of maritime economics.

Within the Department of Applied Economics we owe large debts to Miss Marion Clarke and her assistants for carrying out a great deal of computing work, and to Mrs. Lilian Silk and her staff for typing several versions of our manuscript with the utmost patience and goodwill.

Dr. L. J. Slater and Mr. B. Shearey gave us valuable specialised advice and help with the application of our computable price model to a substantial quantity of data, and also with other statistical problems. A special word of thanks is due to Mr. E. Bougourd for his very painstaking and competent work in gathering data in the field

1 The results were published under the following title. B. M. Deakin and T. Seward. *Productivity in Transport. A study of Employment, Capital, Output, Productivity and Technical Change.* Department of Applied Economics, University of Cambridge, Occasional Papers 17, Cambridge University Press, 1969.

and in collating and preparing it for use, and also for the help he has given us in preparing the final manuscript with great care and accuracy. Miss A.M. Cook also gave us assistance with statistical research and analysis and we are very grateful for her help.

Mr. K.D. George read some sections of our manuscript and gave us comments and suggestions which have enabled us to make better use of our material. Professor W.B. Reddaway, who was Director of the Department of Applied Economics for much of the period of this research, gave us the very great advantage of his general guidance and advice at the start of our work. On particular aspects his help was also invaluable in enabling us to avoid pitfalls and improve our analysis.

Any errors and shortcomings which remain in this book are entirely our responsibility.

This research was carried out with the indispensable financial support of the Social Science Research Council which we gratefully acknowledge.

T.S.
B.M.D.

1   Introduction: Study Methods, Treatment and Scope

There are about 360 shipping conferences in existence to-day. Membership can vary from 2 to 40 or more shipping lines. Some conferences are inactive; these are chiefly the 'short sea' conferences covering routes between the United Kingdom and various European countries, but a large number of 'deep sea' (long distance) conferences are at present in full operation. These organisations are associations of owners of freight liners which are suitable for the carriage of 'general', i.e. non-bulk cargo. These owners act together to make common prices for the carriage of goods over the defined routes on which the conference operates. They also act in combination to admit or exclude applicants to conference membership, to share the trade in various ways amongst themselves, to make a common policy on such matters as setting the level of shippers' discounts and rebates (which are so arranged as to 'tie' shippers of goods to a particular conference), combatting competition from non-members, pooling and sharing earnings, and enforcing these and other agreements which conference members have made with each other.

What has been outlined above is the 'closed' type of conference. New members can join 'closed' conferences only with the consent (usually a unamimous vote is needed) of existing members. 'Open' conferences may be joined by any shipowner without the consent of existing members.[1] Both these types of conference exist to-day on different routes in various parts of the world. The 'closed' conference is more common. The 'open' conference prevails chiefly on routes which connect the United States to other parts of the world. In both types of conference a common, agreed tariff of rates of freight is normally charged.

This study is concerned with why and how shipping conferences came into existence towards the end of the 19th century, how they changed and developed under the influence of new technologies which greatly altered both the vessels and the character and volume of the goods they carried across the world, and how they are organised and how they operate to-day. Following this historical approach particular attention is paid to methods of price formation, price trends, and to some of the economic and financial consequences of conference membership.

---

1 Provided that the shipowner who joins can meet the criteria laid down by the Federal Maritime Commission. See particularly the FMC Code of Federal Regulations title 46, part 533, points 1 and 2. The regulations amplify Section 15 of the USA Shipping Act of 1916, and they require the aspiring new conference member to give evidence of ability to maintain a regular service in the trade covered by the 'open' conference. The regularity of the service will be precisely defined in each case, e.g. one vessel sailing every 14 days, or whatever is considered necessary.

1

Other workers[1] in this field have suffered a handicap which we did not suffer in that they were generally unable to gain access to information and records of conference activities at first hand. We have been more fortunate in that we have been given a very full measure of collaboration from three groups of 'closed' conferences, and this has been coupled with very considerable freedom of access to records of these conferences, and to those of a number of British shipowning companies who are members of many conferences.

The aspect of shipping conferences which is perhaps of greatest interest to an economist is the vast mechanism of administered prices. The conferences are 'price makers' on an enormous scale. In the United Kingdom-Australia Conference for example, there are an estimated 7,125 commodities in the freight tariff, and they are located into a range of 150 separate prices and price classes. There are many fewer commodities in the tariff for the homeward conference in this trade but more prices. New products, and products not previously shipped, are continually coming forward for shipment and prices must be made for them. How is this done? What principles guide the price-makers? It is these and similar questions which have particularly engaged our attention. ˙

Our method has been to try to discover first how the system developed, how it works now, and then to build a model of the pricing machinery to try to discover why it works in the way it does, and which of the several factors involved are more important and which are of less importance in determining price. It is of course impossible to resist the urge to compare 'what is' with 'what ought to be'; but what ought to be raises a host of speculations. Among economists the controversy about pricing rules has a very long history and many distinguished names have been involved in it: Dupuit (as long ago as 1844), Edgeworth, Marshall, Pigou, Pegrum, Meade, Hotelling, Lerner, Andrews, Coase, Hicks and Houthakker to name only a few at this stage and to allow only a mention of the 'old' and the 'new' welfare theorists in the shape of Pareto, Little and Graaff who, among others, have also contributed to greater understanding of the wider, social implications of pricing policies and of pricing rules of various types. Some economists would agree that there is such a thing as a theoretical, ideal pricing rule named 'marginal cost pricing', hedged about though it is with definitional controversy, immeasurable social implications, and pre-conditions of a virtually unattainable idealism. Although a *general* theory (in several versions) of 'the second best' has been devised in order to enable monopolistic conditions and taxes in the rest of the economy to be recognised and allowed for in constructing an ideal pricing rule, its application to *particular* industries is hedged about with still more controversy.

Any pricing rule must relate to cost and must therefore take at least some account of these conditions. An attempt is made here to study the price and cost structure of freight liner operation and to consider appropriate pricing rules.

---

1 Daniel Marx, *International Shipping Cartels,* Princeton University Press, 1953. E. Bennathan and A.A. Walters, *The Economics of Ocean Freight Rates,* F.A. Praeger, New York, 1969. Proceedings of the United Nations Conference on Trade and Development, *Trade and Development,* Volume 5, *Financing and Invisibles.* Institutional *Arrangements,* chapter on 'Ocean shipping and freight rates and developing countries' p. 212, E/Conf. 46/141, New York, 1965. UNCTAD 1969, *Freight Markets and the Level and Structure of Freight Rates,* UNCTAD publication reference TD/B/C 4/38/Rev. 1. (1969), and others.

At this point we set out our approach to the analysis contained in later chapters and at the same time explain, in concise terms, the methods employed at the various stages of it.

There are four principal stages to our analysis before the conclusions. These are now discussed in the sequence in which they occur in later chapters.

1. History and development of the conference system, 1875-1939

We have started our learning process on shipping conferences by using the early records opened to us. We examine in Chapter 2, the historical development of three groups of conferences:[1]

UK/Continent-Far East
UK/Continent-Australia
UK/Continent-India/Pakistan

In all cases the conference outward and the separate[2] conference, or conferences, homeward are included. It is these three conference groups which form the basis for the analytical work which follows in later chapters, although not all of the component conferences and their individual members are included in all the analyses made.

An exhaustive history from the start of the conference system, which is generally agreed to be 1875 in the UK-Calcutta tea trade, is not attempted. What has been done is first to examine the principal factors in the circumstances which led to the formation of the early shipping conferences, and second to trace the salient features of conference development from 1875 to 1939. The features judged to be salient are those which appear to have been most influential in present conference organisation, and the more transitory and ephemeral aspects have been omitted.

An examination is made of factors influencing the supply of shipping capacity in the second half of the nineteenth century, for example, the advent of major technical change in the shape of the steamship and the Suez canal. Changes in the flow of trade in both directions over the specified routes, major alterations in the area pattern and commodity composition of this trade and changes in the freight rates charged by shipowners for operations on these routes are all examined for the light they shed upon the causes and consequences of conference formation. These aspects are dealt with concisely, but they are regarded as an essential study of the circumstances attendant upon the start of the now widespread conference system.

Against this sketch of the background and of the more powerful determinants in it, is set next a description of conference development up to 1939. Many of the features of present day conference operation, such as a common tariff, cargo sharing, loyalty rebates, and 'pooling' agreements came into existence before 1939, and the causes and circumstances of their introduction are studied here. The ability of conferences to maintain the loyalty of their customers and their members, the type and importance of outside competition and the ways in which conferences have dealt with over-capacity and over-tonnaging problems are also examined.

---

1 The present composition of these groups of conferences, the 'cross trade' conferences which are contiguous with them, and their recent membership are given in Appendix A.

2 With different membership from the outwards conference, but with many lines belonging to both conferences. In a few cases a conference covers both directions of trade on a particular route.

2. Recent and present organisation and practices in shipping conferences

The sequential examination of conference development is continued through the post-war period and brought up to date in Chapter 3. An attempt is then made to give a more comprehensive and detailed answer than has previously proved possible to the general question: 'How do the member lines of shipping conferences arrange among themselves to provide regular freight shipping services to meet the fluctuating demand for such services?' An answer is given in four parts.

First, the methods and practices of delimiting and defining the geographical scope of a conference are examined. This includes the way in which a choice is made of particular routes and ports to be served by a conference and to be subject to a common agreed freight tariff: also described are the arrangements and methods of pricing the services to 'outports' (ports not included in the regular sailing schedules of the conference), and the services of transhipment to ports outside the geographical area of the conference. The sometimes subtle differences between base ports, direct ports, wayports and outports are explained.

Second, a study is made of conference policies on membership in the post war period, in an attempt to discover the determining factors which govern admission to a conference. Also included are methods of checking a member's performance in relation to existing conference practice. For example:

    a. meeting obligations to shippers as regards sailings and calls.
    b. ensuring that weight and volume measures correspond correctly with freight rates charged and, more generally, that members charge the agreed common tariff.

Third, the activities of non-members, 'outsiders' as they are called, are examined in terms of the scale of their activities on conference routes and the bearing this has upon the actions of the conference in deciding to fight the competition or admit the competitor to conference membership. Two case histories are given.

The fourth section is concerned with the various methods adopted by conferences to share out the total trade among their members. The methods include limits on the number of sailings allowed to each member, tonnage sharing, geographical limitations on the basis of ports of loading and discharge and 'rationalisation' schemes of various types. Sometimes a combination of these methods is employed. Also explained are the ways in which these shares are changed to meet fluctuating and peak demand, and for other reasons.

The fifth and last section deals with agreements to pool gross revenue earned in a particular trade and to share out the pool according to agreed principles. These agreements are currently much employed and they have a long history. Agreements of the 'joint purse' type even pre-date the formation of conferences.

These detailed studies were made with the close collaboration of a number of conferences and shipowners. The results provide a basic knowledge of how the specific conferences organise themselves to meet the demand for regular freight liner services on the routes they cover. Given the conference, its membership and organisation as described, we now turn attention to the way in which shipping conferences price their services.

3. Price formation

A brief description is given below of the economic nature of shipping conferences. This seems to be a necessary background to the description which is given next of the methods used to analyse price formation by conferences.

A shipping conference is a loosely organised collective monopoly. It fixes common prices with a considerable degree of differentiation for the same service. It also arranges to share output and uses several different methods to do this. The product is freight shipping services, and in general terms these are fairly homogeneous within a conference with some, not very important, differences between and within member lines in the speed of ships and in passage time, and between lines in terms of the services which are associated with the service of shipping and which are provided by the shipowner. There is also some 'spatial' monopoly which arises historically from the origins of some conferences, and it can also be created to-day by some methods of ouput sharing, for example, where this is done by sailings on a territorial basis.

Opportunities for price differentiation exist because the aggregate demand curve for freight shipping services over a specified route is not smooth and continuous. There are likely to be many discontinuities in it, and in the case of *some* products the demand for shipment may be almost completely inelastic. This is because of the relatively very high unit value of some commodities and also because the market for shipping services is fragmented; the buyers of such services have little knowledge of or interest in the rates charged for shipping commodities which are not manufactured by themselves or their competitors. So buyers rarely make comparisons of the rates charged by the conference for transporting over the same route commodities which are completely different from their own. There are barriers to entry into this sector of the shipping industry. Some of these are in terms of the fairly large minimum size of investment necessary to maintain regular services over the long route distances involved in the 'deep sea' type of conference examined here. Other barriers are institutional; conferences generally admit new members only by unanimous vote. A shipowner aspiring to conference membership would normally have to show that he has the resources in terms of ships and working capital to cover and serve regularly the 'share of the trade' he would be allotted if he were admitted. A further factor, which governs admissions to membership in some cases, is whether the applicant is in a position to gain a share of the export carrying trade of his own country.

Given the circumstances of conference development, organisation and practice (described in Chapters 2 and 3) an answer is attempted to the question 'What are the principal factors which govern price formation by shipping conferences?' This very large question is broken down into several parts and is dealt with in the following ways in Chapters 4, 5, 6 and 7.

a. Conference procedures and practices for changing freight rates

This is in turn broken down into sub-sections which deal with various aspects of price formation.

    (i) General, 'across-the-board' rate changes.

   (ii) Exemptions for individual freight rates from changes under (i) above.

  (iii) Changes in individual tariff rates of freight which take place, for a
        number of different reasons, independently of a general rate change.

  (iv) Policies for rebates, discounts and contract rates viewed as aspects
       of pricing.

(v) The 'open' rate and its applications. These rates are not fixed by the conference but by individual shipowners acting on their own judgment of particular market conditions.

b. Price differentiation

Estimates are attempted of the extent and degree of price differentiation in various conference 'trades'. The number of prices quoted and the number of commodity types and groups separately distinguished in the tariff are compared.

c. A discussion of theories of price formation in relation to the empirical situation in shipping generally

Five aspects are examined.

(i) The cost characteristics of ship owning and operation. Attention is directed to the high proportion of fixed to total costs in the short run, and the consequent rapid decline of average costs as output increases up to the *full capacity of a vessel.* In the short run the costs which vary with output are those of selling, handling, stowage, transhipment and some ship's time costs due to waiting for cargo. As the size of vessels increases, and this is occurring rapidly with the introduction of container ships into the liner trades and bulk carriers into non-liner trades, the costs which are fixed in the short run become an even higher proportion, and the costs which vary with output an even lower proportion of total cost. The behaviour of costs in the long run, when all are variable, is also considered, and a study is made of the implications of discontinuities in the cost structure as an expanding demand over time entails a successive supply of vessels on the berth.

(ii) A distinction is drawn between the cost structure in ship operation generally, which is dealt with under paragraph (i) above, and the cost structure of a liner freight shipping 'industry' serving a particular 'trade'. The long run cost structure of liner shipping in this context, whether or not organised into a conference, is examined for its implications for pricing policies, and for the light it can shed upon the extent of cross-subsidisation between the shippers of commodities.

(iii) The implications for pricing of the cost characteristics found under paragraphs (i) and (ii) above are studied next. The significance of the capacity utilisation ratio becomes apparent, and this leads on to further consideration of differentiation in the pricing policies of conferences.

(iv) There are discontinuities in the demand curve for liner freight transport services, and the reasons for these are examined for the light they can shed on the price policies which are in fact adopted, and also on the pricing rules which are considered for this industry on theoretical grounds.

(v) Systems of price differentiation which do not violate 'marginal conditions' are examined in relation to the pricing practices of shipping conferences.

In an empirical study which follows these more theoretical discussions, comparisons are made between conference prices (both 'block' prices and individual prices) and average cost (AC). The extent by which the prices made by the conference exceed or fall short of AC are shown. No wholly accurate measure of marginal cost (MC) is practical, but the 'escapable' costs of selling, stevedoring and marginal ship's time costs, named average incremental cost (AIC), may usefully be compared with the lowest 'price classes' in the tariff in order to detect whether losses are being made by charging less than AIC (regarded as an approximation for MC at the actual output level) for some cargo. This essentially short run analysis is carried out, and it enables a conclusion to be reached on whether conferences, in their understandable anxiety to enable their members to fill their ships, charge less than this proxy for MC for low value, but often high volume, cargo.

In the long run AIC will include the cost of putting additional ships on the berth. It will also reflect the economies which may be found to arise from operating a larger fleet. It is likely that short-run average incremental cost, SRAIC, would be below LRAIC until output expands to the point where the shipowner has to find an additional ship by adding to his fleet. More usually an additional ship is 'put on the berth', where it is needed to meet the demand for its service, by the shipowner. Sometimes the conference asks a shipowner who is a conference member to provide an extra sailing. The conference can and does call upon one of more of its members to provide an additional sailing and the member concerned is usually able to switch vessels between conference routes in order to match such changes in demand fairly smoothly in terms of both time and cost. This will *tend* to make for constant long run average incremental costs within any single 'trade' served by a conference, although the *probability* of an additional sailing being needed may be introduced for greater refinement in the cost estimates.

To charge less than MC in transport, or other activity, in either the short or long term, is widely deplored.[1] In conference liner operation the gaining of low value high quantity cargo, the so called 'base' cargo, is regarded as important in the purely practical sense of making the vessel more manageable at sea. In other words such cargo is useful as ballast. It may also be worth obtaining such cargo at less than MC if it prevents the cargo from being secured by the non-conference competition which would also use it as base cargo, and thence as a 'foundation' for higher value and higher rated cargo. Arguments for a cross-subsidy for such cargo to an extent that it pushes the rates for it below MC are possibly tenable on commercial grounds and from the viewpoint of the shipowner concerned. On the other hand, too much may be given away for the sake of this 'ballast cargo'. This aspect is examined in Chapter 4 where consideration is also given to the wider implications of this practice.

d. Analysis of price trends, pricing and price elasticity in individual cases

(i) Price trends. A test is made of two hypotheses.

    A. That conference liner freight rates in three specified 'deep sea' trades have risen faster than time-charter tramp shipping rates over the period 1948-1970

    B. That conference liner freight rates in three specified conference groups have

---

1   Much of the literature is clear on this point, even though it is far from unanimous on pricing policies which involve setting price at or above MC. See M.J. Farrell, 'In defence of public-utility price theory', *Public Enterprise,* R. Turvey (Ed.) pp. 45, 46 and 47, Penguin Books, Harmondsworth, UK.; and also G.J. Ponsonby *Transport Policy: Co-ordination through Competition, Hobart Paper* 49, IEA, London 1969. pp. 61, 62. It should however be noticed here that a price less than MC may be justified if a substitute for the service in question is causing strong external diseconomies to arise, for example, charges below MC for public transport where private motor vehicles are causing heavy congestion in urban areas.

been more stable than time-charter tramp shipping rates over the period 1948-70.

The method of measuring the exponential rate of change of freight rates under hypothesis A is by least squares regression calculation, which makes allowance for the wide swings in rates (found particularly in tramp freight rates), and thus reduces the problems involved in finding an unobjectionable base year. From these calculations of movements in rates we get a differential rate movement, viz., liner rates (LR) *less* tramp rates (TR). In this differential rate there is a 'bias factor' against liners. This is in part due to two elements (i) the exemptions made for particular rates when 'across-the-board' liner rate changes are made by the conference, and (ii) the reductions in individual liner rates (or sometimes groups of rates) as a result of bargaining between individual shippers (or groups of shippers) and the conference. We have been able to construct a weighted index of movements in conference liner rates in one trade. In this case, movements in individual freight rates are weighted by the relative importance, in terms of freight revenue earned, of the cargo carried. In the case of other conference trades we have gathered information about changes in freight rates, surcharges and the rates for individual commodities where these have been altered independently of a general rate change or have been exempted from one. Not all but nearly all exemptions from a general rate increase, and individual rate changes due to bargaining, are downward changes, and this will tend to make any weighted liner rate index rise at a slower and decline at a faster rate than the corresponding unweighted indexes we have constructed.

(*ii*) *Pricing and price elasticity*. The demand for freight shipping services is a derived demand, derived from the demand for the goods shipped into the markets in the areas of destination. The price elasticity of demand for the goods shipped is to some extent reflected in the price elasticity of demand for their transport. This relationship is examined for its implications for price formation in liner freight services.

In Chapter 6 an examination is made of individual rate bargaining which takes place between an individual shipper, or a shippers' association, and a conference. These bargaining processes are analysed in terms of a number of case histories of these negotiations. The salient features are defined and the factors which appear to have been most influential in reaching the final decision to change, or not to change an individual liner freight rate are isolated. These factors are compared with the results of a multivariate regression analysis of relative freight rates which are given in Chapter 7.

To this extent we are able to examine from two separate viewpomts the factors which influence and, to some degree, explain the structure of relative prices. Furthermore, the evidence of the case histories lends *some* support to relationships between the elasticity of demand for liner shipping services and the elasticities of supply and of demand for the commodity shipped, and the proportion of the freight charge of the total c.i.f. value of the commodity shipped. These relationships have been developed by A.A. Walters, and are examined here for the degree of support which the results of our studies afford them, and also for the light that they can shed upon factors which are influential in price formation in conference freight liner services.

8

The expression given in the footnote below[1] formalises three relationships. *First,* that the price elasticity of demand for the shipping service will vary directly with the elasticity of demand for the goods shipped. *Second*, the elasticity of demand for shipping service will be lower the lower is the proportion of the freight charge of the total c.i.f. value of the commodity shipped and *vice versa. Third,* the more inelastic the domestic supply of the commodity shipped, the lower will be the elasticity of demand for freight shipping services, and *vice versa.* It is of course necessary to add in respect of each relationship a *ceteris paribus* assumption in respect of the values of the remaining variables in the expression.

The meaning of the foregoing paragraph may be clearer if the service of shipping is seen as a factor of production involved in the output of goods delivered to distant markets. Much of what Alfred Marshall writes[2] about derived demand is applicable here. For example, where the outlay on a factor of production is small in relation to total costs of production then the elasticity of demand for that factor tends to be lower than it is for a factor on which the outlay is a higher proportion of total cost. The same principle applies to the term T in Walters' expression. Where the freight charge payable is a small proportion of the total c.i.f. value of the commodity shipped, then the elasticity of demand for the shipping service is low, and *vice versa.* This characteristic of the demand for freight shipping services is *one* condition which enables shipping conferences to 'charge what the traffic will bear', but it is not the only condition.[3] Charging on this principle depends upon the elasticity of demand for the service and on the ability of the price maker to judge elasticity with some accuracy. This elasticity depends, not only upon the proportion of freight charge to the c.i.f. value of the commodity shipped, but also upon the elasticity of demand for the commodity shipped to the markets in the area of destination, and upon the elasticity of domestic supply of the commodity shipped. In each of these three cases the elasticity of demand for the shipping service varies directly with the determinant named.

e. Price structure and the construction of a price model

An examination is made of relative prices (liner freight rates) within two specified conferences. We have constructed a price model (which is described below) in order

1 A.A. Walters, 'A Development Model of Transport', *Papers and Proceedings of the American Economic Association,* May 1968, p. 360. His relationships may be expressed as follows

$$\epsilon_{trans} = T \left[\frac{\epsilon_s \cdot \epsilon_d}{\epsilon_s - (1-T)\epsilon_d} \right]$$

where: ϵ_{trans} is the price elasticity of demand for freight liner shipping services
   ϵ_d the price elasticity of demand for the commodity shipped by the service concerned to markets in the area of destination
   ϵ_s the elasticity of domestic supply of the commodity shipped
   T the proportion of the freight charge of the total c.i.f. value of the commodity shipped

2 Alfred Marshall, *Principles of Economics,* Book V, Chapter VI. Joint and composite demand, particularly the section on the law of derived demand.

3 *Report of the Committee of Inquiry into Shipping,* Chairman Lord Rochdale, (H.M.S.O., Cmd. 4337, May 1970) reported that this condition was 'the main factor influencing the level of freight rates in the short run... thus low value goods are carried at cheaper rates than high value goods', para. 411, p. 119.

to seek to isolate and evaluate various factors which are influential in price formation in conference liner freight shipping.

The purpose of constructing this price model is to seek to explain *relative* prices (rates of freight) in terms of eight factors which are set out below.

1. The unit value of each commodity shipped. It will have been shown by work under paragraph ld (ii) above, on pricing and price elasticity, that the unit value of the commodity shipped and the price elasticity shipping service rendered vary inversely with each other, and that unit value seems likely to be an important consideration when prices are made. By putting this factor into our price model we are able to assess its importance as a factor which is explanatory of relative prices.

2. The weight (or measurement) tonnage of each consignment. Conferences give discounts to their customers, the shippers, for loyalty but not for large quantities shipped. However, there is some evidence from other sources that commodities shipped in large tonnages do get lower rates when these are negotiated, and this factor is included in our model.

3. The ratio of measurement tons to weight tons of each consignment. Again there is some evidence, which is presented in Chapter 7, that consignments which are by their nature very bulky or of awkward shape involve a 'loss of stowage' which varies directly with their measurement/weight ratio. This proposition is tested.

4. The price model also includes five variables which represent cargo types with various different characteristics which involve special handling or stowage treatment, and which therefore cause differential costs to arise. These types of cargo are as follows.

   a. Hazardous cargo (e.g. explosives, dangerous acids, etc.).
   b. Cargo which requires deep refrigeration.
   c. Cargo which requires 'cool chamber' stowage.
   d. Cargo of very high unit value which requires specially secure locker stowage.
   e. Cargo of very low unit value which is subject to 'open' rates of freight.

In Chapter 7 the construction and particulars of this model are further explained and it is then applied to five whole ship samples. The vessels concerned were operating at the time concerned in the Far Eastern and Australian trades on main conference routes. Outward and homeward bound cargoes are included in the sample, as are conventional and container vessels.

The price model is arranged as a multi-variate regression equation.[1] It is computable and from its application to the data described above estimates are made of the relative importance to price formation of each of the terms in the model.

It has been widely argued,[2] with some supporting evidence, that conference liner freight rates are predominantly 'demand based'. Our model includes both cost-based and demand-based factors and an attempt is made to assess their relative importance.

1 In the form FR (rate of freight) $= a + a_1B + a_2C + a_3D + \ldots \epsilon.$

2 Chiefly D. Marx, *International Shipping Cartels*, 1953, op. cit., and S.G. Sturmey, 'Economics and International Liner Services', *Journal of Transport Economics and Policy*, May 1967.

4. Some economic and financial consequences of active conference membership

In Chapter 8 an analysis is made of the economic and financial performance of individual shipping lines, which are members of a particular conference. A parallel and comparative study is also made of the performance of the conference as a whole.

This analysis covers the period 1958 to 1968 and is divided into three parts.

First, an examination is made of the extent to which the conference cargo capacity which is available[1] on specific routes has, in the event, been utilised by revenue-earning cargo. The conference aggregate result in terms of load factors is compared with the corresponding ratio of individual conference members. Time utilisation is then considered separately and the amount of idle time incurred within the conference trade itself, or attributable to it, is estimated. Load factors and time utilisation are then combined into a measure of physical *capital* utilisation, which is compared with the average performance of nineteen British industries in respect of the degree of utilisation of their employed capital.

The conference freight liner shipping industry employs substantial quantities of capital and its utilisation of scarce resources is *one* measure of economic efficiency and minimisation of waste. The results under this *first section* are a basis for some conclusions about resource utilisation under conference operation. It is widely known that conferences of the 'closed' type considered here restrict membership while organising the supply of liner freight shipping services so as to 'serve the trade'; by this is meant the provision of regular, advertised sailings and the acceptance of all cargo offered for shipments at common tariff rates laid down and agreed by the conference secretariat. 'Does such a system', it may be asked, 'lead to a consistently high or low level of capacity utilisation on particular trades which are served by the ships of the conference'? An answer is forthcoming.

Second, an investigation is carried out into the conference membership links which shipowners have in the Eastern and Australian trades which comprise the scope of this study. With a few important exceptions a conference covers a single direction of trade only. So, for example, a member of the conference which covers trade from the United Kingdom to Australia needs a membership link in the conference from Australia to the United Kingdom, or to the continent of Europe, or at least a cross-trade link into another trade, e.g. from Australia to India and from India back to the United Kingdom. In the absence of such links ballast voyages and loss of utilisation are inevitable. This question is explored here and a considerable quantity of data, brought together in Appendix A, is examined. A further matter of interest is the extent to which long-established conference members differ from the more recently admitted members in respect of these linkages, and whether the links which the newer members have are viable in the sense just described..

In the *third* and final section of Chapter 8 an analysis is made of the financial consequences of conference operations. This is done on an aggregate basis for a

---

1 This concept is defined as the capacity of each vessel, as measured by its 'bale' in cubic terms, *less* capacity 'vacant unavailable' which is known only after loading and is due to 'broken stowage', or the limitation imposed by the vessel being loaded down to permitted 'marks'. The measure thereby takes account of both volume and weight constraints of a ship in relation to its cargo.

whole conference group (covering both directions of a trade), for individual conferences covering one direction of a trade, and for individual conference members in respect of their performance in each direction of trade. The financial results of operations by each member line are compared, in respect of several different measures, with the conference average and computations of correlation, deviation and variation are then introduced in the form of a 'range analysis'. By these means we are able to examine the range of financial performance of conference members in relation both to the average performance of the conference as a whole and to the performance of each other member, and with particular reference to the most profitable and the least profitable member lines.

It has been widely conjectured that shipping conferences make arrangements for agreeing prices and regulating output which allow the weaker members just to survive while the stronger members prosper. The work in this section enables some tests to be applied to this thesis, and some comparisons to be made between the percentage return to actual capital employed in conference shipping in the trades studied here with returns found by Rochdale[1] to exist more widely in British freight liner shipping, in other sectors of the shipping industry and in British industry generally.

The conclusions from the earlier analysis (section 1 of Chapter 8) of the degree of utilisation of capital are then drawn into relation with the results of the analysis of profitability to provide a more comprehensive measure and assessment of the economic performance of freight conference shipping services.

The results of the whole study, which are briefly stated at the end of each chapter, are brought together in Chapter 9 to form an integrated assessment of the economic performance of shipping conferences as it emerges from the wide range of data assembled and analysed in the course of this research.

---

1 *Report of the Committee of Inquiry into Shipping,* Chairman, Lord Rochdale, H.M.S.O., Cmd. 4337, May, 1970, Ch. 18.

2 History and Development of the Conference System, 1875–1939

1. The background

There are now about 360 conferences operating in international frieght transport. Not all of these are fully operative or fully independent; some are in the short sea trades and are virtually defunct while the more well-known conferences are in the deep sea trades with membership varying from between 2 to 40 or more shipping lines. Most of these conferences are closed conferences, i.e. their membership is restricted. We could not hope to cover the individual developments in each of these conferences, and we will therefore have in mind when considering the conference system those conferences which serve the eastern trades — mainly those between the UK/Continent of Europe and China, Japan, Malaya, India and Australia. Many of the factors which were present in those trades also existed in others (for example, technical factors affecting the design and speed of ships) and many of the methods used by conferences in the Eastern trades were common to all conferences.

A notable feature of shipping services in the Eastern trades in the latter part of the 19th century was not only the growth of the trades but the dominance in these trades of British shipowners. This can be seen from Tables 2.1 and 2.2; Table 2.1 shows the total tonnage of ships entering and leaving the ports of the main areas of destination in the East while Table 2.2 shows what proportion of these entrances and clearances was made by British-owned ships. (The figures include, of course, tramp vessels as well as ships on a regular liner service.) Given the dominance of British-owned ships in these areas in the period 1870-1900, it is perhaps not surprising that British shipowners were the originators of the conference system.

a. Demand for shipping

The direction of trade was influenced by political factors and the interests of British manufacturers. That is to say, a flourishing trade grew up in those manufactures which the British colonies, as they then were, needed to buy from the British manufacturer and in return, the colonies (and other countries in the Far East) supplied the UK and the Continent of Europe with raw materials and food.

Some indication of the pattern of trade with Australia and the Far East is given in Table 2.3. This shows the importance of certain commodities in the total export trade with the UK in Australia, India and China, from 1870-1900.

Table 2.1 *Total tonnage (entrances and clearances) of vessels in Australian and Eastern trades (excluding coasting trade), 1870–1900 (selected years).*

'000 net registered tons

	1870	1875	1880	1885	1890	1895	1900
Australia	3,702	5,613	7,733	11,532	14,246	16,848	23,704
India (a)	4,009	4,826	5,703	6,650	7,316	8,256	8,627
Ceylon	1,424	2,216	2,907	3,561	5,118	6,543	8,488
Straits Settlement (b)	1,651	3,164	4,808	6,964	8,642	10,054	13,354
Hong Kong	2,640	3,894	5,079	7,699	9,772	11,526	14,022

Notes:
(a) Figures are for years ended 31st March
(b) Exclusive of trade between the Settlements
Source:
Accounts and Papers: Statistical Tables for the Colonies, various volumes.

Table 2.2 *Share of British-owned vessels in total tonnage (entrances and clearances) in Australian and Eastern trades (excluding coastal trade), 1870–1900 (selected years).*

Per cent of total tonnage of vessels

	1870	1875	1880	1885	1890	1895	1900
Australia	92.2	93.9	94.1	89.1	87.6	89.3	85.2
India	86.7	78.9	84.2	84.6	87.4	87.2	84.3
Ceylon	86.0	84.6	84.8	83.0	84.3	85.4	71.8
Straits Settlement	66.7	69.8	69.7	66.2	70.6	71.4	57.3
Hong Kong	62.5	71.7	74.0	78.1	71.6	74.5	65.3

Source:
Derived from *Accounts and Papers: Statistical Tables for the Colonies,* various volumes.

The dominance of tea in the China trade from 1870–1890 can be seen clearly from Table 2.3 while silk became an increasingly valuable commodity. The importance of tea in the China trade declined as China tea was replaced by that from India and tea became an increasingly important commodity in the Indian trade in the 1880's.[1] In terms of actual shipping tonnage required, jute, rice and linseed were the most important commodities but tea, because of its special shipping requirements and its value, was the commodity which affected the development of shipping conferences in this area. In terms of both tonnage and value, wool was the most important commodity in the Australian trade and played a major part in the operation of the Australian shipping conference. In terms of cargo from a single area, India and Australia were more important in volume terms while the Straits Settlement,[2] Hong Kong, China and Japan provided a volume of trade (imports and

---

1 See Table 2.3

2 Malaya and Singapore. Singapore became an important coaling station after the opening of the Suez Canal and an important entrepôt trade grew up there in the late 19th century.

exports) equivalent to the Australian trade up to the 1900's (see Table 2.4),[1] after which the Australian trade grew faster than trade in the Far East. The Indian trade was larger in volume terms than either Australia or the Far East in the period under consideration.

Total trade from the Eastern and Australian areas was growing rapidly in the 1880's. Table 2.5 shows the total volume of imports and exports from these areas. The volume figures in cols. (1) and (2) are the value series which have been translated into volume terms by the use of a price index while col.(3) gives imports from these areas in tonnage terms (exports cannot be calculated on a tonnage basis). The tonnage figures are given because it is important in assessing the demand for shipping space to try to estimate the weight or measurement of the cargo. Ideally, we should like to have been able to apply a stowage factor to the commodities moving to and from the areas with which we were concerned but this was not possible. The nearest indicator is the tonnage figure given in the trade statistics of the period and this has been adjusted to take account of the commodities for which no weight was given. A comparison of the import constant price volume figures with the tonnage figures shows that the tonnage figures moved at a faster rate than the constant price volume series.

b. Supply of shipping

Against this background of the demand for shipping space, it is important to look at the supply which was available. In the 1870's, the sailing ship was still numerically the main type of ship in use, but it was being rapidly replaced by the steam ship. Of the ships registered in the U.K. the gross tonnage of steam ships had overtaken that of sail by 1885, although the number of sailing ships still registered was nearly three times that of steam ships (Table 2.6). This indicates that steam ships had more cubic capacity than the sailing ship; later the compound engine was introduced and this reduced fuel consumption leaving more space available for cargo. In the 1880's the triple expansion steam engine was introduced and was universally accepted in the 1890's. This meant not only increased speed but more economical operations in terms of fuel consumed and time taken for voyages. Shipping space was therefore increasing on two counts; (a) through the absolute size of the ship and the economy of fuel both of which gave greater hold capacity, and (b) through the faster speed of the steam ship which enabled ships to complete more voyages per year. The steam ship also has the advantage of being more independent of the weather than the sailing ship and it was possible for a ship-owner to introduce and maintain a regular scheduled service. The combined quantitative effect of these factors is difficult to determine with accuracy but it is estimated that the voyage to Australia was shortened by 15–16 days between 1873 and 1897; that to China by 11 days and that to India by 7 days in the same period. This meant that if the same number of ships were used in the Australian trade the supply of shipping space would increase

---

1 Volume of imports and exports have been obtained by deflating value figures by a price index. This is a very imperfect method in itself and even more so, from the point of view of estimating shipping space required. It is used here to give a general indication of trade and does not claim to be a precise measurement of tonnage moving. Some commodities have a high stowage factor (e.g. wool) which means that more shipping space would be required to ship a given quantity of wool than for the same quantity of wheat. See Appendix 1 for more detailed description of the method used to obtain volume figures.

Table 2.3 *United Kingdom commodity imports from Australia, China and India, 1870–1900*

	1870			1875			1880		
	Weight	Value	Value of specified commodity as % of total value of all imports	Weight	Value	Value of specified commodity as % of total value of all imports	Weight	Value	Value of specified commodity as % of total value of all imports
	Tons '000	£'000	%	Tons '000	£'000	%	Tons '000	£'000	%
AUSTRALIA									
Wool	64.4	9,375	78.5	84.4	12,936	75.8	107.0	14,852	72.8
Ores	15.5	163	1.4	2.1	48	0.3	3.9	49	0.2
Unwrought Copper and Pig Lead	4.5	269	2.3	11.4	562	3.3	9.4	681	3.3
Tallow and Stearine	23.2	969	8.1	12.2	470	2.8	19.2	651	3.2
Fresh Meat and Dairy Products	.0	2	.0	.0	0		0.2	13	0.1
Total of specified items	107.6	10,778	90.2	110.1	14,016	82.1	139.7	16,246	79.7
TOTAL OF ALL IMPORTS FROM AUSTRALIA		11,943	100.0		17,070	100.0		20,391	100.0
CHINA									
Tea	54.6	8,557	90.2	70.6	10,642	78.2	65.2	7,702	65.1
Silk (all kinds)	0.2	650	6.9	1.5	2,334	17.2	1.4	2,650	22.4
Total of specified items	54.8	9,207	97.1	72.1	12,976	95.4	66.6	10,352	87.5
TOTAL OF ALL IMPORTS FROM CHINA		9,482	100.0		13,608	100.0		11,826	100.0
INDIA									
Corn	–	–	–	66.7	670	2.2	161.5	1,759	5.8
Raw Cotton	152.0	9,944	39.6	170.7	9,173	30.4	92.1	4,782	15.9
Jute	118.3	2,317	9.2	170.3	2,571	8.5	231.7	4,015	13.3
Rice	172.3	1,960	7.8	323.3	2,881	9.6	328.2	3,135	10.4
Seed (Linseed etc.)	150.9	2,462	9.8	218.4	3,056	10.1	211.4	2,897	9.6
Tea	5.8	1,131	4.5	11.4	2,192	7.3	20.2	3,073	10.2
Total of specified items	599.3	17,814	71.0	960.8	20,543	68.2	1045.1	19,661	65.3
TOTAL OF ALL IMPORTS FROM INDIA		25,090	100.0		30,137	100.0		30,117	100.0

Source:
U.K. *Annual Statement of Trade*, various volumes.

16

Table 2.3 *(continued)*

1885 Weight (Tons '000)	1885 Value (£'000)	1885 Value of specified commodity as % of total value of all imports (%)	1890 Weight (Tons '000)	1890 Value (£'000)	1890 Value of specified commodity as % of total value of all imports (%)	1895 Weight (Tons '000)	1895 Value (£'000)	1895 Value of specified commodity as % of total value of all imports (%)	1900 Weight (Tons '000)	1900 Value (£'000)	1900 Value of specified commodity as % of total value of all imports (%)
123.9	12,332	67.9	144.2	14,832	70.7	186.2	13,808	55.3	111.7	11,518	48.4
1.8	16	0.1	4.0	89	0.4	34.4	115	0.5	21.9	228	1.0
8.6	446	2.5	43.7	549	2.6	44.7	702	2.8	69.9	1,408	5.9
13.5	739	4.1	21.0	574	2.7	76.9	269	1.1	42.7	398	1.7
2.7	133	0.7	6.9	273	1.3	62.3	3,408	13.7	60.7	2,451	10.3
150.5	13,656	75.3	219.8	16,317	77.7	404.5	18,302	73.3	306.9	16,003	67.2
	18,137	100.0		20,992	100.0		24,955	100.0		23,801	100.0
58.6	6,045	70.2	30.6	2,617	54.2	15.3	1,249	37.3	8.4	615	26.1
0.6	955	11.1	0.5	711	14.7	0.4	400	12.0	0.3	329	13.9
59.2	7,000	81.3	31.1	3,328	68.9	15.7	1,649	49.3	8.7	944	40.0
	8,614	100.0		4,831	100.0		3,344	100.0		2,360	100.0
608.5	4,559	14.3	455.6	3,461	10.6	440.1	2,342	8.9	0.3	2	.0
64.7	2,890	9.1	106.5	4,740	14.5	23.0	759	2.9	15.6	657	2.4
285.2	3,236	10.1	369.5	4,917	15.1	390.0	4,331	16.4	278.3	4,101	15.0
242.4	1,798	5.6	240.1	1,984	6.1	203.5	1,352	5.1	–	–	–
369.2	4,187	13.1	216.0	2,535	7.8	124.4	1,198	4.5	168.3	2,279	8.3
28.7	3,732	11.7	45.4	4,768	14.6	55.1	5,096	19.3	68.6	5,576	20.4
1598.7	20,402	64.0	1433.1	22,405	68.6	1236.1	15,078	57.1	531.1	12,615	46.1
	31,882	100.0		32,638	100.0		26,431	100.0		27,388	100.0

17

Table 2.4 *Value (in constant prices) of imports and exports in Australian and Far Eastern trades 1870–1913 (selected years)*

Constant 1880 prices £m.

	1870	1875	1880	1885	1890	1895	1900	1905	1910	1913
U.K. IMPORTS FROM:										
Australia	10.3	15.9	20.4	21.3	25.9	24.9	31.2	27.0	46.1	45.7
India	21.7	28.0	30.1	37.4	40.3	38.4	35.8	48.3	51.2	58.1
China	8.2	12.7	11.8	10.1	6.0	4.9	3.1	2.3	5.0	5.2
Japan	.8	.3	.5	.6	1.3	1.7	2.0	2.5	5.8	5.3
Hong Kong	.2	1.1	1.2	1.1	1.5	1.1	1.4	.5	.8	.8
Malaya	2.2	2.9	3.7	5.2	6.4	6.8	9.2	9.2	13.9	23.2
Philippines	1.0	1.3	1.7	1.1	2.0	2.3	2.2	2.5	2.0	2.6
U.K. EXPORTS TO:										
Australia	7.6	14.2	15.6	23.7	24.6	20.8	25.7	23.2	34.4	39.0
India	16.9	21.3	32.0	35.3	39.9	33.4	33.8	52.8	52.1	74.0
China	5.4	4.2	5.5	5.5	7.7	7.0	6.1	15.8	10.3	15.5
Japan	1.5	2.2	3.8	2.3	4.7	6.3	10.8	11.7	11.2	15.3
Hong Kong	3.0	3.2	4.0	4.1	3.1	2.3	3.2	4.6	4.2	4.7
Malaya	2.0	1.7	2.5	2.5	3.4	2.7	3.5	4.0	5.2	7.6
Philippines	.7	.8	1.3	1.0	1.2	.6	1.3	2.9	1.3	1.1
TOTAL TRADE										
Australia	17.9	30.1	36.0	45.0	50.5	45.7	56.9	50.2	80.5	84.7
India	38.6	49.3	62.1	72.7	80.2	71.8	69.6	101.1	103.3	132.1
Far East (a)	25.0	30.4	36.0	33.5	37.3	35.7	42.8	56.0	59.7	81.3

(a) The Far East includes China, Japan, Hong Kong, Malaya, Philippines

Table 2.5 *U.K. trade with the Eastern and Australian areas, 1880–1900*

	U.K. Imports Constant prices, Index, 1880 = 100	U.K. Exports	U.K. Imports ('Adjusted' tonnage)[a] Index numbers 1880 = 100
	(1)	(2)	(3)
1880	100.0	100.0	100.0
1881	106.0	110.3	117.9
1882	116.3	108.5	132.7
1883	116.0	114.8	148.7
1884	117.5	117.4	128.1
1885	110.5	123.8	140.4
1886	114.3	124.4	129.4
1887	114.4	125.0	118.9
1888	118.2	142.6	124.6
1889	126.6	128.2	138.7
1890	120.1	130.9	127.5
1891	123.7	128.5	150.1
1892	120.8	112.3	141.0
1893	114.2	104.1	125.1
1894	126.6	113.6	139.2
1895	131.5	113.7	148.9

Source:
Annual Statement of Trade and Imlah *Economic Elements in the Pax Britannica.*
Cambridge, Mass. 1958.
(a) See Appendix I to this chapter

Table 2.6 *Ships registered in the United Kingdom at 31st December each year*

	Total Vessels		Steam Vessels	
	Number	'000 net tons	Number	% of total *net* tonnage
1850	25,984	3,565	1,187	4.7
1855	25,948	4,349	1,674	8.8
1860	27,663	4,659	2,000	9.7
1865	28,787	5,760	2,718	14.3
1870	26,367	5,691	3,178	19.6
1875	25,461	6,153	4,170	31.6
1880	25,185	6,575	5,247	41.4
1885	23,662	7,430	6,644	53.5
1890	21,591	7,979	7,410	63.2
1895	21,003	8,989	8,386	68.1
1900	19,982	9,304	9,209	77.5
1905	20,581	10,736	10,522	84.4
1910	21,090	11,556	12,000	90.4
1915	20,790	12,427	12,771	93.7
1916	20,074	11,752	12,405	93.9
1917	18,720	10,232	11,534	93.9
1918	18,190	10,101	11,334	94.0
1919	18,346	10,928	11,791	94.6

Source:
B.R. Mitchell in collaboration with P.M. Deane *Abstract of British Historical Statistics,*
Cambridge University Press, 1962

by roughly 30 per cent,[1] and if it is borne in mind that the size and carrying capacity
of ships was also increasing it is possible to get some idea of the increase in the
supply of shipping space at the end of the 19th Century.

1 The voyage to Australia by steamship is estimated to have taken 60-65 days in 1870.

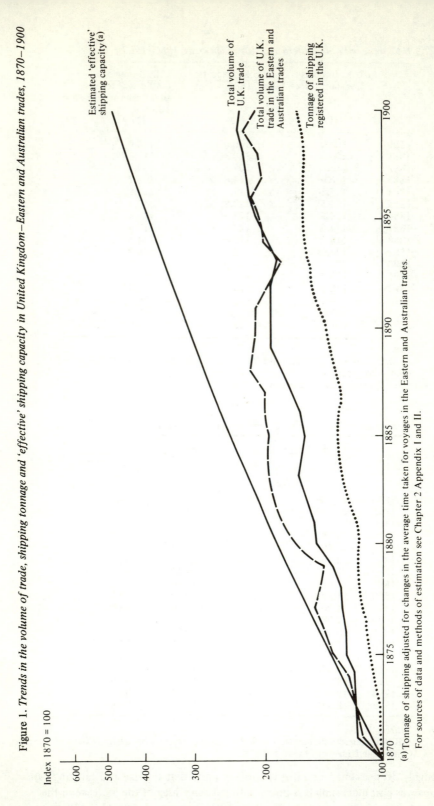

Figure 1. *Trends in the volume of trade, shipping tonnage and 'effective' shipping capacity in United Kingdom–Eastern and Australian trades, 1870–1900*

Index 1870 = 100

Estimated 'effective' shipping capacity (a)

Total volume of U.K. trade

Total volume of U.K. trade in the Eastern and Australian trades

Tonnage of shipping registered in the U.K.

(a) Tonnage of shipping adjusted for changes in the average time taken for voyages in the Eastern and Australian trades. For sources of data and methods of estimation see Chapter 2 Appendix I and II.

The importance of the increase in the supply of shipping is its relation to the demand to move goods by sea. In Figure 1, we try to show the way in which shipping space was increasing in relation to its demand. As can be seen, the total volume of U.K. trade moved at a faster annual rate than the supply of shipping as measured by the tonnage of ships registered in the U.K. When however, some account is taken of the increase in the speed of ships and other factors, the 'effective' capacity of the shipping tonnage can be shown to be increasing at a faster rate than the volume of trade. In the period 1873–1897, it is estimated that the total volume of U.K. trade increased at the rate of 2.62 per cent per annum while the volume of U.K. trade with the Eastern areas and Australia was increasing at a somewhat slower rate at 2.18 per cent per annum. Tonnage of ships registered in the U.K. increased at the rate of 1.80 per cent per annum but if the reduction in voyage time is taken into account, the growth in 'effective' capacity is 5.33 per cent per annum,[1] over twice as fast as the increase in the U.K. trade and 3.15 per cent faster than the growth in the Eastern and Australian trades. As reference to Table 2.5 will indicate, however, the increase in the demand for shipping space may be under-estimated by the use of trade volume figures for the reasons explained on p.15, footnote 1.

c. Freight rates

In a free market when supply is in excess of demand for a commodity or service it is expected that, other things being equal, the price of that commodity or service will decline. The price of shipping services is of course the freight rate and the trend of freight rates, at least in the homeward direction of the Eastern trades, was in a downward direction throughout the 1870's. It has not been possible to compile the composite index of freight rates in the Australian and Eastern trades for these early years because of the lack of data. Information concerning the freight rates is not easy to obtain but a certain amount of information is given in the Report of the Royal Commission on Shipping Rings, 1909. From the evidence submitted to the Commission, it has been possible to compile Table 2.7 [2] which shows freight rates in the China trade in 1874 and again in 1878; the rates show a substantial fall in the period. In the Australian and Indian trades the continuing use of the sailing ship is thought to have contributed to the competition for cargo. Sailing ships were prepared to carry cargo at rates well below those which were profitable for steamships and this accentuated the decline in freight rates. Insofar as costs could not be reduced in line with the fall in freight rates, it is to be expected that the profits of shipping companies would decline. Annual reports of shipping companies at this time indicate that this was so.[3] Other factors will, of course, affect the profitability

---

1   This is a very crude measure of the increase in capacity. The time spent in port may – or may not – have also changed over the period; if there was little change in this factor then by taking voyage time only into account we may be over estimating the increase in 'effective' capacity. On the other hand, we do not have any quantitative information on the effect of increased size of ships or of the extra hold space made available by improvements in engine design and performance.

2   Other information is contained in 'Fairplay' – Fifty Years of Freight Rates – but it was not possible to build up a *consistent* picture of liner cargo rates from the published data.

3   See F.E. Hyde *'Shipping Enterprise and Management 1830–1939, Harrisons of Liverpool'*. Liverpool University Press, 1967.

of companies and no definite relationship can be established between the fall in freight rates and the profitability of shipping companies. We put it forward, however, as one of the possible reasons why shipping companies should have been induced in the 1870's to form combinations among themselves to raise prices (freight rates) and to regulate the trade.

Table 2.7 *Homeward rates of freight from China, Japan and Malaya 1874 and 1878*

| | Per ton of 40 cubic feet | | | |
	1874		1878	
Japan	s.	d.	s.	d.
Tea	105	0	80	0
Waste Silk	108	6	80	0
General Merchandise	108	6	45	0
China (Shanghai)				
Tea	70	0	45	0
	80	0	70	0
Waste Silk	75	0	40	0
	80	0	55	0
Hong Kong				
Tea	80	0	65	0
Waste Silk	90	0	80	0
Singapore and Penang				
Gutta Percha	100	0[a]	70	0
General Merchandise	100	0[a]	60	0

(a) 1875
Source:
Report of the Royal Commission on Shipping Rings, 1909

d. *Early Conference formation*

It was this combination of circumstances which led shipowners to combine to 'protect their interests'. They formed what have since become known as shipping conferences. These conferences were regional organisations of cargo liner operators and, in general, they had two main aims. The first was to regulate the traffic and to fix the carrying rate and, following from this, to combat competition from shipowners who were not conference members.

The methods used to achieve these aims varied from region to region but, in general, the conference members would agree among themselves the rate to be charged on certain commodities and in addition they might impose restrictions on the number of sailings or limit a member's right to call at a port for loading and discharge of cargo. Some shipowners went further and made arrangements for pooling their earnings on the freight carried. Whatever arrangements they made for traffic sharing, however, they were concerned to combat competition from shipowners who were not parties to the agreement. The main weapon used was the system of rebates on the freight rate; this could be a straightforward rebate payable at the end of a period if a shipper declared that he had shipped his goods by conference vessels only during that period. Alternatively, the discount on the freight rate could take the form of a deferred rebate, which meant that if a shipper sent his goods by conference vessels only for a certain period he would receive a rebate on the freight rate but only if he continued to use conference vessels for all his business in the following period; the rebate on the first period would be paid at the end of the second period. When the loyalty of the shippers was broken (e.g. if a non-conference member was consistently charging freight rates below the conference level) then conference members might agree among themselves to conduct a 'rate-war', i.e. to reduce rates below those charged by the 'outsider' for so long as it was necessary to persuade the 'outsider' to offer his services elsewhere or to charge the conference rate.

The Royal Commission on Shipping Rings investigating shipping conferences in 1909 has given insight to the way in which the early conferences were formed. 'At the time conferences were formed, some lines were identified with particular ports while others despatched steamers from several ports. The tonnage of some lines was small, that of others large. In most cases, the original conference was based upon the recognition of interests existing at the time.' This recognition of interests developed further as conference organisation became more formal and some conferences formed what might be called sub-divisions – for example, in the Indian trade, the main Calcutta conference divided into two sections known as West Coast Lines and East Coast Lines. These sections often had power to fix rebates locally (this was true in the Calcutta trade) provided that they were fixed in such a way 'that the percentage of rebate allowed shall equalise the rates at the respective ports, it being a principle of the conference that the same minimum local rates shall rule at London, Liverpool and Glasgow.'

We will now look at the three main conference areas in the Eastern trade more closely – China and Japan, (including the Straits Settlement), India and Australia. In the development of the conferences in these areas certain features were common to all but there are differences and certain special features which cannot be dealt with adequately in a general context.

2. The Indian trade

Although it was in the Indian trade that the earliest combination of shipowners was formed, the amount of information which we have been able to obtain on the early developments in this trade is less than that available for other trades. Most of the early records were destroyed during the Second World War and little information is available about the development of the conference in the inter-war period.

What we do know is that in this trade the conferences were based on ports and not on the whole area. That is to say, the first conference which was formed was the UK–Calcutta conference (in 1875) and this was followed in later years by separate conferences for Madras–U.K., Bombay/Karachi–U.K. This type of conference continued and as Continental European shipowners also began to participate in the Indian trade so separate conferences were formed for trade between individual ports on the Indian coast to specified European countries. In the post-1948 period (following independence) there were over 100 different conferences operating in the Indian trade.

1875–1914

Calcutta seems to have been the main trading port in the early years; it was certainly the most important terminal port in the Indian trade. When excess capacity became acute in the Calcutta trade in the 1870's, seven British shipowners operating a regular service in the trade at the time joined together and agreed to take concerted action to deal with the problem. Up to this time, competition among shipowners had led to freight rates being varied according to such factors as the amount of cargo offering and the size of the parcels; large shippers were given concessionary rates, the amount of the concession depending on the degree of competition from other shipping companies.[1] Shipowners would also delay the sailing date of their ships in order to ensure that they had a full cargo; often they would act as merchants and carry goods on their own account to obtain a full loading. In 1875, however, the seven British shipowners agreed among themselves (a) to regulate the number of sailings which each would make and (b) to fix equal minimum rates from all ports in the U.K. to Calcutta and from Calcutta to U.K. ports regardless of the size of the consignment or of the shipper. With the formation of the conference the members undertook to sail on a given date regardless of whether they had a full cargo and the fixing of equal minimum rates of freight was meant to compensate for this. No rebate of any kind was offered to the shippers at that time.

This early agreement between the shipowners was not popular among the shippers of Manchester cotton piece goods — the 'fine' cargo of the outward trade. They claimed that there was no incentive for them to go on using the vessels of the shipowners within the conference and in 1877 the merchant shippers of Manchester threatened to charter their own vessels (they were powerful enough to do this); the conference members were therefore forced to allow a rebate on Manchester piece goods to those shippers who regularly used conference vessels.

The arrangements made by shipowners in the Calcutta trade were soon extended to cover other ports on the Indian coast including Bombay, Madras and Karachi. In 1885 ten shipping lines came to an agreement on sharing the trade from the UK; the agreement laid down the number of sailings which each line was permitted to make from UK ports (Glasgow, Liverpool and London were the named ports) to ports on the Indian coast — six lines had rights in the Bombay trade and one of these called at Karachi and the sailing rights of nine lines were recognised in the trade to Madras and Calcutta. Rates of freight were to be agreed by all members and a distinction was made between 'rough' and 'fine' cargo; special arrangements were to be made for the carrying of government stores and railway material. Although the agreement appeared to cover the outward trade only, a clause concerning freight rates also specifically mentioned rates of freight in the homeward direction; these homeward rates were to be fixed at weekly meetings[2] of the agents of each of the lines. The lines also agreed to pool the freight earnings[3] on certain 'fine' cargo (Manchester cotton piece goods) and on the division of such earnings between the lines. An unusual feature of the agreement was the naming of an arbitrator to deal with any claims which lines might make against one another if the agreement was broken.

1 F.E. Hyde: *Shipping Enterprise and Management 1830–1939, Harrisons of Liverpool*, op. cit.

2 There is nothing to indicate that rates in the homeward trade were as volatile as to require a weekly meeting to fix the rates. It may be that the agents met to discuss the rates to be fixed for 'open-rated' cargo and this might depend on the number of tramp ships available and ready to drive down the rate.

3 Referred to as the 'joint purse'.

It has not been possible to discover how this agreement worked in practice but it appears to have been the basis for the future working of the trade up to 1948 with the possible exception of the trade to and from Calcutta.

In the Calcutta trade, a new agreement covering the outward trade from Glasgow, Liverpool and London was drawn up in 1892. This agreement made formal what had been operative in practice — the demarcation of 'spheres of influence' between East and West coast lines in the outward direction. That is, the lines operating mainly from Liverpool and Glasgow agreed not to load at East coast ports and the lines operating from London agreed not to load from the West coast ports. The East coast included any ports between Newcastle to Southampton inclusive and all continental ports from Hamburg to Bremen down to Cherbourg; West coast ports were all the ports west of Southampton and round the west and north to Newcastle.

This agreement meant that lines operating from the East coast would have little or no opportunity to carry the remunerative 'Manchester cargo' of fine cotton piece goods and yarn. The new agreement therefore made provision for the East coast shipping lines to share in the net freight earnings pool when the rates were higher than a prescribed amount. A similar provision was made for the homeward tea trade pool the revised terms of which were included in the same agreement. In the case of the tea trade, it was the East coast lines which obtained the bulk of the trade as practically all the tea was carried to London. Contributions to the tea pool by the carrying lines were to vary between 12½ per cent and 20 per cent depending on the gross rate of freight which was fixed for the season.

An interesting feature of this agreement was the curious provision it made for the payment of rebates to shippers in the outward direction. Such rebates were to be agreed locally and not by the conference members as a whole, in order that the percentage of rebate allowed should equalise the rates at the respective ports. In the homeward direction, rebates were decided by all the members of the conference as a body — for tea and other homeward cargo. It is from the Calcutta tea trade that we have been able to gain insight into the working of the conference agreements not only from the point of view of the shipowning companies but also from the shippers' angle. In the homeward trade from Calcutta, by far the most valuable item of liner cargo was tea. The tea merchants, in turn, were dependent on the liner service, and it is from the evidence given to the Royal Commission on Shipping Rings by one of the tea merchants' associations that much of the information concerning the early working of the conference system in the Calcutta trade has been obtained. Tea had two important characteristics which made it eminently suitable as liner cargo: (a) the importers required shipment in small quantities at regular intervals and (b) it is a commodity which could easily become contaminated if it came into contact with other cargoes.

In 1881 the Indian Tea Association was formed.[1] By this time, the Calcutta conference seems to have become well established and not only were rates of freight fixed by the shipowners but a loyalty rebate was given to shippers in return for exclusive dealing with conference members. The freight rate on tea was fixed for the whole of the season and the rebate was payable at the end of the season. A

1 This was one of a number of organisations which seemed to represent the tea growers. There was an Indian Tea Districts Association situated in London and the Calcutta Tea Traders' Association operating in Calcutta.

relationship between the rate on tea and the rate on 'rough' cargo was expected by the shippers, and it was because this relationship had become unacceptable that the Indian Tea Association protested to the conference. That is to say, it was felt that the rate for tea in 1886 was fixed too high in relation to that for rough cargo. The members of the Association also protested against the use of rebate, on the grounds that all tea shippers should receive the same terms.

The conference members, who presumably felt themselves to be in a strong position, would not give way on the question of rebate (although they offered to increase the amount) nor were they prepared to reduce the rate of freight. The tea planters therefore made the first attempt to found an independent line. They made arrangements with a firm of Glasgow shipowners to provide a sufficient number of steamers during the tea season to carry the cargo at a much lower rate than that offered by conference lines. The name given to the steamers provided was the Planters' Line. Its existence was short-lived, however, for the conference members cut the rate for tea to well below that agreed by the growers with the Planters Line, and they were able to attract the trade away from the 'intruder'. Negotiations ensued between the conference members and the tea shippers on rates to be charged and an agreement was reached. In 1892, when this agreement came to an end, the shippers made a further attempt to get a more favourable rate together with the abolition of the rebate system, the latter to be replaced by an agreement (or contract) between the conference and the shippers who could be penalised for any breach of the agreement. The conference members on the other hand, wished to introduce the *deferred* rebate system into the new agreement and it was this innovation which the members of the Tea Association felt they could not accept. They asked for the new agreement to include immediate rebate payments and in addition dispensation for f.o.b. shipments.[1]

The conference members were not willing at that stage to amend the terms of the new agreement. It so happened, however, that a British shipowner, (the Brocklebank Line) not a conference member, began to accept tea cargoes at well below the agreed conference rate of freight. In addition, one of the members withdrew from the conference and reduced the rate of freight on tea. Later in 1892, the conference members also reduced the rate of freight on tea and abolished the deferred rebate clause. At the end of 1892, the Brocklebank Line joined the conference but further negotiations between the Indian Tea Association together with the Calcutta Tea Traders' Association and the conference members to obtain more favourable rates broke down.

The tea merchants negotiated to set up an independent Line (the Mutual Line) but before the new line got under way, the conference members reduced the rate on tea to below what was being offered by the new line. The line withdrew and a new agreement negotiated between the conference and the tea merchants associations came into operation in 1895. The deferred rebate was not put into operation and a sliding scale relationship between 'rough cargo' and tea cargo was adopted.

Although the tea merchants were not happy with the new arrangement – they accused the conference members of artificially inflating 'rough' cargo rates – it did

1 Shipments for which the purchaser specifies the ships or shipping line which must be used if the purchase is to be made.

26

in fact last until 1907 when the tea merchants were sucessful in negotiating a rate for tea without any reference to other types of cargo. The rebate system remained but no further attempt was made to introduce the deferred rebate.

1919–1939

A feature of the Indian trade in the years up to 1914 was the almost complete dominance of the trade by British shipowners. One German line obtained membership of the conference in 1907 with loading rights from Middlesbrough only.[1] After the 1914–1918 war, other continental lines (namely German, Scandinavian and Dutch) began to participate in the Indian trade although their share remained relatively small.

The participation of continental lines was formalised in agreements drawn up in 1925 and 1926. These agreements were between the British East coast lines and the continental lines and these lines formed a conference quite separate from the UK conferences known as the North Continental Conference. The UK conferences continued to be organised on the lines of the 19th century agreements but in a period of slow growing (or even declining) trade, British shipping companies combined in a different way, that is, this was the period of mergers of British shipping lines. The biggest merger of the period and the one which created most interest in the shipping world was that between the British India Steam Navigation Company and the Peninsular and Oriental Steam Navigation Company, but other mergers also took place between lines engaged in the Indian trade, for example, the Ellerman and Hall lines merged to become the Ellerman Line.

The sharing of the trade in the outward direction continued to be organised as it had been before 1914 with sailings circumscribed for some members (while for others the number of sailings was left quite open) and a percentage earnings pool in operation in the outward trades. The division of trade between the East and West coast lines also continued to be observed. In the Bombay/Karachi trade there was no general formal agreement between lines but certain 'spheres of influence' were recognised. The rates of freight for the outward trades were set by reference to the rates to Calcutta and the deferred rebate continued to be used. One curious feature concerned membership of the outward conference. In the period of mergers, a small line which had held rights in the East coast trade under the supervision of one of the larger shipping lines, was acquired by one of the West coast lines. The earlier arrangement was cancelled, but the acquiring line agreed not to apply for full membership until advised by the larger East coast line. Application for membership was duly made in 1929 but the West coast lines would not agree to membership being granted except on conditions which were unacceptable to the applicant line. The application for membership was withdrawn and the line continued to operate in the trade under the wing of the two larger East coast lines. The participation of the line was such that a 15 per cent earnings pool among all the three lines (the two large East coast lines and the non-member line) was instituted of all trade from the East coast to Calcutta.

---

1   Membership was not granted easily; the German line competed with the British lines by cutting freight rates and it was aided in this by a small British line which was endeavouring to gain conference membership at the same time.

In the continental outward trade, the agreement with the continental lines laid down that rates of freight from the UK and the continent should be the same. In practice, however, continental rates were lower and this seems to have become accepted by the British members of the conference. A 25 per cent earnings pool operated among the lines on cargo obtained from Dutch and Belgian ports but not from German ports. A cargo sharing agreement operated from German ports but this was permissive only, i.e. the shipping lines, which were divided into groups for the purposes of the earnings pool and the cargo sharing pool, were entitled to a share of the cargo emanating from German ports, but if any group was not sucessful in obtaining its share, there was no compensation from the other groups nor any penalty on a group which exceeded its entitlement. The earnings pool did give rise to some difficulty in the 1920's in that a complaint was made by the continental groups that British lines were not berthing sufficient tonnage to carry their quota of cargo to Bombay and Karachi.[1] It was eventually agreed that unless a minimum number of steamers were berthed monthly by each member, such a month could not count for pool puproses.

In the homeward trade, the conference organisation was much less formalised. From Calcutta, for example, there was no agreement among the lines on which ports of discharge individual members would serve although continental lines seem to have undertaken not to load for UK ports either direct or for transhipment. Rates of freight from Calcutta to the UK and Europe were net (i.e. no rebate system was operated) and although the rates were intended to be the same whether cargo was moving to the UK or the continent of Europe, in practice – as in the outward direction – rates to the continent were lower than those to the UK.

In other Indian ports arrangements varied; only certain 'choice' items were regarded as 'conference' items in Madras, and the British lines tried to keep the trade in 'choice' items to themselves; one French line was granted the right to carry 'choice' items to Marseilles so long as it did so at conference rates. German and Scandinavian lines operated regular services from Madras but presumably carried open-rated 'non-choice' cargo. Trade from Bombay and Karachi remained 'open' in the pre-war period. An attempt to form a conference in the 1920's – or at least to stabilise rates – was unsuccessful. The reason seems to have been the existence and active operation of merchants who were large enough to charter vessels in opposition to the regular lines if they considered freight rates were too high. Despite the fact that Bombay and Karachi were open ports, however, regular lines operating from the port adhered fairly closely to the ports of discharge laid down for lines operating from other Indian ports.

One further development in the Indian trade in the 1930's which must be noted for its significance in the post-1948 period is the admission to conference membership of an Indian line. This 'line' was in fact one ship (owned by a cotton manufacturer) and was called the Scindia Navigation Company of Bombay. This was the beginning of participation in the trade of Indian national flag lines and this was to increase after 1948.

---

1 It is interesting to note that although there seems to have been no formal agreement among British lines in the Bombay/Karachi trade in this period, there was a formal agreement between the continental lines and the British East coast lines.

This survey of developments in the Calcutta trade and trade from other Indian ports can be summed up briefly. The combination of shipowners in 1875 became a permanent arrangement despite attempts from within and without to break the combination. From an early arrangement to agree on freight rates, the shipowners introduced the rebate system, a pooling arrangement, and agreed on concerted action (in this instance competitive cutting of rates) to combat competition from 'outsiders'. These methods were to be used later, perhaps even more forcefully in othe conferences in the Eastern trades.

3. The Far Eastern trades

There are now numerous conferences under this heading operating between Europe and the Far Eastern area. These conferences grew up in the 1880's but the system began with the China trade — which at that time was the most important area in the Far East for European traders. The main commodities on which the trade was based in the homeward direction were tea and silk (see Table 2.3) and they continued to be important until the mid 1880's.

1875–1914

It was the China trade which was the main concern of John Swire, the chief architect of the conference system in the Far East; indeed, he has sometimes been called the 'Father of Shipping Conferences'.[1] John Swire, among his many interests in the China trade, acted as the Agent for Alfred Holt & Company (The Ocean Steam Ship Company). His first attempt to form a conference in both homeward and outward directions was made in 1879. The participants at that time included five British lines and one French together with three firms of brokers or agents; the six lines were those who were at that time providing a regular service to the area. The formation of a conference was not an easy matter — particularly in the homeward trade — and John Swire had to battle long and hard (not least with his own company — Alfred Holt) to get the conference established and accepted.

The outward and homeward trades operated as separate entities, although members of the outward conferences were likely to be members of the homeward conference. As the conference developed, the overlapping of membership in the outward and homeward direction continued but more shipping companies were admitted to the conference in a homeward direction only.[2] In the outward direction, the short term agreement made in 1879 continued to be renewed by the companies concerned until 1887 but in the homeward trade the conference agreement broke down at the end of 1879 (the first agreement was drawn up for four months only) and lapsed until 1881 when a new agreement was reached. This was also short-lived, however, and lasted only until 1882; no further agreement was reached until 1885. In 1887 there was a complete breakdown of the conferences in both outward and homeward directions because of a legal action brought by the Mogul Line on the grounds that the conference constituted a conspiracy.[3] The action was unsuccessful

1 S. Marriner and F.E. Hyde: *The Senior: John Samuel Swire, 1825–1898. Management in the Far Eastern Shipping Trade.* Liverpool University Press, 1967.

2 See Chapter 8 for a description of the present position.

3 See Marriner and Hyde, op. cit.

but there was no new agreement among the shipping companies until 1893 when new outward and homeward agreements were drawn up and accepted. Apart from a temporary upset in 1897, the conference became from that date an established concern in the Far East trade accepted by both shipowners and shippers alike. Conference arrangements were accepted not only in the China/Japan trade but also in the Philippines and in the Straits Settlement (Malaya and Singapore).

Membership of the conferences had also expanded by this time; two more British companies had been admitted to membership by 1890, and by 1900 three German companies and a Japanese line had also been admitted. The criteria for membership seems to have been that the applicant lines should be able to show that they had a stake in the trade, i.e. that they were running a regular service with owned tonnage from their own country to the Far East throughout the year. Shipping lines which tried to come into the trade at peak periods and 'take the cream of the trade' were not accepted. Nor did membership of the conference mean unlimited and unrestricted rights at all ports in all parts of the conference area. New entrants were given limited loading and discharging rights in both the UK and on the Continent of Europe.

The inevitable question arises, of course, as to why the conference agreements worked amicably in the outward direction (at least up to 1914) but not in the homeward direction. One of the reasons for this was the lack of balance between the outward and homeward trades; another, as we have seen (p.21) was an excess supply of shipping space in relation to the amount of trade in this period which meant that not only liner vessels but also tramp vessels were looking for cargo in the homeward direction. Up to the 1880's there had been more demand for shipping space from China than in the outward direction, but in the 1880's the situation was reversed. In evidence to the Royal Commission, Richard Holt stated that the outward cargoes were the principal part of the trade and this was not overtonnaged. Certain items which were not in the conference tariff (and need not therefore be confined to shipment by conference members) were also shipped to the Far East in very large quantities; there were no restrictions on the number of sailings which members of the conference could make. Holt also pointed out that no goods from China and Japan were capable of being shipped in whole cargoes — 'regular steamers do not get a third full on the homeward voyage from China and Japan'. For all these reasons, there was a tendency in the homeward trade towards a scramble for cargo — and not only in China and Japan but also in Singapore and Malaya where shipowners with half full ships hoped to obtain enough cargo to fill their ships. It is interesting to note that Holt estimated the proportion of tramp vessels to regular liner vessels in the trade at that time (1908) to be 2:1.

John Swire fully appreciated the problems of the trade and felt that even if trade were completely balanced in any one year in the outward and homeward directions, the problem of seasonal fluctuations and of lower and higher rated cargo would remain. Marriner and Hyde in their biography of Swire have said the he was passionately convinced that the only means by which shipping companies in this trade could survive was through co-operation among themselves. Even before his attempts at forming a conference, Swire had been instrumental in securing agreements between shipping companies for the sharing of trade on the China coast. He tried to bring the same agreements into more general use in the deep sea trade. His main aims were to regulate competition among shipowners and to raise freight rates.[1] Swire himself was very much in favour of an earnings pool and he was finally successful in instituting such a pool for certain commodities in the China trade.

The attempt to regulate freight rates was through the fixing of a maximum rate. It seems odd to contemplate now, when conference members agree to abide by the agreed tariff, that although the maximum rate was agreed, members of the conference were permitted under the terms of the agreement to quote a rate lower than the maximum rate in order (a) to obtain a full cargo *homeward*, or (b) to compensate for a 'poorer quality' service i.e. if a line had slower ships than those employed by other lines in the trade. Such a system not unnaturally, was abused and there were constant complaints at conference meetings of undercharging by certain members. There were also differentials in rates in the outward direction, but these differentials were more concerned with shipment from e.g. Liverpool and London, or from the Continent and the UK. It was not until the 1930's that equal rates and conditions of shipment were agreed among conference members in the UK and in Europe.

On the other hand, the agreement on rates extended not only from the Far East to European ports, but it was laid down in 1895, after complaints had been lodged that one member had been charging an 'all-in' rate to America, that the conference agreement specified not only cargo for Europe but for foreign ports *via* Europe. It had been customary for the conference to agree rates to America because it was important for their members that they should do this.

There were of course disagreements on rates among conference members in both outward and homeward directions. Members were allowed under the freight rate agreement to quote a special rate if they were able to obtain enough cargo from one client to fill a ship, or if they undertook to carry railway material. There seems to have been no agreement between Continental and British lines on the level of rates to be charged for these special contracts. The hope was expressed at one of the meetings of lines in 1899 that a German line would soon be able to raise their contract rates to the British level. It should be noted here that individual rates were fixed by a brokers' committee. The conference meetings, which the owners or principals attended, rarely discussed individual rates but they did discuss tariff rates in general terms, i.e. how much per ton on average was required for each of them to break even — or better.

In the outward conference there was a scheme in the early days for shipowners to accept forward cargo and this raised many difficulties for members of the conference. Forward business seems to have been undertaken for many months ahead, and this caused difficulties when rates were changed in an upward direction. Many complaints of underquoting on tariff rates were made but were defended by the shipowners concerned by reference to forward booking, and although conference members as a whole felt that 'floating engagements at a fixed maximum rate only were detrimental to the interests of all lines' no action was taken until 1900 when it was agreed that no forward bookings would be made at any port more than six months in advance for weight and three months (later changed to six) for measurement cargo.

1 S. Marriner and F.E. Hyde, op. cit., p. 137 et seq.

A further differential in rates grew up with the admittance of Continental members, and this was the differential between measurement rates as per the metric system and those as per the linear system. Agreement was finally reached on this in 1900 in the outward trade. In the homeward trades, underquoting through the declaration of false measurements had become very prevalent in the 1890's and early 1900's, and in 1906 a committee of Sworn Measurers was set up in Kobe and in other Japanese and Chinese ports. This committee of Sworn Measurers still exists in the homeward trade.

As mentioned earlier, one of Swire's aims was to regulate the trade and this included the regulation of ports of loading and discharge for conference members. The 'founder' members of the conference felt themselves to have full rights in the trade, and although the UK lines came to an agreement in the early 1890's over the division of the loading rights in the outward direction on the East and West coasts, the French line maintained exclusive loading rights at north coast French ports. When other lines were later admitted to the conference their admission was subject to their not interfering with the trade of existing members. Their rights to load or discharge from certain ports was severely circumscribed although they could of course claim the right to load and discharge at ports within their own national territories. Antwerp was the one open port; the Belgians had no deep sea shipping line.

From the beginning, the Far Eastern Conference instituted pooling arrangements. In the outward trade, the pool was confined at first to British lines and to trade in Lancashire and Yorkshire cotton and woollen goods. As new members from Continental Europe joined the conference, attempts were made to set up a pooling arrangement for cargo lifted from Antwerp. This was in response to complaints of undercharging but there was a good deal of reluctance, particularly by the German lines, to enter into any pooling arrangement. As the other members would not adopt a pooling system which left out some of the most important carriers from Antwerp, the negotiations for setting up such a pool were long and protracted. In the homeward direction, pooling agreements existed from the very early days for certain commodities which were the mainstay of the trade.

The deferred rebate was introduced into the Far Eastern trade when the conference was first formed in 1879. When first introduced it was at the rate of 5/- per ton with the exception of certain commodities which were regarded as 'open' (e.g. rice) and of commodities which would in any case be shipped by liner vessels (e.g. silk and treasure). The percentage rebate system was introduced at a later stage; it was certainly in existence in 1909.

There was some discrepancy in the method of applying the deferred rebate. The French line did not use it at all, because as a government-regulated concern, it was not allowed to do so. Similarly, there were some differences between the way the German owners applied the rebate system (which in effect meant a higher rate of rebate) and the way it was applied in the UK. The rebate system grew out of the old system of primage, and in fact primage was still part of the conference tariff up to the end of the 19th century. The conference tariff quoted so much per ton plus primage, usually 10 per cent. Five per cent was returned to the shipper at the time of shipment and a 10 per cent deferred rebate was given after six months. The question of the type of rebate system to be used was not settled until the 1930's (see p. 35).

It has been noted earlier that as trade with areas in the Far East expanded so a conference organisation was set up, often with the same membership as in the China/Japan Conference. The two principal conferences which developed from the China/Japan Conference were the Philippines Conference and the Straits Settlement (Malaya and Singapore) Conference. The latter is interesting because of the special circumstances of the port. Singapore was developed after the opening of the Suez Canal. It became a very important coaling station and for this reason there was no shortage of ships calling at the port. This meant that if the shipowners providing a regular service were to obtain the cargoes they required — at the rates they had fixed — they would have to obtain the loyalty of the shippers.

The first Straits Settlements Conference was formed in 1885 and incorporated the rebates system. This agreement lasted until 1887 and no further attempt at co-operation among shipowners was made until 1893 when the conference was re-formed. This combination lasted until 1895, but as no rebate was offered to the merchants it is perhaps not surprising that they did not give their exclusive support to conference vessels. In the scramble for cargo the conference lost its attraction for its constituent members and it again broke up in 1895. In 1897 it was again re-formed but this time a special inducement was offered to the merchant firms, some-times called freight agents, to give their exclusive support to conference vessels and to refrain from chartering. These freight agents, who were no more than seven in number, were sufficiently well organised to be able to threaten to charter ships on their own account on a group basis, and as it appears that they represented approxi-mately 60 per cent of the trade they were a considerable threat to conference mem-bers. In 1897, therefore, the conference members finally agreed (although there was a good deal of disagreement in the early stages) that they should offer special terms to the freight agents in Singapore in return for their exclusive support. These special terms were linked to the freight rate level so that the merchants had an interest in maintaining the rate at a level which the shipowners thought remunerative. The special terms were in return for 'loyalty' to the conference and 'assistance'[1] in maintaining rates at what was considered to be a profitable level; they did not apply to all merchants, but only to those who were strong enough to use the threat of chartering a vessel on their own account.

This special agreement with the merchants at Singapore lasted until after the publication of the Report of the Royal Commission on Shipping Rings, which con-demned this type of agreement. The agreement was terminated on the initiative of the shipping companies and on payment of a lump sum in compensation to the merchants. After this, the Straits Settlement Conference fell into line with the China and Japan conferences and adopted the same type of agreements and arrange-ments with shippers. The rebate system adopted in Singapore, however, was that all rebates due to the shippers would be paid within the same year.

It is not possible to give details here of the year by year operations of the con-ferences in the period up to 1914. Suffice to say that despite disagreements among

---

1 It is not clear how this assistance was to be given. It was part of the agreement that the Singapore merchants should 'do their best to prevent opposition', but it is not clear how this would be done. What is known is that as well as being merchants in their own right the merchants concerned in the agreements also acted as forwarding agents for smaller merchants and it may be that pressure was exerted in this way.

the members over freight rates, pool shares, sailing rights and other matters, as well as opposition from prospective members of the conference, the organisation survived — and expanded — up to 1914.

1919–1939

In 1918 the conference members regrouped themselves ready to take up the organisation again. The co-operation among shipowners which John Swire had striven so hard to bring about was put to severe tests in the inter war period, and it is indicative of the resilience — or perhaps flexibility — of the organisation that it survived this very difficult period intact.

Apart from a short period immediately after the end of the war, the period 1919–1939 was one of declining world trade and an excess supply of shipping space. Small wonder perhaps that in these circumstances some shipowners found the conference organisation restrictive and they tried to evade the rules. The conference records of this time show constant reference to the payment of illicit rebates (particularly from Belgian and German ports), and even direct under-quoting of the tariff. A means of evasion of the conference rate was the under-quoting of weight or measurement of a particular cargo and at one time it was suggested that a panel of Sworn Measurers should be set up at Continental conference ports. The German shipowners seem to have found conference rules and regulations particularly irksome. When they were re-admitted to the conference in 1921 (on the same terms as they had enjoyed before the war with the exception that their loading rights in the UK were discontinued) they wished to be allowed to fix their own tariffs. Other members of the conference quickly pointed out that commodities which were shipped from all countries must have the same rates under the conference agreement; the German rate fixing committee could only have jurisdiction over those commodities coming exclusively from Germany. The Japanese lines made a similar request in 1922, but again the other conference members felt that it would create a dangerous precedent.

The conference members felt that the only way to deal with the problem of under-quoting the tariff rate was to draw up an earnings pool agreement. Although this was first put forward in 1921, it was not until 1931 that an outward pool agreement covering the continent and the UK was agreed. The evasion of tariff rates had by then become so serious a matter that in 1930 a penalty scheme was adopted by conference members. The scheme adopted attempted to cover the malpractices which had come to light during the 1920's as the following quotations will indicate:

(a) 'All measurements on the quay to be taken according to methods at present in force at the port of loading. Any cases of doubt to be referred to conference secretary.

(b) Freight to be charged on measurements taken after reception of the goods by the ship's agent on the quay and in no circumstances to accept figures furnished by f.o.b. suppliers or any other parties.

(c) No action to be taken by parties to the agreement or their agents which could be construed as equivalent to a reduction in ocean rates either for the purpose of equalising insurance or of reducing mail or lighter rates or premature payment of rebates or any other reason.

(d) Agents or parties to agreement not to pay any charges on goods ex-railway or ex-lighter which should be borne by shipper. No rates to be quoted which cover transit, handling, or any other charges or part thereof from any point to the loading point or at the loading port except those already agreed and/or provided for in the tariff.

(e) No commission, brokerage or forwarding agency fee of any kind to be paid.'

The penalty clause was on the following lines. 'Any infringement or deliberate breach of conference regulations or conference tariffs shall be subject to a fine. In order to secure payment members give an undertaking to guarantee payment of any fine up to £2,500.' Machinery was set up to deal with complaints through the conference, including provision of an arbitrator. The onus was on the members against whom complaints were made to prove innocence. Mistakes or inadvertencies were not deemed a breach but would also be fined.

It has not been possible to establish whether any action was ever taken by the conference under this penalty arrangement, but it did continue in existence until the beginning of the Second World War. In 1937, there was some attempt to revise the provisions of the document but this was not sucessful.

A second problem for conference members in the 1920's and 1930's was the existence of outside competition. This did not for the most part involve conference members in a long and bitter rate war; the situation was usually resolved by admitting the 'outsider' to the conference but this meant of course that other members had to accept a smaller share of a trade which was not growing very fast and in part of the period it actually declined.

The most noteworthy event as far as shipping conferences as a whole were concerned in the 1920's, was the enquiry undertaken by the Imperial Shipping Committee in 1921 on representation from Commonwealth governments. One effect of the publication of the Committee's findings on the Far East conferences had to do with the deferred rebate system, although the Committee was set up to enquire into all aspects of transport from Commonwealth countries. The Committee did not in fact condemn the rebate system; it recognised that if conference lines were to maintain a regular service, provide sufficient tonnage for the 'ordinary' requirements of the trade, and maintain stable freight rates with no distinction between large and small shippers, then some *quid pro quo* from the shippers was not an unreasonable demand. They did recommend, however, that an alternative to the rebate system should be offered by shipping companies, and the contract system, used at that time in the South African trade, was suggested.[1]

The result of the Committee's recommendations as far as the Far East Conferences, were concerned was that the conference members, despite opposition from some of them who did not see the necessity to change the system, agreed to introduce the contract system as an alternative to the rebate system as from 1st January 1931. The contract system means that a shipper contracts to ship by conference vessels only for a period (e.g. 12 months), and in return he is quoted a net rate on all his shipments which is more or less equivalent to the rebate. The advantage as far as the

1 The ISC also recommended greater consultation with shippers before freight rates were increased. The setting up of Shippers' Associations to represent shippers' interests in various trades was recommended, as indeed it had been by the Royal Commission on Shipping Rings in 1909.

shipper is concerned is that he does not have considerable sums of money held by the shipping companies. As far as the shipowner is concerned this was felt, in the 1930's, to be a disadvantage of the contract system because the deferred rebate was held as security for the shippers' continued support.

It should be mentioned here that the contract system was introduced in the Philippines Homeward Conference as early as 1920, because it was acknowledged that the rebate system was illegal under American law. The contract system was substituted and accepted.

Despite these difficulties, the Far East Conference continued to operate and to meet up to 1940 but the arrangements were then suspended until the end of the war.

4. The Australian trade

In an unpublished thesis, Keith Trace[1] has commented that Australia is a terminal point on one of the world's longest trade routes, and this has always been recognised by the shipping lines which served the trade. Comparative sea distances estimated by Trace for the routes between the UK (London), Australia and various other trading destinations are shown below.

Australia	Brisbane	11,961 miles (via Suez)
	Fremantle	9,537 miles (via Suez)
Canada	Montreal	3,000 miles
U.S.A.	New Orleans	4,000 miles
South America	Buenos Aires	6,250 miles
India	Bombay	6,220 miles (via Suez)
South Africa	Cape Town[a]	5,947

(a) From Southampton

The UK—Australia trade suffers from other disadvantages, more particularly in the homeward direction, in so far as the commodities entering trade are concerned. For example, wool is and has been since the late 19th Century the most important single commodity in the trade (see Table 2.3), from Australia to Europe, and wool in terms of shipping space is a low capacity loading commodity which means that a large amount of shipping space is required. A large proportion of the trade from Australia to the UK also consists of primary products which not only need refrigerated shipping space (ships for which are costly to build and to run), but these products have large seasonal and annual fluctuations in the amount to be shipped.

1875–1914

The disadvantages of the Australian trade do not appear, however, to have discouraged shipowners. Before 1900, eleven British, one French and two German lines were operating a *regular* service to Australia. They operated both sail and steam ships (there was not the same urgency for quick delivery of wool as there was for tea in the Indian and Chinese trade). In 1906, of the general cargo ships in the

---

1 K. Trace, 'Shipping Conferences on the Australian Route'. Unpublished Ph. D. thesis, available in Essex University.

Australian trade 120 were steam ships and 54 were sailers, excluding sailing ships carrying such cargoes as phosphates and pig-iron.[1]

The organisation of shipping in the Australian trade was a 'free for all' in the 1870's and early 1880's. Individual shipowners and brokers made agreements with merchants in London and producers in Australia for exclusive shipment of cargoes to and from Australia. These agreements gave the shipper the lowest rate on similar goods in the same ship or the lowest rate quoted by the shipowners or, alternatively, in return for a certain quantity of cargo (e.g. 600 tons) they would receive the consignment of a vessel, commission on the total freight of the vessel or a discount on their freight bill. This is the kind of situation where large merchants or merchant shippers could use their bargaining strength and also could play off one shipowner against another in an attempt to get better terms, and according to evidence given to the Royal Commission this frequently happened.

With the experience of shipwoners in other trades to guide them (in many cases they would have been the same shipowners), the lines operating a service to Australia from the UK decided in 1884 to join together to agree freight rates among themselves. The description given by Sir Thomas Sutherland, Chairman of the P & O Steam Navigation Company in the 1880's, of the arrangements among shipowners in the Australian trade runs as follows:

> 'This is controlled by a combination of owners and brokers popularly known as Davis.[2] Davis, I believe, was the name of the house or office wherein this combination many years ago commenced existence in the days when the Australian trade was principally carried on by sailing ships. The various members of the conference hold their interests in it by means of shares which are supposed to be allotted in proportion to their importance in the trade. The agreement under which the trade is worked is definite until the 1st March, 1911, and thereafter until terminated by a two-thirds majority but any single signatory may retire on giving two months' notice. This combination works on the whole for peace and if there were none such shipowners would be worse off than they are now, while as regards the shippers they would not have such fine fleets at their disposal as they have now with regular and well understood rates of freight to work by. Shortly stated, all the cargo steamers owners pay into the association account on the basis of 12½ per cent of their freight and there is now no chartering except an occasional sailing vessel in the event of the steam tonnage being insufficient for the requirements of the trade. Contributions to the association are divided amongst the members according to their shares and the cargo steamer owners have a pool among themselves. The association has a fixed tariff of freights which applies to all cargo steamers; the mail steamer rates are higher than this tariff (except for weight) and vary according to the demand for space. They can quote the same rates as the cargo steamers if they wish to do so, but it is understood that they will not quote less. The rates of freight are fixed by the rates committee of Davis very often after consultation with the Merchants Committee in the Australian trade.'

1 See p. 21 for the possible effect of this on freight rates.

2 Davis was apparently the name of the first Secretary of the Australian Associated Owners and Brokers and his name continued to be used in the trade up to the early 1960's.

It is not possible to obtain a more detailed account of how the early Davis agreement worked or how successful it was. From the description by Sir Thomas Sutherland it would seem that a freight pool was operated in the Australian outward trade from an early date as well as a minimum tariff. From other evidence by merchants and others, further pieces can be added to the story. For instance, a London merchant in his evidence in 1909 maintained that 'until recently' (he put the date at about 1900) there were no regular sailings. Ships were put on the berth and sailed when they were full. The same merchant maintained in his evidence that the rates of freight of the conference members fluctuated according to the amount of cargo offering but this does not correspond with Sir Thomas Sutherland's evidence unless the merchant concerned was referring to the mail steamers or to the rebate system, which was in fact used in the outward trade from the earliest formation of the conference.

In the northbound or homeward trade, there may well have been some justification for this merchant's complaint. It has been said of the northbound trade from Australia that it was 'ill organised' and participants in it 'aggressive and mutually mistrustful'. Although there were attempts to form a conference (in particular among the British shipowners), these were not very successful in the early days, for much the same reasons as in the Far East trade. That is to say, the commodities being shipped from Australia were bulk commodities such as wheat, ores, wool and skins and as such, tramp shipping was as acceptable to the shipper as the regular liner service. With the introduction of refrigerated ships, which were costly to build and to run, shipowners in the trade did enter into an agreement for the shipment of butter and fruit, but no details of the agreement or the circumstances of its introduction are available.

The first formal agreement between shipowners in the Australian homeward trade for non-refrigerated cargo seems to have come as late as 1909. It was made by British shipowners and covered the charging of minimum rates of freight and an attempt to rationalise sailings. It laid down that agents of the conference lines were to avoid the clashing of sailing dates as far as possible consistent with giving shippers the best service. The agents handling conference vessels were required not to load for shipowners who were not parties to the agreement − with the exception of sailing ships. The shipping companies tried to 'cover the berth' with vessels belonging to, or chartered by the signatories to the agreement. Parties to the agreement were asked to declare the number of vessels they intended to load with details of the space available for the following three months, and the conference then undertook to charter ships to cover any additional space required . In addition there was to be an earnings pool among members each paying one third of their net[1] rate earnings into the pool and the division being made among the participants in proportion to the number of 40 cubic feet which each had had available in the accounting period.

The Australian conference trade in the outward (southbound) direction had employed the rebate system to gain the loyalty of the shippers. The rebate was in the form of a fixed percentage (e.g. 5 per cent) for exclusive dealing with conference members. Sailing ships were excluded from this agreement until 1895, when the rebate system was extended to all vessels in the Australian trade. (By this time the

1 Net rate in this instance being defined as gross rate less forwarding charges at both ends, dumping charges, rebates, and other minor charges.

number of sailing ships in the trade was declining).[1] In the homeward trade it was much more difficult to impose the exclusive dealing arrangements, (although by 1906 in the coastal trade of Australia it was successfully in operation), partly for reasons of over supply of tonnage, but also because by the time the first formal agreement was entered into in the homeward trade the Australian Industries Preservation Act of 1906 had come into operation. This Act came on to the Statute Book as a direct result of the rebate system being used by shipowners in the Australian coastal trade. Under the provisions of the Act if a company 'gives, offers or promises to any person any rebate, refund, discount or reward upon condition that that person deals, or in consideration of that person having dealt with, [the company], to the exclusion of other persons dealing in similar goods or services' then that company would be liable to heavy penalties.

This was the first occasion on which the Australian government intervened to pass legislation which would directly affect shipping interests in Australia — but it was not to be the last time.

Despite their shaky beginnings (at least in the homeward trade) conferences continued to operate in the outward and homeward trades up to the First World War. The outward trade had some difficulties in 1903/1904 when one of the British lines withdrew from the conference agreement because they were dissatisfied with their share of the trade. Other conference members took action against the defaulting member by (a) quoting special rates on ships which were sailing from the berth at the same time as the ships of the ex-member (i.e. 'fighting' ships), and (b) making a general overall reduction by as much as 50 per cent (and more) on all commodities. The ex-member, the line operating on its own, had not sufficient financial resources to combat this sort of retaliation and it rejoined the conference later in the same year; it managed to negotiate, however, an increased share of trade.

Not much has been said so far about new members entering the conference in the early years of development, and indeed little direct information is available. It is evident, however, that new members were parties to the agreements in the early 20th century. The principle of admittance seems to have been that so long as new participants did not encroach upon the interests of existing members they were allowed into the trade.

1919–1939

In the period between the wars the Australian trade was to become much more closely regulated than it had been hitherto. This was due to a number of factors; first, with the slump in primary product prices the freight rate from Australia to Europe became of vital importance; second, costs at Australian ports increased more rapidly than in other parts of the world, with adverse effects on shipowners' profits; and third, trade in the outward direction to Australia grew more rapidly than in the homeward direction.

At the end of the First World War, there was a considerable shortage of shipping space and this inevitably led to an increase in freight rates which reached a peak in 1920. The rise in rates stimulated shipbuilding but the increased tonnage came into use just as the rate of growth of trade was beginning to slacken. Up to that

1 See p. 37

time, in any case, trade had been increasing faster in the southbound direction than in the northbound[1] with the result that an excess of tonnage was available in the northbound direction. In an effort to obtain a full cargo load for the northbound voyage ships called at several ports. One shipowner wrote in 1928: 'shipowners compete so actively that expensive ships follow each other round the coast from port to port taking longer over their voyages than the slower ships took pre-war and then finally sail 12,000 miles without a full load'. This contention is partially verified by statistics available of the number of ships loading at the different ports in 1913 and in five years in the 1920's. The figures are given as a percentage of all loadings made, and it will be seen that in 1913 it was common for ships to call at 4 or 5 ports. This situation continued in the early 1920's but in addition a growing number called at 6 or 7 ports in an attempt to obtain cargo.

Table 2.8 *Ports of call of liner ships, 1913 1924–1928–Australian trade*

	1913[a]	1924	1925	1926	1927	Per cent 1928
Loading at 1 port	. . .	–	2	1	1	1
Loading at 2 ports	3	4	10	8	8	6
Loading at 3 ports	14	23	21	24	24	17
Loading at 4 ports	36	27	31	25	32	30
Loading at 5 ports	38	31	24	21	22	28
Loading at 6 ports	8	13	8	14	7	14
Loading at 7 ports	–	2	3	4	5	2
Loading at 8 ports	–	–	. . .	1	. . .	2
Loading at 9 ports	–	–	–	. . .	–	. . .
Loading at 10 ports	–	–	–	–	. . .	–

(a) 1913 figures cover returns from five companies covering half the steamers only and are not therefore strictly comparable with the later figures.
Note to Table 2.8:
. . . = less than 1 per cent; – = zero.

Figures are also available of the capacity utilisation of refrigerated and general cargo space, and these are shown in the Table 2.9. The under-utilisation of capacity averaged over 10 per cent for ships of six British Lines over the period as a whole, but for refrigerated vessels the monthly percentage average of unused space was as high as 61 per cent in 1927. It was said by one shipowner that the excess of tonnage in the Australian trade was not caused by tramp shipping – 'tramps had learned to avoid Australia by the late 1920's'.

Freight rates in these conditions were difficult to maintain even for the members of the conference. The conference was forced by the pressures of the freight market to reduce their rates in 1925. It was estimated that liner freight rates as a whole fell by 17 per cent in the trade to Australia and by 19 per cent in the northbound trade between 1924 and 1928. Costs at the Australian end of the trade route did not fall, however, and in fact by 1928 costs of bunkering in Australia had about doubled over the 1913 level while in the UK the costs of bunkering had declined by about

1 The following estimates of the increases in the tonnage of trade were made at the time

	Exports from Australia	Imports into Australia
1919–1925	+ 3.8%	+ 38.7%
1922–1926	+ 29.0%	+ 60%

40 per cent between 1924 and 1928. (See Table 2.10). In these circumstances, it is not perhaps surprising that shipping companies were making losses in the Australian trade. Figures prepared by six British companies operating in this trade showed that expenses exceeded earnings by 21 per cent, 17 per cent and 13 per cent in 1926, 1927 and 1928 respectively.

Table 2.9   *Percentage of unused space (1925–28), Australia to Europe – summary for 6 British lines*

	Refrigerated and General Average for year, per cent.	Insulated Space (Monthly Average) per cent
April to December 1924	8.03	53.6
1925	12.04	30.6
1926	15.24	53.8
1927	10.40	61.7
1928	9.23	42.8

Table 2.10   *Bunker prices, UK and Australian ports, 1913, 1920–1928*

	1913	1920	1921	1922	1923	1924	1925	1926	1927	1928
UK ports										
Average of Hull, Liverpool, Glasgow	100.0 (14/-)	n.a.	221.4	178.6	196.4	171.4	142.9	142.9[a]	135.7	125.0
Australian ports										
Sydney	100.0 (13/6)	185.2	229.6	222.2	196.3	196.3	196.3	209.2	216.7	222.2
Melbourne, Adelaide, Fremantle (average)	100.0 (25/-)	160.0	168.0	172.0	174.0	174.0	174.0	174.0	176.0	172.0

(a) Up to the UK coal strike.

In 1928 the conference members raised freight rates in the outward trade to Australia and the producers in Australia, fearful that this increase was a prelude to an increase in rates in the homeward trade, asked the Australian Government to intervene. The government did so by calling a meeting of overseas shipowners and representatives of producers, importers and exporters in Australia.

From this meeting a general agreement seems to have emerged that because of the requirements of the Australian trade – covering both the type of commodities and the seasonal factor – special arrangements would have to be made in order to provide a regular liner service which would be acceptable to both shipper and shipowner. After the meeting therefore, State committees and a Federal committee of Producers, Importers and Exporters were set up simultaneously with State committees and a Federal Committee of Overseas Shipowners. Representatives from these bodies formed the Council of the Australian Overseas Transport Association (AOTA). In addition, Producer Boards were set up and came into operation during the 1930's.

The shipowners agreed to enter into separate agreements for different classes of freight; broadly, these were:

(a) General cargo (excluding bulk cargo such as wheat and flour)
(b) Wool of all kinds
(c) Meat, Eggs and other refrigerated cargo
(d) Dairy produce
(e) Fresh fruit
(f) Citrus fruit

There were two types of freight agreement — the one used for wool was the deferred rebate system, and for all other commodities a contract system was used. This meant that shippers contracted to ship by conference lines exclusively for a given period and they were given a net rate on all shipments. If they broke the conditions of the contract they could be fined.

At the same time shippers agreed to provide forecasts of their requirements for shipping space for 'some time ahead', while on their side the shipowners undertook to provide tonnage for the 'reasonable needs' of the shippers.

A further feature arising out of the meeting was the agreement reached concerning freight rates. It had been customary for shipowners to announce, without consultation with the shipper, when an increase in the freight rate would take place. Under the new arrangements, however, when shipowners in the conference wished to obtain a general increase in freight rates they had to put their case to the AOTA executive, they then had to negotiate with each commodity section, after which there was consultation with the State committees of producers, exporters and importers; finally, the council of AOTA was consulted. By giving its blessing to these arrangements, the Australian government not only gave tacit recognition to the existence of a conference but in addition it agreed to amend the 1906 Industries Preservation Act to allow the rebate and contract agreements to come into operation legally.

The troubles of the Australian trade did not come to an end with the institution of this new found co-operation between members of the shipping conference and the producers and shippers of Australia. There were two main sources of concern for the shipowners. First, the homeward trade continued to be over supplied with tonnage. Throughout the 1930's there are frequent references at meetings of conference members to a 'rationalisation of tonnage' and in 1935 the British lines set up a special committee 'to examine and make recommendations on questions affecting the future rationalisation of tonnage'. In 1936 'all lines agreed to co-operate' and it was reported in October 1936 that 'some lines had reduced their despatches'. There were some lines, however, which did not reduce the number of their ships in the trade and there was little action — apart from exhortation — which other conference members could take. The number of ships despatched to Australia was determined to a certain extent by a member's share in the wool pool, but because ships carrying wool also needed other weight cargo, the conference members attempted to control the 'wool despatches' of individual members.

The second problem still faced by conference members after 1929 was the problem of outside competition. The most well-known example is that of Westralian Farmers, a group of farmers in Western Australia who did not agree with the setting up of AOTA and started an independent line. Despite negotiations with conference members they continued to operate throughout the 1930's. There were two other major competitors to the conference in this period — one of whom finally came to terms with the conference members for the carrying of certain cargo and the other became a full member of the conference.

The conference in its revised form continued to operate with no major upheaval, however, until 1939 when all merchant ships were requisitioned by the government and the conference agreements were left in abeyance.

Summary

This brief outline of the development of the conference system in the period up to 1939 highlights a number of interesting features. It indicates that the early conference organisation was resilient and also comprehensive. Despite adverse circumstances both inside and outside the conferences themselves they survived and developed, indicating that shipowners as a whole gained advantages from the organisation. Conferences do not appear to have been highly monopolistic, inflexible institutions; alternative means of shipment were available and were frequently used and conference organisations were subject to a number of pressures which brought about changes in their organisation. There is no doubt, however, that shipowners felt the need to combine in order to protect their interests, and in such a heavily capitalised industry they felt that their interests were best protected by regulating the shipping space available and the terms which were offered to shippers. Although, as we have seen, conferences developed in different ways, they had certain features in common including:

    (a) maintenance of a fixed minimum tariff for the majority of goods shipped;

    (b) control of the supply of shipping space through the use of sailing restrictions, tonnage restrictions or port restrictions or a combination of all three;

    (c) the use of a revenue pool or a cargo sharing pool so that each member of the conference met his obligation to other members of the conference and to the shippers to carry low-rated as well as high-rated cargo;

    (d) the use of the rebate or, alternatively, the contract system which put a reward on shippers' 'loyalty' to the conference members;

    (e) the use of similar methods to keep 'outsiders' from breaking into the trade while yet maintaining a certain flexibility in the membership of conferences.

As conferences developed so they became accepted not only by shippers but also by governments and, in some cases, governments took an active part in encouraging conference organisation.

In the next chapter we shall see how far the system was maintained or modified in the very different postwar conditions.

APPENDIX I

Volume of UK trade in the Australian, Far Eastern, and Indian areas

Two methods were used to estimate the volume of UK trade in the Far East, Australian, and Indian areas.

Method One

The Annual Statement of Trade for the UK gives details of the total value of UK imports and the total value of UK exports. It also gives the same information for each country of the world. It was therefore possible to extract the figures of UK imports from and exports to Australia, India and the Far East. (For this purpose the Far East was taken as Japan, China, Hong Kong, Malaya and the Philippines). These figures were then collated to give a total value figure for the Eastern and Australian trades.

These value figures for both total UK imports and exports and for imports and exports in the Eastern and Australian trades were then divided through by A.H. Imlah's net import price index and export price index published in *'Economic*

Elements in the Pax Britannica' (pp. 94—98). The disadvantages of using this composite index were unavoidable; such an index cannot take full account of the different commodities which entered into the Eastern and Australian trades as compared with the total of UK trade, but it was a consistent series and provided a rough estimate of the volume of trade in the period. The volume figures of exports and imports were then added to give an estimate of (a) the total volume of UK trade and (b) the volume of UK trade in the Eastern and Australian areas. The results are shown in Figure 1.

Method Two

In Table 2.5 the results of the second method of calculating the volume of trade in the Eastern and Australian trades are shown (the column referred to as 'adjusted tonnage'). Unfortunately, this second method of obtaining volume figures could be applied to imports only.

The Annual Statement of Trade gives details not only of the value of UK imports but also, where possible, a weight in tons or other appropriate measurement. The weight figures for UK imports from the Far East, Australia, and India were converted to a standard measure and summed to give a total weight in tons of UK imports from these areas.

The value of the commodities making up this total weight was then obtained and the proportion which this represented of the *total* value of UK imports from these areas was calculated from 1880 to the mid-1890's. This proportion was over 90 per cent in the 1880's, declining to just under 90 per cent in the 1890's.

On the assumption that the average weight/value is not very different for commodities for which a weight figure was available from those where it was not, the weight figure obtained from the Annual Statement of Trade was adjusted by multiplying the figure so obtained for each year by the ratio of total value to the value of goods included in the tonnage figure for that year. The figure so obtained is the 'adjusted tonnage' figure shown in Table 2.5.

References: A.H. Imlah. *Economic Elements in the Pax Britannica. Studies in British Foreign Trade in the Nineteenth Century.* Cambridge, Mass. 1958.
Annual Statements of Trade of the United Kingdom. HMSO.

APPENDIX II
Supply of shipping capacity

The estimated rate of growth of shipping capacity shown in Figure 1 (p.20) was obtained by adjusting the increase in the net tonnage of ships registered in the UK to take account of the decrease in the average number of days taken per journey in the Eastern and Australian trades.

1. Sources of data used

a. Average number of days per voyage by steam and sailing ships. In the period 1870—1900 very little data are available on the number of days taken per voyage for steam and sailing ships, but for the years 1873, 1887 and 1897 figures are available for the contract times for mail steamers and our estimates are based on these figures. For the year 1897 estimates are also available of the number of days less than the contract times which, on average, ships took for the voyage. These estimates have been subtracted from the contract times to obtain an estimate of the average voyage time in 1897. The same information is not available for either 1873 or 1887 and it is possible that ships took, on average, less than the contract time in these years also; if so, then our estimate of the decrease in the average voyage time could be an over-estimate.

The time taken for a voyage by a mail steamer is likely to have been shorter than that for the ordinary cargo vessel. We are interested, however, not so much in the absolute, as in the rate of change of voyage times. Evidence which we found for the China trade seemed to indicate that the rate of change in the voyage time was similar both for mail and for cargo steamers.

Very little information was available on the length of time taken for voyages to the East and to Australia by sailing ships, and this is not surprising as the voyage time would be variable depending on weather conditions. It was assumed that on average there was no decrease in the time taken for voyages by sailing ships between 1887 and 1897. By 1897 the amount of sailing ship tonnage in total shipping tonnage was relatively small.

b. *Proportions of steam and sail in total tonnage.* Data for Australia and India on total tonnage of steam vessels entered and cleared are contained in Accounts and Papers: Statistical Tables for the Colonies, 1899. No separate figures are given for steam vessels in 1873 and the proportion was therefore estimated by extrapolation. The proportion for China was estimated from data for other countries.

c. *Volume of UK exports and imports.* The value figures for imports and exports contained in the Annual Statement of Trade for the years 1873, 1887 and 1897 were deflated by using Imlah's export and import price indices (see Appendix I).

2. Methods of estimation

Our aim was to obtain an estimate of the increase in speed (or decline in the average journey time) for the Eastern and Australian trades taken together. The following method was used.

    a. The separate estimates obtained for each of the three areas (Australia, China and India) of the average number of days taken for the voyages by steam and by sailing ships were weighted to give combined estimates for each area of the average length of journey taking both steam and sailing ships into account. The proportion of steam and sailing ships in use in the trade in each year were used as weights.

    b. The overall average voyage time for each area was then weighted in accordance with the importance of the trade to and from the area (i.e. by volume of trade – see 1c. above). This gave a weighted average voyage time for the whole area for each of the years 1873, 1887 and 1897.

    c. The decline in the average voyage time between these three years was then expressed as an annual rate of increase in average speed. The rate was calculated separately for the period from 1873 to 1887 (showing a faster rate of increase in speed) and between 1887 and 1897.

d. The annual rate of increase in the tonnage of ships registered in UK was also calculated for the same periods.

e. An estimate of the increase in the supply of shipping capacity, between 1873 and 1897, taking into account the increase in the speed of ships, was obtained by the addition of the annual average rates of growth in c. and d. The result is shown in Figure 1.

The main source of data on length of voyage time is R.J. Cornewall-Jones *'The British Merchant Service'*, 1898.

Recent and Present Organisation and
Practices in Shipping Conferences

1. Developments in the post-war period, 1945–1970

a. The Australian trade

In the second world war, as in the first, British shipping was requisitioned by the War Office and although the conference system remained in existence, the actual machinery was not in operation. In the outward trade, the conference organisation was resumed soon after the end of the war; that is to say, shipowners in the conference came together to agree freight rates and shippers were expected to confine their shipments to conference vessels if they wished to obtain 'contract' terms. Increases in rates were negotiated from time to time in consultation with the Australian and New Zealand Merchants' and Shippers' Association and with other manufacturers' associations. The importance of manufacturers' associations in the Australian trade is illustrated in Chapter 6 which gives a number of case histories of conference rates and policies being adopted on representation from the manufacturers' associations.

The conference arrangements in the homeward trade were not resumed immediately after the end of the war. The continuation of bulk food buying by the Ministry of Food until the mid-1950's meant that the conference was not fully operational in the sense that homeward freight rates for the major commodities were agreed with the Ministry and not with the Australian producer. The contracts for the supply of foodstuffs were made between the two governments on a f.o.b. basis and the UK Ministry of Food then contracted with the shipping conference to carry the food to the United Kingdom. For the most part refrigerated ships were required and the direct bulk purchasing by the Ministry continued until 1954. During this period, the conference negotiated with the Ministry for three increases in rates of freight and in the early 1950's the AOTA became anxious that the Ministry of Food would agree too easily to pay increased rates which would then have to be accepted by Australian producers and exporters when the arrangements for bulk buying ceased. Assurances by the Ministry and an agreement to include AOTA in future negotiations over rate increases pacified the Australian producers somewhat and the general level of rates when the Ministry of Food had withdrawn (in 1954) and the old AOTA organisation was in full operation once more, was 36 per cent above the 1948 level of rates.

As was indicated in Chapter 2, however, the most important commodity in the Australian homeward trade is wool and the bulk buying agreements of the UK Ministry of Food did not extend to wool. The wool pool of the interwar period was revived by the conference members in 1946; the German and Italian lines had not at that time been re-admitted to the conference and their share of the wool pool was divided amongst the other members. (The Italian lines rejoined the Conference in 1948 and the German lines in 1954.) There have been considerable 'ups and downs' in the Australian/European wool trade in the postwar period; it increased rapidly in the immediate postwar years but two factors contributed to its decline in the 1950's and 1960's: (a) the growth of synthetic fibres in European markets and (b) the growth of Australian/Japanese trade; Japan is now the largest single buyer of wool. There has been considerable manoeuvering in the basic wool shares of members in the Australia/Europe trade since 1946; not only have the German lines pressed for an increased share of the trade but a Russian State line and a Yugoslav State line have been admitted to the wool pool.

The organisation and operation of the conference in its prewar form was not destined to last long after the withdrawal of the Ministry of Food. As a result of a proposed increase of 10 per cent in homeward rates by the conference lines in 1955, the Australian government was once more asked to intervene. The shipping lines had asked for an increase on the grounds of increased costs, and although both shipowners and shippers made separate assessments of costs they could not come to any agreement. In the end, the Australian Government was able to force agreement on both sides and a rate increase of 7½ per cent was settled. Neither side was satisfied, however, and further meetings were held the final outcome of which was an agreed 'Formula' which was to be the basis of all future negotiations on freight rate increases. The Formula was an arrangement whereby the actual operational and financial accounts of all voyages were supplied to independent accountants by all members. The ships to be included were those which made a direct cargo voyage to and from Australia; i.e. if a ship was carrying goods to Australia as part of a multistop voyage, it could not be included in the returns, nor could ships carrying more than 200 passengers.

The Formula not only took into account the variable costs of each voyage, such as crew's wages and stevedoring charges, but also made allowances for the replacement of capital and for a return on capital estimated to be that rate which would keep shipowners in the industry. The Formula did not lay down any requirements on ports of call, regularity of service, or type of service; it was assumed that these would continue as under the previous system of contractual agreement. Although the agreement on the Formula lasted until 1968, with modifications in 1959 and 1964 to the rate of return on capital employed in the trade, there was growing dissatisfaction on the side of conference members, and with the advent of container ships a new agreement was negotiated.

In the meantime, however, the Australian government had passed the Australian Trade Practices Act of 1966. This Act was extended to shipping in 1967 and lays down that shippers in Australia are to form themselves into a single central body to be known as Australia/Europe Shippers Association (AESA). The new AESA replaces AOTA; it includes representatives from all the old producer boards but now also includes metal producers. It is for shippers only, but shipowners who wish to trade in Australia have to give an undertaking (which has to be filed with the Commonwealth Government in Canberra) that on the request of the AESA they will enter into negotiations with that body on rates or other matters. If such negotiations are opened, the shipowners (in this case the conference) must provide all 'reasonable'[1] information as a basis for the negotiations.

In addition, the Australian government brought considerable pressure to bear on shipowners to bring about a rationalisation of services. 'Rationalisation' in this context meant that fewer liners should call at each Australian port and the shipowners felt that this could not be achieved except by some sort of revenue pooling agreement among themselves. The reason for this is that if, for purposes of rationalisation, liners belonging to some conference members are prevented from going to certain ports, it could mean that one or two shipowners would get the 'cream' of the trade and the others would get the low-yielding, seasonal or awkward cargo.

A comprehensive agreement was therefore drawn up by conference members. This agreement covers both ports of loading and discharge (in the UK and Europe) of conference vessels, the number of sailings of each conference member, the amount of cargo to be carried in both outward and homeward directions, and arrangements for an earnings (or revenue) pool among all members of the conference. The agreement was scheduled to last for six years and with the exception of a few special items it covered all commodities, including refrigerated cargo, and all ports.[2] The Australian Government gave the agreement its blessing.

The existence of the AESA does not mean that a central contract is negotiated for all commodities. The agreement on such matters as freight rates and services to be provided is made with the individual shipper or with the Producer Board concerned. Any agreement so made, however, has to have the approval of the AESA. The conference has agreements with all the main Producer Boards, and most of the agreements include the provision of estimates by the Producer Board of the cargo likely to come forward in the next year so that the conference can then make plans to 'cover the trade' which is part of their obligation under the agreement. Penalty clauses affecting both sides are included. The working of the new arrangement depends a good deal on the forecasts of the cargo coming forward.

The first three years of operation of this type of agreement cannot be said to have been entirely satisfactory, particularly for some products. For example, the forecasts of the amount of shipping space required for certain products has been wildly inaccurate and the shipping companies have been forced to charter additional vessels to meet their obligation to cover the trade; alternatively, they have found that the produce coming forward is less than that forecast and ships are under utilised.

b. The Far East trade

The British and French member lines began to operate the Far Eastern Freight Conference again immediately after the war. The Dutch and Scandinavian Lines recommenced their services in 1948. The German and Japanese merchant fleets had been requisitioned and they were in no position to take up their pre-war membership as early as 1948, but the lines of both the latter countries rejoined the conference in 1952/53.

---

1 It has not yet been clearly and unambiguously established what is meant by reasonable.

2 The pool is described in detail later in this chapter at Section 2. e.

The basic arrangements of the Far Eastern Conference in the postwar period have not been so closely controlled as in the Indian and Australian trades. There is, even now, no revenue pool of any kind and the trade is regulated by means of (a) restrictions on the number of sailings which members can make in any one period; (b) restrictions on the amount of cargo which members can carry in any one period; and (c) restrictions on the ports which any one member can serve. All members are subject to one or a combination of these restrictions which were not relaxed even when there was a shortage of shipping space in the immediate postwar years. Instead, vessels were chartered on conference account in an attempt to deal with the cargo coming forward[1] but there was a good deal of dissatisfaction among shippers in the early years. Certain of the cargo sharing arrangements which had been in operation in the pre-war period were revived in 1946, at first as an interim arrangement, but later on a more permanent basis. These pooling arrangements have since been modified to take account of changing conditions in the trade but they have not been carried as far as a revenue pool and a complete rationalisation of shipping tonnage.

In other ways this conference has, however, moved in the same direction as the Australian trade; for example, in regard to its relations with shippers. We have seen that as far back as 1909 the Royal Commission on Shipping Rings recommended the setting up of shippers' councils to represent the interests of shippers in various trades and this recommendation was endorsed by the Imperial Shipping Committee in the 1930's. In the mid-1950's a Shippers' Council was established in the United Kingdom, and similar organisations were set up in Europe with a European Shippers' Council forming the apex of the pyramid. The conference members recognised that it would be in their interests to establish good relations with the shippers' councils on a national and international level, and by 1961 they were consulted over the terms and conditions of the contract entered into by the conference and shippers as well as the length of notice which should be given before rate increases come into effect. It was also agreed that the intention to increase rates would be communicated to shippers' councils in advance to enable them to be in a position to make representation to the conference. This informal consultation was formalised after discussions among West European Transport Ministers in 1963 which culminated in the conclusion of a Note of Understanding. The Note provided for regular meetings between shippers and shipowners in the conference and provision was made for the settlement of differences which could not be solved by mutual discussion by an independent panel.[2] The conference shipowners are represented in their discussions on general principles with European Shippers Councils by CENSA.[3] The application of those principles to individual conference trades is a matter for the conference concerned and not CENSA. Of course CENSA and the Shippers' Councils are not concerned only with the Far Eastern Freight Conference, but this conference is the one in the three which we have studied which has had a dispute referred to CENSA. On the homeward side, shippers' councils or similar associations have also been formed in Hong Kong, Malaysia, Singapore, and Japan,[4] as well as in India and Ceylon.

1 Each conference member would contribute towards the cost of any chartered ships.

2 This does not extend, however, to general across-the-board freight rate changes.

3 CENSA also has machinery for dealing with disputes between conference and non-conference shipowners. For further details see Section 2.C.(iii).

4 In Japan, the organisation concerned is an exporters' association known as the Freight Commission of All Japan Exporters' Association.

It has been mentioned that in particular the discussions with the shippers' councils on the new form of contract which this conference introduced in the early 1960's were valuable and informative to both sides on points of detail. The conference still offers the shipper the choice of a contract or a deferred rebate, with the exception of the Japan homeward trade and the Philippines trade. As in the Philippines trade in the inter-war period, the Japanese trade in 1950 came under the influence of American anti-trust law, and the conference had to adjust its practices and agreements accordingly. The Japanese trade came to be governed by separate conferences in the outward and homeward directions, and certain documents relating to conference activities have to be lodged with the Japanese Ministry of Transportation. There was apparently no objection to the deferred rebate system provided it did not exceed 10 per cent. One of the difficulties which conference members experienced in the Japan homeward trade, however, was the use of the f.o.b. 'escape' clause. During the early 1960's, it was found that more and more shippers were using non-conference lines and the reason given was that the goods were f.o.b. shipments, i.e. that the buyers, who have the legal right to specify the method of shipment, were asking for shipment by non-conference lines. This had come to such a stage by the mid-1960's that conference members felt that action had to be taken. It was therefore decided after much discussion to introduce a special inducement to shippers in the form of an extra discount payable so long as they eschewed the use of the f.o.b. clause in the existing contract. This in effect gave three rates in the Japan Homeward trade — (a) the non-contract rate (b) the contract rate giving shippers a discount of 9½ per cent and (c) the special contract rate offering a discount of a further 2½ per cent. However, complaints were made by shippers to the Japanese Fair Trade Commission and, after a full enquiry the conference was forced to drop the special contract rate; this was replaced by a fidelity rebate arrangement whereby shippers who did not invoke the f.o.b. escape clause over a 4 month period were entitled to claim 2½% deferred rebate on shipments made during that shipment period. The essential difference between the two arrangements was that in the first case the conference was entitled to terminate shippers' entitlement to 9½% discount if they were in breach of the special contract whereas if they failed to qualify for the fidelity rebate under the revised arrangements they merely forfeited their claim to the 2½% rebate but did not in any way prejudice their entitlement to the 9½% discount under the shippers' contract.

One special feature of the Far Eastern Freight Conference deserves a mention. As we have seen, in the early years of its development the Far Eastern Conference was very much concerned in trade with China. Even between the wars the China trade was still important for conference members. In the post-war period this trade had declined. Nominally the China trade is still part of the conference and the Chinese Government uses some conference members' ships, but rates and increases in rates were negotiated with the Chinese Government by those lines, known as the China rate agreement Lines, which still wish to service the China trade. These rates are nett and are lower than conference rates from Hong Kong, since neither shippers nor carriers have contractual obligations towards each other.

The Far Eastern Freight Conference has also had considerable changes in its membership, and has had difficulties with non-conference members. These problems are dealt with more fully in Section 2.c.

c. The Indian and Pakistan trades

The major development in the Indian trades in the postwar period was the division of the continent into India and Pakistan. With the achievement of independence from British rule, the Indian and Pakistan governments also wished to obtain greater independence from British shipping which had until the postwar period been dominant in the Indian trades. There had been an Indian shipping line in operation before 1939,[1] but after independence two Indian lines became members with full rights in the India/Pakistan-Europe Conference (with performance limitations in different areas) and it was not long before the National Pakistan Line joined the conference and obtained similar rights. In the agreement now in operation, the Indian lines have the preponderant share in their national trade and similarly the Pakistan line in their national trade.

With the partition of the continent, the direction of trade has also been affected. For example, tea which was grown in Assam and was routed via both Chittagong and Calcutta began to move, after partition, almost entirely through Calcutta; the tea which was grown in the area which had become East Pakistan was adequate for the home consumption of East and West Pakistan and little remained for export. This has raised difficulties for members of the conferences. We have seen that the Indian trades developed as port conferences; shipowners serve a port so long as there is profitable trade to be had at that port. When that trade is diverted to another port for political (or other) reasons, the shipowners who have lost the trade claim that they have loading rights in the port to which the trade has been diverted even though they have never called at that port in the past; their justification for such a claim is that they are serving the trade and not the port. There has been a good deal of dissension among conference members on this issue since the 1950's. The Calcutta/ Chittagong problems were settled, however, by member lines broadly following their previous trades. Thus certain previously dominant lines in the Chittagong trade entered the Calcutta trade and conversely, the dominating lines in the Calcutta trade entered the Pakistan trade. This result seems to have been obtained more by pressure than negotiation but a reconciliation was finally achieved.

Although little is known about the working of the conferences in the Indian trades in the pre-war period, regulation of the trade in the immediate postwar period was by means of control over the number of sailings each line could make in any one period, by the division among conference members of loading and discharging rights at various ports, and by tariff agreements. After 1948 these arrangements became increasingly unsatisfactory for the European shipowners operating in the trade. The Indian and Pakistan national lines wanted to obtain more of the carrying trade for their own ships, and these members engaged in 'malpractices' such as rate cutting and flag discrimination. The Indian government at one stage decreed that all government cargo should be carried in Indian ships to save foreign exchange. These 'malpractices' led to members sending ships one way or the other with little or no cargo.

1   See Ch. 2, p. 28

52

In the late 1950's and early 1960's it was agreed by member lines that this state of affairs could not continue. Capacity utilisation of ships was falling steadily, and as the British Lines still had over 50 per cent of the trade they were becoming increasingly concerned over this. A meeting of all member lines was therefore held in 1960, and in 1961 a new ten year agreement among all members came into effect. This is a comprehensive revenue pooling agreement. There are four main conferences: UK-India/Pakistan Eastbound, India/Pakistan-UK Westbound, Continent of Europe-India/Pakistan Eastbound and India/Pakistan-Continent Westbound. Within each main conference there are various subsections (reflecting the historical development from port conferences) and membership of these sub-sections varies. Members have carrying rights and obligations within each section and an overall share of the trade. The overall share is also an obligation, i.e. each member is obliged to carry his share of the trade and a financial adjustment is made at the end of the year between the over-carriers and under-carriers. The original basic shares were broadly determined by reference to the trade of the individual lines in the Indian or Pakistan trade as a whole or, in the case of the Indian and Pakistan lines, as the outcome of negotiation on what should be the entitlement of the national lines in their national trade. An interesting feature of this conference is that it makes allowance for the national lines to increase their share of the trade over the ten years period. That is to say, lines of other countries serving the trade will gradually reduce their overall share while the national lines will carry more.

As in the Far Eastern Freight Conference, the national lines are collected into groups, i.e. the British group, French group, Indian group, Pakistan group, and so on, and the share of the trade is allocated to the group as a whole. The division of trade within the group is a matter for the lines within each group. An adjunct to the pooling agreement was that the conference agreed to a fixed notice period and a period of stability in respect of freight rate increases. It was also agreed to consult with Shippers' Councils and other interested parties before a rate increase was implemented. The working of the 1961 agreement seems to have been satisfactory for the majority of the members, and although it was open to any member to give notice of a desire to renegotiate the Agreement, this was not done and it has continued in operation subsequent to the initial ten years.

2. Organisation of shipping conferences

The development of the conference system has now been traced up to the present day. In this section a general description will be given of the methods used by conferences to organise international freight transport and only occasionally will reference be made to specific conferences. The following aspects of conference operation will be dealt with in this section.

 a. Geographical coverage
 b. Membership
 c. Competition from 'outsiders'
 d. Output sharing
 e. Revenue pooling

a. Geographical coverage

From the description given of the early development of shipping conferences it will be realised that geographical organisation of conferences grew from the patterns of

53

trade and ports of call existing at the time of conference formation. As trade patterns changed, new areas and new ports were added and ports which had been important previously declined and were no longer regarded as conference ports, i.e. ports which although remaining within the conference sphere no longer commanded a volume of cargo which justified a direct service.

The present coverage of the conferences we have been studying are shown in Appendix A., but we now examine how a conference –
    a. Decides on the limit of its area.
    b. Determines whether a port should be a conference port.
    c. Deals with shipments which are not destined for a conference port.

On the first point it is partly a matter of shipping economics and partly a gentleman's agreement that members of one conference do not encroach on the preserves of another conference. It is obviously more economical to be able to obtain full capacity loads with as few calls as possible, but a ship which was half empty might be tempted to call, for example, at Singapore on its return from Australia to Europe to pick up cargo and thus, for the greater part of its journey, it would have a full load. A shipowner would of course have to calculate the loading time[1] and port dues (particularly if there was no cargo to discharge) and weigh these costs against the additional revenue which he would obtain from the call. It should be borne in mind however that membership of conferences is overlapping, that is, any one shipowning company could be a member of a number of conferences and therefore, shipowners who are members of all conferences operating in the East have only economic constraints to prevent them from calling at several ports in different continents.[2] Conferences have devised various definitions and classifications for different ports; they are as follows.

    (a) *Base ports*. These are ports which are served regularly and frequently both for loading and discharge of cargo. The tariffs quoted are for shipment to or from these base ports, and the reason they are base ports is almost invariably because of the large amount of cargo coming forward (coming into the port for shipment outwards). It is not quite as straightforward as this, however, for a port can be a base port for one particular type of cargo but an outport for all other types of cargo. An example of this is Dundee which is a base port for jute from East Pakistan but an outport for all other types of cargo. This does not mean, however, that all the vessels in the conference serve all the base ports on every voyage. What it does mean is that when cargo is accepted for a base port it is charged at the tariff rate even though the carrier may have to arrange transhipment.

    (b) *Direct ports*. These are ports which would be served at tariff rates or at tariff rates plus a small additional charge if there was sufficient cargo coming forward. If the cargo is insufficient to justify a direct call it would be dealt with on a transhipment basis at a 'transhipment additional' based on costs incurred, as for outports.

    (c) *Outports*. These are ports which are not on the itinerary of the normal ports of call of conference members, but members provide a service to

1 This may also be to the detriment of a shipowner's base trade because time spent in a way-port could affect services provided in the main trade.

2 See Chapter 8. Section 2.

54

them when required so that they can discharge their obligation to 'meet the requirements of the trade'. Because the amount of cargo coming forward is insufficient to warrant a regular direct service to outports, conference members arrange to load and discharge cargo at outports by transhipping in coastal vessels and charging a transhipment fee. This fee scale is agreed by all conference members and is roughly equivalent to the cost of the cheapest method of on-carriage.

Sailing rights of members in various ports differ; for example, in the UK, non-UK, members reach agreement with the UK members on the extent of their participation at UK ports, and a similar position exists in Scandinavia.

The classification of ports as base ports or direct ports depends very much on the amount of cargo coming forward and on the loading and unloading facilities available at a particular port. The first factor will differ according to the direction of trade. Thus in one trade provision may be made for direct calls at Dublin while in another, provision may be made for direct calls at Dundee.

If a shipper requires delivery to a port other than a conference port, an additional charge for transhipment is made. Maximum transhipment rates are also laid down as part of the conference agreement and whether the shipowner does the transhipment in his own ships or employs coastal vessels to do it the charge is the same; conferences usually try to establish that carriage with transhipment is not less than carriage direct. The most frequent type of transhipment arrangement is from the Antwerp/Hamburg range of ports to Scandinavian outports, or transhipment in the UK to, for example, the West Indies. Since 1963 the transhipment trade outward from Scandinavia has been subject to special regulations by the conference in the Far East trade, following complaints from the Scandinavian lines within the conference that indirect price cutting was taking place. The conference now has an arrangement with pre-carriers, i.e. coastal shipping lines in UK, North Continent, and Scandinavia, in respect of the rates and the coverage of the berth. At one time rates were traditionally an agreed percentage of ocean freight rates and the conference had a special committee which maintained a balance between the precarriers rate and the ocean freight rate percentage. This percentage arrangement no longer applies and pre-carriage rates are now quoted. The individual shipper is not affected by this arrangement, the conference rate for port additional or transhipment rate is quoted in the tariff and is subject either to nett terms or to the deferred rebate.

There is one other type of port which should be mentioned and this is the so-called wayport. There is no clear definition of a wayport. From its name it might simply be thought to be a port 'on the way' between two terminal points on the main trade route, but a wayport on one main trade could be the terminal point of another. For example, Accra would be a wayport in the UK/Continent-South Africa trade, but it is a terminal port for the UK/Continent-West Africa trade. Wayports can be categorised in various ways such as —

(1) A wayport pure and simple which is a minor port and/or minor trade *en route* between main ports at which lines call, and to which ultimately there is some recognised regulation of the trade from that port by conference

members. An example of this would be Red Sea ports to ports in Europe (before the closure of the Suez Canal).

(2)A wayport which is a geographical definition of a port (such as Accra) which technically is a wayport but then in itself becomes large enough to become a terminal port.

b. Membership

In the early years membership of the main conferences was dominated by British shipowners, and although they are still important members their dominance is not now quite so evident.

It was explained earlier[1] that there are two types of conference, 'open' and 'closed'. In an open conference, there is no restriction on entry into the conference. Any shipowner trading along a particular route may become a member of the local conference so long as he agrees to charge the common tariff rates and to observe any other conditions which may be laid down such as the ability to provide an agreed minimum service. In a closed conference, however, membership is not automatic. A shipowner must make application for membership if he is to run a service without opposition on a particular route. In this section we try to summarise the factors which have governed membership and note any changes in emphasis which have taken place.

In the evidence which we were able to examine concerning applications for membership, it has been clear that the shipowner must have a permanent interest in the trade he seeks to join. For example, an American shipowner operating from the United States would find it difficult to gain admittance to the UK-Australia Conference. There are exceptions to this, however, in that two Japanese shipping companies have been for many years members of the Outward Continent-Australia Conference. Their membership is of long standing dating back to the 1890's. It does mean, however, that national shipping lines have a strong case to be admitted to membership. The trend in the last fifteen years has been towards the admission to the conferences we have studied of national lines from India, Pakistan, Philippines, Malaysia, Singapore, Italy, Poland, Russia, among other nations to one or other of the conferences. On the other hand, membership has been refused to at least one Greek line which wanted to deploy its ships in the trade between UK/North Continent-Far East trade.[2] The reasoning behind this is that if a 'cross trader', or a ship operator who uses mainly chartered vessels, is admitted then he will have no permanent interest in the trade and will discontinue his service if his ships can be employed more profitably elsewhere. For the same reason it has normally been made a condition of membership that members own the vessels they use and do not rely on chartered ships. Here again, however, there is an exception to this rule in the Far Eastern Freight Conference in that one of the new national lines has been given dispensation to use chartered vessels for a limited period.

1   Chapter 1.

2   This line was in fact later offered a limited number of sailings in the trade, but negotiations about this were still proceeding in 1971.

A right to be in the trade in the sense that the shipping line is a 'national'[1] of one of the countries concerned in the trade is often a necessary but not always a sufficient condition to be admitted to membership of a particular conference. Another factor which may be taken into account is whether there is adequate (or perhaps more than adequate) coverage of the trade by the existing members of the conference. There was a period immediately after the war in both the Australian and Far Eastern trades when in fact the 'coverage of the berth' by the existing conference members was insufficient for the trade that was coming forward. Applications for membership were refused to several shipowners on the grounds that pre-war members, i.e. German and Japanese shipowners, would shortly be re-entering the trade and the admission of new members at the earlier date would have led to over-tonnaging later. Conversely, in recent years, new members (mainly national lines) have been admitted to these conferences even though the berth was already sufficiently well supplied with shipping capacity for the needs of the trade at that time. In these instances, existing members had to accept a smaller share of the trade and either run their ships at less than full capacity or re-deploy them in another trade.

Another important factor in the admission of new members is the financial strength of the potential member. That is to say, if the applicant has sufficient financial strength to force his way into the conference if membership is refused then it may be granted without recourse to 'fighting'. More often than not, however, a trial of strength does take place.

The admission of new members to a conference requires in most conferences a unanimous vote in favour. The reasoning behind this is that if a new member is accepted, then all members will be affected in some way and they must feel confident of the new member's ability to adhere to the rules of the conference and to meet the obligations of a conference member. This is one of the few instances in which a unanimous vote is nearly always required. For other matters, such as freight rate increases, a majority vote (varying from 51 per cent to a two-thirds majority depending on the conference) is sufficient.

c. Competition from 'outsiders'

This aspect of conference operation is closely linked with applications for membership. There have been cases where the only way in which a shipping company could gain entry to a shipping conference was by setting up a rival service and persuading shippers to use it. Alternatively, there have been producers who have successfully set up their own shipping lines and by this means have gained membership of, or at least association with, the conference operating in their area.

In the early days of conference formation, competition to conferences came mainly from lines which had previously been members and from the tramp vessels. In the 1920's and 1930's when the conference system had become established, the competition tended to come from shippers who were dissatisfied with conference rates or arrangements or both, or producers who were also shipowners and wanted to deploy their ships to the best advantage. An example of the latter type of competition occurred in the late 1920's/early 1930's in the Far Eastern and Australian

---

1 It would be difficult to give an unambiguous definition of a 'national' line, but in this context it is meant to indicate a shipping line which is financed and operated by nationals of the country concerned.

trades. A large British firm of meat producers and shippers tried to enter the Australian meat trade and to re-deploy some of their refrigerated ships from the Far East. They gave notice to the conference that they would be entering the trade from Australia to the UK/Continent in 1934. The Australian Tonnage Committee (as the conference was called) accepted the inevitable and admitted the line to membership with each of the then members slightly reducing their share of the trade. Trade in the 1930's was not growing in the way it has in the post war years, but the new British line was accommodated and even given an allocation of the wool tonnage pool.

A further example in the inter-war period of a large shipper setting up a shipping company in opposition to the conference is the case of the West Australian Farmers. After the setting up of OSRA in 1929, the West Australian Farmers continued to protest at the rates charged by conference members which they considered to be excessive. The line set up by West Australian Farmers ran a service of chartered vessels, and it was not until 1937 that agreement with the conference was reached. This agreement gave associate membership of the conference to the line.

A factor which perhaps accounted for much of the competition to the conference in the pre-war period was the slow growth in trade. One independent line which gave members of the Australian conference considerable trouble was one which was originally carrying copra in bulk (an 'open rated' cargo) from the south sea islands. The independent line which did in fact charter vessels in the open market was itself encroached upon in its copra trade (by a conference member) and in turn it looked for other cargo with which to fill its ships. The most convenient cargo was wool and the independent line offered rates which were below the conference tariff in order to cover the cost of its chartered ships. The conference dealt with this problem by agreeing to provide a certain amount of cargo for the independent line on the understanding that the company would abstain from carrying any other Australian cargo with the exception of copra and a limited amount of wool. The arrangement was for five years and covered the northbound direction only, i.e. the company said it had no intention of carrying cargo *to* Australia; and its ports of call were limited by the agreement.

In the post-war period conferences have experienced competition from three main sources:

(i) 'National flag' lines (state-owned or state-subsidised lines).
(ii) Lines already established in other trades and wanting to enter new trades.
(iii) Incidental outsiders — lines which do not provide a regular scheduled service but operate in a way similar to tramp vessels.

(i) *National flag lines.* Included in this section are the shipping lines which the emergent countries have now developed, for example, India, Pakistan, Singapore, Malaysia and the Philippines each run a national line now, and they have become members of conferences with a defined, and in some cases, a growing share of the trade. In most instances there is only one national line, but in some cases a second national line has tried to enter the trade and conference members have regarded the second line as an 'outsider', and where necessary have taken action to combat such competition.[1]

1 See Section 2c(iii) for a summary of action which conferences can take in such cases.

58

A second group of national flag lines which have encroached upon conference shares of the trade are the lines of East European countries, including the Soviet Union. The Soviet Union has been most prominent in the Australian trade where it despatched its own ships to lift cargoes of wool. But the Russians found that in some cases the ships despatched had space available which could be used to take general cargo and they therefore offered to carry general cargo at rates below that quoted by the conference. Similarly a Polish National line, which had become an associate member of the homeward conference from the Far East in the 1960s, remained outside the conference in the outward trade and was lifting increasing amounts of conference cargo from conference ports to the Far East to supplement their carryings from their national ports which were outside the conference. The conference members did not pursue a rate war against these national flag lines but protected their interests in the normal manner under their contractual arrangements with shippers. In 1968 the Russian line became a full member of the Europe-Australian conferences outward and homeward, and the Polish line (Polish Ocean Lines) became a full member of the Far Eastern Freight Conference in 1971, having been an associate member since 1963.

It is interesting to note that those national flag lines which have operated as outsiders have usually in the end become members of a conference. The reason for this is not too difficult to find. In all cases the national lines have gained access to ports and markets which they did not have when operating outside the conference system. For example, the Russian shipping line now has limited rights to lift and discharge cargo from North Continental ports.

It is also noteworthy that the conferences have in some instances relaxed one of the 'rules' of membership in the case of national lines; that is that a member must use owned tonnage in the trade and not chartered vessels. One Eastern national line, when it first became a member of the conference, had no vessels of its own and was allowed to use chartered tonnage for a period. The service also operated on a very irregular basis for some considerable time and while there is no obligation on members to mount the specific number of sailings to which they are entitled, there is an unwritten obligation that a conference member should be able to run a regular scheduled service.

National flag lines which are owned by or strongly supported by their governments are, of course, in a very strong position vis à vis the conference. It has been shown in the case of India[1] that where a relatively large proportion of the cargo is government controlled, it is possible to influence the use of ships for transporting the cargo to the detriment of the other lines in the trade. National flag lines often have entirely different objectives from a commercial shipping line. These objectives may be (a) the maintenance of a low rate of freight for their exports (which makes if difficult for the conference as a whole to obtain increases in rates of freight when they are commercially necessary) or (b) the acquisition of foreign exchange irrespective of the profitability of running the national line.

Not all national flag lines have been admitted as members of the conference system, however, and there are instances where, although national flag lines have represented very real competition, conference members have been very unwilling to give way and to grant membership to yet another line of the country concerned. A case of this kind occurred in the early 1950's when a Japanese shipping line which

1   See p. 52

59

had been operating in the American trade, tried to gain admission to the UK/Continent-Far East trade. There were at that time two other Japanese lines in the Far East conference and, although the trade was a fast growing one, the members were reluctant to admit a third Japanese line. The situation was complicated by the fact that the line applying for membership had government backing, and eventually the line was given limited rights in the trade.

(ii) *Lines already established in other trades.* Competition from lines already established in other trades have perhaps presented the conferences which we have studied with the most troublesome kind of competition. Because of the continuing nature of this competition, and the light which it throws on conference action in combating such competition, we give 'case histories' of two of the most important of these 'outsiders'.

Case One. The line concerned in this case was one which was already running a scheduled service one terminal of which was within the area of the conference it aimed to join. One reason given for its application was the high cost of repairs at one end of its scheduled route relative to costs in Europe; the line therefore wished to bring ships back to Europe, off its scheduled route, and not unnaturally it wished to carry cargo when doing so.

The application for membership came at a time when conference members were finding it difficult to provide sufficient tonnage to cover the trade; not all pre-war lines had at that time rejoined the conference and conference members felt at that time that when membership was back to its pre-war strength, they would be more than capable of covering the needs of the trade. If the applicant line wished to bring ships back to Europe, there was sufficient 'open rated' cargo which could be carried, but there was some doubt among conference members whether this was the real reason for the application, as the line had indicated that it intended to run a monthly service. Conference members had no wish to admit a 'cross trader', which they felt the applicant line to be to the trade. The application was therefore turned down.

The applicant line accepted the decision at that time but in the course of the next few years it made four further attempts to gain admission to the conference. There was still a shortage of tonnage in the trade as a whole but conference members were reluctant to admit new members until all pre-war members had full scheduled services in operation. It is interesting to note that this reluctance to admit new members was not confined to the main conference but applied also to associated conferences; it was felt by most members that admission to an associated conference would give 'back door' entry to the main conference.

The line's fourth attempt to gain admission to the conference was, however, successful, in that certain limited rights in particular parts of the trading area were granted to the line which then concentrated its efforts in trying to increase these rights. The reasons given by the conference for the exclusion of the line from full rights in the trade were as follows:

(1) Steady contraction in volume of general cargo.
(2) There had been some expansion of traffic in the trade but a large part of this had originated in a particular area and had been followed by increased participation of the national lines in that area.

(3) In several territories short and long term prospects of production and trade were overshadowed by political uncertainties and indeterminate factors, such as the extension of OEEC and intra-regional economic activity.

(4) National flag lines would be entering the trade in the near future.

(5) The style and scope of sea carriage on these routes was likely before long to be drastically changed and probably contracted by the introduction of new methods. (The conference no doubt had in mind the use of container ships).

Late in the 1960s the line again made a formal application to inaugurate a full service to and from the conference area. The conference members realised that the line could be a serious threat and that, in view of its financial standing the conference could well be the loser in any rate war which might develop. The matter was brought to a head and one way out of the difficulty which was suggested was that the whole dispute should be referred to CENSA.[1] The applicant line itself was not willing to refer the dispute, however, and finally, after protracted negotiations it was admitted to the conference in both outward and homeward directions with a limited number of sailings and a limited amount of tonnage which could be lifted.

The whole episode stretched over a period of nearly 20 years and it is interesting to note that it seems to have been important to the applicant line that they should 'have the blessing' of the conference. This was so important that the idea of starting a service was dropped when conference membership was refused. It is also interesting to notice conference members' reluctance to start a rate war, even though they had grave doubts about the over-tonnaging of the trade, doubts which, incidentally, were not realised.

Case Two. The second case of competition from a line which had been refused membership of a conference started in 1962. The outside line operated a trans-Pacific service between the Far East and the East coast of the U.S.A. It now wished to extend this service to Europe in what would virtually be a 'round' voyage. In this case, however, the refusal of conference membership — on the grounds that the applicant line did not have a 'stake in the trade' — did not deter the line from implementing a monthly service from the East to Europe via the Panama Canal. Much of the cargo obtained by this line came from Japan and from Hong Kong.

It was estimated in 1964 that 50 per cent of the cargo which the 'pirate' line obtained was shipped on f.o.b. terms. This means that the purchaser of the goods had named the carrier and there was no action which the conference could take to alter this. There was a certain type of commodity which the line was known to carry in large quantities from Hong Kong, the tonnage rate on which was an important proportion of the final price of the commodity. The conference members therefore reduced their rate on this commodity, and their action had the desired effect in part, i.e. the competitor lost some of his cargo to conference vessels. The conference policy at this time, however, was not to enter into a general rate war but to try to stop any incursion into the trade by taking action under the contract system

1 Committee of European National Shipowners Associations. The Committee has conciliation machinery which was set up to 'find means of resolving disputes between conferences and independent lines'. For this purpose a three man Conciliation Committee could be established, the members being drawn from a panel of liner operators nominated by each national association.

against known supporters of the non-conference line.

The shippers' response to this, however, was to use a 'cover' name and this practice developed to the extent that the non-conference line itself established a number of trading companies in whose name the conference contractors could make shipments by non-conference vessels. Successive applications for admission to the conference in 1964, 1966 and again in 1967 were refused, but conference members were beginning to realise that their policy of trying to contain the 'outsider' had not been very successful. The operations of the line had by 1967 been extended to the outward (eastbound) trade, and the line considered that it was established in the trade.

The outcome of the further refusal of membership in 1967 was that the line asked the CENSA Conciliation Committee to look into the dispute. This committee's enquiry took place in 1968 with both sides putting their case to it. In 1969 the conference expressed willingness to give the independent line certain limited rights in the trade and associate membership of the conference from the Far East to Europe, but in the outward trade (Europe to the Far East) the conference was unwilling to grant the applicant line's request for loading rights at London and discharging rights at two specified ports in the Far East. The line considered that unless it was given these rights its trade would be unbalanced and possibly uneconomic. By 1970 there was still no agreement between the line and the conference; the Conciliation Committee expressed willingness to continue negotiations but it could not impose a solution on either side and the dispute was left unresolved.

*   *   *

These two case histories illustrate two different policies of conference members on outside competition. Also shown is members' unwillingness to enter into rate wars, which had been a feature of early conference development.

(iii) *Incidental outsiders.* The idea that has grown up that conferences operate a monopoly in international shipping and that it is impossible for non-conference lines to enter the trade is not borne out by the events of the postwar period. Indications have been given above of some of the ways in which shipping lines have entered a conference in the last 25 years, but throughout this period there have also been a number of small independent shipping lines operating irregular services which have obtained general cargo (not open rated) in competition with conference members.

In some of these cases the conference has thought it worth while to cut rates on certain commodities in order to confine the trade to its own members but in others it has allowed the trade to pass to the independent line. One such case occurred in the Indian trade when a Greek Line began to compete with the conference over the carriage of gunny bags from Calcutta. The Greek line was offering rates so far below the conference tariff rate that conference members withdrew from the trade; the Greek line then raised its rates of freight. The final outcome was that the trade declined and the Greek line also withdrew.

With primary products, the world market price can vary enormously over quite short periods of time and the proportion of the freight rate in the final price of the product will also vary widely. With a product such as timber, for example, which is being sold in competition with timber from other parts of the world, the rate of freight could have powerful effects on the market for a particular type of timber from the Far East. Similarly, rubber is sold on the open market and fluctuates widely in price, whereas the rate of freight remains relatively very stable.[1] The dissatisfaction of the timber and rubber merchants is such that it provides an opportunity for an independent line to offer to carry these products at reduced rates.

There have been other cases. An Italian line used to run a service from Italy to the Far East, a Japanese line from Japan to the Red Sea area, and an East German line from Singapore to Europe. The conference was aware of the operations of these independent lines and endeavoured to keep a check on the amount of cargo which they lifted. So long as the service provided was not a regular one and the amount of cargo obtained was relatively small, the conference has been content in the postwar period to let the independent lines obtain what cargo they can.

It remains to ask what courses of action are open to conference members to deal with an independent shipping line which is considered to be a threat to the 'orderly conduct' of the trade. The main methods which a conference could adopt and has in fact adopted are:

> Rate wars
> Further inducements to shippers to remain loyal to the conference.
> Conciliation machinery
> Action against shippers

Rate wars. This means that the conference deliberately cuts its rates to below the rate at which the independent line is offering to carry cargo. This rate cutting could be a general 'across the board' cut, or a cut in the rate on selected commodities from which the independent line gets most of its cargo. The idea behind this is that either the independent line will also have to cut its rate to compete with the conference, in which case the conference could cut its rate again, or, if the new lower rate proves to be uneconomic, the independent line would be forced to withdraw from the trade. The 'success' of such rate wars will, of course, depend on the financial resources of the independent line, and whether it can 'subsidise' the trade which it is trying to enter from other trades in which it is engaged. The rate war has been used with reluctance by conferences in the postwar period.

Further inducements to shippers. This could take the form of an increased rebate or an additional discount for those shippers on contract terms. In addition, one conference introduced what was called a Fidelity Rebate Scheme. This allowed for a further rebate to shippers who did not accept importers demands for f.o.b. shipment.[2]

Conciliation machinery. It has been possible since 1966, when the CENSA Conciliation Committee was established, to refer disputes to this committee. The committee has no legal powers and cannot impose a solution on either party, but it can bring both sides together and help to negotiate a compromise solution.

Action against shippers. Lastly, there is the action that the conference can take against the shippers who use the independent lines. In order to get the best confer-

1 See Table 4.9 in Chapter 4.
2 See p. 51

ence terms a shipper either contracts to ship all his goods by conference vessels subject to a period of notice of termination), or he claims a deferred rebate at the end of a period on all shipments he has made provided that he has used conference vessels exclusively.

In the case of a shipper who has used non-conference vessels, a conference could (a) under the contract system suspend a shipper's entitlement to immediate discount and/or appoint a trustee to investigate the alleged breach of contract. If the shipper admits the breach of contract, or if the trustee confirms that one has been made then the conference can claim damages as specified in the contract; or (b) under the rebate circular withhold rebates over both the shipment and the qualifying periods. The difficulty with these procedures, however, is first to obtain evidence that a shipper has used non-conference vessels (other shippers' allegations may not be regarded as sufficient) and, second, whether it is worthwhile alienating a large conference shipper for possibly only one breach of contract. In the Far East trade this method of combatting competition has been used, but the first step is usually for the conference to write to the shipper concerned with a warning before any direct action is taken. There have been a number of instances, in the post war period however, when a shipper's entitlement to discount has been suspended.

A shipper may claim in his own defence that a conference vessel was not available at the time of shipment, and another device which the conference has used has been to 'blanket' the ports. That is to say, the conference has made sure that there is at least one vessel belonging to a member line available in the port or ports where the independent line is known to lift its cargo. This, however, is an expensive method for the conference, and if the independent line has a wide range of ports it could be impossible for the conference to blanket all of them completely.

d. Output sharing

Output sharing or regulation of the trade has been a feature of 'closed' conferences since their inception. The regulation of the tonnage 'on the berth' was considered essential by the founder members of the conference if they were to avoid an over supply of tonnage in a particular trade or the possibility of one member gaining more of the trade at the expense of other member lines. Output sharing, cargo sharing, or regulation of the trade (whichever term is used) is therefore employed in conjunction with the common tariff to try to ensure an 'equitable' distribution of trade among the members. The practices used in order to share the trade are: (a) limitations on the number of sailings each member can make, (b) restrictions on the ports of loading or discharge, and (c) restriction on the amount of cargo which each member can lift either in the total trade or from certain ports or a combination of both. These practices are also used in conjunction with revenue pooling agreements as will be shown in the next section. The Far Eastern Freight Conference, however, has no revenue pool and therefore uses a combination of sailing restrictions, port restrictions and tonnage sharing.

(i) *Limitations on sailing.* This method is seldom used on its own but it takes the form of limiting the number of sailings which each member may make in a specified period of time or from any one port, or group of ports (e.g. the North Continental ports such as Amsterdam, Antwerp and Hamburg) in a given period. The limitation of sailings is purely in terms of number of sailings and no size of ship or hold capacity is specified. There are, of course, certain physical limitations to the size of ship that can be used in some trades because the port facilities are not suitable for ships above a certain size. There are also economic limitations on the size of conference liners. Some members of conferences are not subject to any limitation on sailings because they are founder members of the conference.

(ii) *Restrictions on ports of loading.* In addition to specifying the number of sailings which a member line can make in a given period, conference members seek to limit direct loading from their ports to their own national shipping lines and they try to sustain this position in their negotiations with other conference members seeking access to their ports. UK ports are for the most part served by UK shipping lines, although other conference members have rights in the UK. On the other hand, member lines have sometimes imposed voluntary restrictions on themselves by refraining from serving certain ports. An example of this is that a number of UK shipping lines who were founder members of conference have the right, in theory, to load at any port in the UK; but in practice a division between East and West coast lines exists on the mutual understanding that East coast shipping lines will not load at West coast ports and vice versa — an early example of rationalisation.

(iii) *Tonnage lifting restrictions.* This form of restriction can be applied to the total trade of conference members, to certain commodities, or to the tonnage coming forward at particular ports. If it is the first case, it is usually applied in conjunction with a revenue pool; an example of the second case is the wool pool homeward from Australia. The members of the Australia-Europe Conference devised a scheme in the inter war period whereby the wool trade (the most valuable single commodity in the homeward trade) was to be shared amongst conference members according to each members's 'stake in the trade'. The system was not altogether satisfactory, because members were dissatisfied with their shares but, in the postwar period particularly, it was claimed by the Australian producers and shippers that too many conference ships were covering the wool sales and were therefore sailing homewards at less than full capacity. This affected the earnings of the conference lines as a whole and, so it was alleged, showed up in the Formula calculations (see p.48). A limitation of tonnage was therefore combined with a 'voluntary' limitation on the number of ships which each member despatched to cover the wool sales.

The most comprehensive cargo sharing arrangement now in use (excluding revenue pooling agreements) is that which is operated in the Far Eastern Freight Conference in the outward direction from North Continental ports.[1] The arrangement has operated since 1946 (at first as an interim measure but later made more permanent). Because the North Continental ports are 'open' ports in the sense that no one national line has a 'right' to the trade, the conference members have tried to 'rationalise' the tonnage on the berth. For this purpose, the conference set up a Berthing Committee which is responsible for estimating (on the basis of information from ship's brokers and other sources) the amount of cargo coming forward in the next period (two months under the present arrangement). On the basis of these

1   Ports in Germany, Holland and Belgium.

estimates, the Committee allocates to the national groups the amount of cargo they will be allowed (or expected) to carry; it also once programmed the rotation on the berth of ships from each national group.

For the purposes of the pool, the conference is divided into national groups, i.e. the British lines form one group, the French another, and so on. Each group is allocated a proportion of the cargo and the way this proportion is allocated to the individual lines within each group is a matter for the group itself. (A similar arrangement was introduced in the India/Pakistan trade from 1961, and in the Australian trade in 1966). A distinction is also made between 'ceiling' and 'non-ceiling' cargo; 'ceiling' cargo is that which is defined as coming within the terms of the cargo which is to be shared in a given proportion among member lines. 'Non-ceiling' cargo is of course still conference cargo subject to the common tariff and the contract or rebate system, but it is not included in pool calculations.

The basic share of the trade (tonnage) allocated to each group was determined in the first instance by the share obtained by the lines in each group over the three years prior to the agreement being made. Homeward a group might increase its basic share if it could show that in the preceding years it had been a consistent over-carrier. In 1965 a revised arrangement was introduced. Under the new arrangement a member may ask for a re-negotiation of shares in the trade if, operating from the year in which shares were last fixed, the total trade of the conference members has increased by 20 per cent. In this way the base year can be altered and account may be taken of a line which has secured a larger proportion of a growing trade.

e. Revenue Pooling

Revenue pooling is not an arrangement which originated with the formulation of conferences; 'joint purse' agreements for some commodities existed in certain trades before the formation of conferences. The object of pooling gross earnings within a conference is to give each member an equitable share of the trade and to avoid competition among individual members, while at the same time maintaining the service to the shipper. Pooling arrangements do not necessarily cover the whole trade but might, for example, embrace only those commodities which are either valuable or, alternatively, very low rated cargo. An example of the first is the tea revenue pool in the Calcutta trade in the early days of that conference in which all conference members shared even though they did not carry any tea cargo, and an example of the second is that which obtained in the Far East trade in the inter war period for so-called Schedule D or 'rough' cargo.[1] A revenue or earnings pool can be varied from a 100 per cent of earnings paid into a pool to a much lower percentage, e.g. 40 per cent. Revenue pools have not always been pools of gross earnings, but in some cases have allowed members of a conference to deduct certain specified items of cost before payments are made to the pool; it then becomes a net earnings pool.

In the Australian trade homewards, revenue pooling agreements have been introduced in the postwar period as a result of pressure for the rationalisation of services, and it has been the Department of Trade in the Australian government which has

1 The pooling agreement from North Continental ports in the Far East Freight Conference was a comprehensive agreement covering most commodities lifted from those ports, but each conference member was obliged to carry a specified amount of 'rough' (Schedule D) cargo.

been prominent in encouraging rationalisation. The members of the UK/Continent-Australia conferences adopted the policy that revenue pooling agreement had to be all-embracing to be successful, and the Indian/Pakistan conference members had come to the same conclusion five years earlier. The revenue pooling arrangements in the Indian/Pakistan trade were introduced in 1961 and those in Australian trade in 1966. The pooling arrangements in both conferences operate in a very similar way, although we give details of the Australian conference only.

The Australian revenue pool arrangement has been described as 'an earnings pool qualified by carryings'. Member lines undertake to provide coverage of the trade in that they will provide 'sailings of sufficient number and with sufficient space and lifting capacity to lift its quota of cargo and earn its share throughout a pool period'. Each line has an entitlement of a *maximum* number of sailings and a *minimum* obligation to provide 80 per cent of their sailings in each pool period. Sailings must be reasonably spread over the period.

If space offered had to be adjusted to the flow of cargo and there is no obvious over carrying or under carrying by any member line, then the issue is decided by a Programming Committee. When additional tonnage has to be provided as a corporate responsibility it is made in accordance with pool shares *or* a sailing rota.

If any line or group does not maintain an agreed minimum number of sailings while at the same time under-carrying by more than 10 per cent of its carrying obligation, then its basic entitlement in the pool is reduced *pro rata* to the number of sailings by which it fell short of its obligations. When the basic entitlement is reduced, carrying obligations are reduced accordingly.

Lines recognise that they have to cover all the trade including 'difficult or onerous' trade, and lines/groups who provide this service are financially compensated from the pool. Qualification for automatic compensation includes discharge at any port in Australia outside the range Fremantle, Brisbane and Hobart.

The way in which revenue pooling agreements operate do vary between conferences but certain basic issues are common whatever the details of the agreement:

(i) *The share of each member in the pool.* In the early pool agreements the basic share entitlement was decided according to the number of ships despatched or the gross registered tonnage of ships. The method now used seems to be based on the average liftings of members over a number of years, e.g. the three years preceding the setting up of the revenue pool. Adjustments to the initial shares would appear to be difficult, given the penalties for under or over carrying, but in the Indian/Pakistan trade a continuous adjustment factor was written into the agreement to allow the national lines of India and Pakistan an increasing share of the trade.

(ii) *Coverage.* Recent developments seem to indicate that conferences are now more ready to include all commodities within an earnings pool. Certain commodities are, however, still considered unsuitable as revenue pool cargo. For example, hazardous cargo would be exempted as would bulk cargo such as wheat, metal ores and sugar. Under this heading can be included the problem of dealing with the 'rough' cargo which is either difficult to load or low rated and therefore not attractive to the shipping lines. The comprehensive 100 per cent revenue pool would apper to deal adequately with this problem as each member line would receive its basic share of the total revenue of all lines regardless of the type of commodity carried.

(iii) *Pool earnings.* The revenue pooling system has developed from the 12½ per cent contribution made to the pool in the early days of the Australian Outward Conference, through the 40 per cent contributions of the Far East Conference in the inter-war period to the 100 per cent earnings pool now operated in the Australia and India/Pakistan trades. This 100 per cent pool means that all earnings are credited to the pool, and at the end of an accounting period each member will receive or pay in such amounts by which his own freight earnings fall short of or exceed his basic entitlement.

Summary

In the first part of this chapter we examined the major developments in conference organisations in the postwar period. It is probably true to say that the present organisation and operation of shipping conferences is a combination of historical development and adaptation to changing conditions.

The geographical limits of conference operation derive partly from historical trading links and partly from a response to changing patterns and conditions of trade. Conferences endeavour to be comprehensive in their coverage of areas and ports while at the same time running economical services, and to this end conference organisations have distinguished between ports which are served regularly and those that are served only with transhipment or on a more 'casual' basis.

Competition from shipowners who are not members of the conference system has continued to be a problem for conferences, but institutional arrangements have come into force in the postwar period which enable negotiations to take the place of rate wars. Membership has grown in the conferences we have examined and a feature of the increased membership has been its composition; it has been predominantly the national flag lines of developing countries which have acquired conference membership.

The system of output sharing, which has always been a part of conference organisation, has progressed even further in some trades in that now not only is 'output' (trade) shared but also revenue. The revenue pool agreements currently operated differ from the 'joint purse' agreements and revenue pooling of the early years of conference development in that their coverage of the trade is much wider (i.e. the pool is not confined to a few major commodities) and they invariably include close supervision of the shipping services (sailings) provided by each member. These revenue pooling agreements seem to have been entered into as a direct result of over-tonnaging in the trade and under-utilisation of capacity, (possibly brought about in one trade by flag discrimination). Shipowners (and governments) in the trade felt that in order to rationalise the services offered it was necessary for them to be sure of obtaining their 'fair share' of freight earnings, and so they agreed on revenue pooling amongst themselves — but with the encouragement (in the homeward trade) of the governments concerned. It could be argued that the closer organisation of shipping services might inevitably lead to a diminution of services in the wider sense that revenue pools provide little or no incentive for an individual shipowner to improve his service or to accelerate the investment which he makes in ships. It has yet to be seen, however, what the full impact of container services will be on conference organisation and development.

In addition to the developments which have taken place within the conference system, the amount of organisation on the shippers' side has grown in such a way that shippers' councils are now an important factor influencing conference decisions. They are consulted on matters which are likely to affect shippers and in turn they can call for improvements in conference operations so as to facilitate the movement of goods. This development has been most noticeable in the Far Eastern trades and to a certain extent in the India/Pakistan trades in the post-war period; in the Australian trade it has existed for a much longer period of time.

4   Price Formation

A full description of conference organisation and practices has been given in Chapter 3. The present chapter is the first of a group of four which are concerned with various aspects of price-making by shipping conferences. The chapter is divided into three parts. The first part is concerned with those aspects of conference organisation which provide the essential context for 'price making' by shipping conferences, and which influence that process. The second part contains a description and analysis of the static and dynamic price-making processes by conferences, and in the third part this is related to aspects of price theory. In the next chapter an examination is made of price trends in the post war period in both conference and non-conference shipping. This is followed in Chapter 6 by a study of pricing and price elasticity in individual cases. In Chapter 7 the structure of relative freight rates in shipping conferences is examined, and a price model is constructed and applied to data assembled in the course of this research; the results are considered for the light they throw upon the relative importance of various factors which are explanatory of the structure of relative prices.

1. The context of conference price making

A shipping conference is a device for establishing and continuing a collective monopoly of a particular type of freight[1] shipping service. In its roles of setting common prices and sharing output, in various ways, amongst member lines a conference functions as a cartel. Other types of *freight* transport service by air[2] and sea are largely unorganised in the sense just described, and they offer competitive services which are fairly close substitutes for conference liner services at the top and bottom ends respectively of the scale of cargoes ordered by freight rate. Air freight transport and independent and, in some cases, specialised (i.e., unitised or containerised) liners outside the conferences offer competition at the top end of the range, and tramps and specialised bulk carriers offer even more effective competition at the bottom end of the price scale. So the collective monopoly of a conference is not complete over the whole range of the overseas freight transport market and some indication of the extent to which it can be broken or seriously encroached upon has been given in the Chapter 3. There does remain, however, a wide band of cargo ordered by price where the conference monopoly is relatively strong and here the absence of any very serious outside competition allows the conference to make prices which

1   Conferences in passenger shipping services did exist at one time, but are now largely inoperative.

2   IATA does 'organise' some air freight transport services, but many such services are operated on a charter basis and are 'unorganised' in the sense explained here.

are differential, that is to say, different prices or freight rates are charged in different sections of the market. This can be done because of the absence of outside competition and because of the nature of the market for freight shipping services and this is described later. First, it seems important to appraise the extent of monopoly power available to shipping conferences.

A shipping conference is a fairly loosely organised collective monopoly with some, not very great intra-conference, non-price competition; but it is important to notice here that this type of competition is somewhat limited by the 'spatial' monopoly enjoyed by some member lines. Traditionally some lines are based on and serve particular geographical loading areas and ports[1] to the exclusion of the ships of other member lines, but the vessels of non-conference competitors may load at these ports.

A conference has some power to raise price above cost for some services, but this power is continuously subject to erosion by outside competition which does in fact make inroads from time to time to 'cream-off' the more profitable parts of the trade. Such market power as conferences have is preserved by various barriers to entry. Some of these arise from the highly-capitalised nature of the shipping industry and the large minimum size of investment necessary to maintain regular services over the long distances involved in the 'deep sea' trades where conferences are particularly strong. A further barrier of this type has arisen in the post war period particularly. This is the marked trend towards the formation of a few large groups of shipowning firms within and across conference boundaries.[2] Some scale economies at the fleet level have arisen from these mergers, and although the extent of these economies are not investigated in this study they cannot but add to the barriers to new entry. Furthermore, there are barriers which are institutional and which are arranged by the conference. New members are generally admitted only by a unanimous vote of existing members. A shipowner aspiring to conference membership will normally have to show that he has the resources in terms of ships and working capital to cover the share of the trade to which he would have access if he were admitted to membership. This is done to ensure that a new member will be able to fulfill the obligation the conference feels to 'serve the trade', and it is also designed to keep out those whose object it is to carrry only the more profitable, higher valued and rated cargoes. So these two barriers are not strictly additive as obstacles. Given the resources to surmount the natural barrier of minimum initial size, the institutional barrier is less formidable. But the door is not automatically opened when these requirements are met. There exists the further requirement that the applicant has to show that he represents a national interest in the trade and that he is in a position to gain a share of it. Despite these rules there have been cases where third flag carriers, who have few or none of these qualifications, have nevertheless in fact fought their way into a conference.[3]

---

1 In some cases a conference member leases an 'appropriated berth' with associated quays and dockside facilities. This type of arrangement confers priority of use on the shipowner concerned, but not exclusive use.

2 This trend was first detected by D.L. McLachlan 'The Price Policy of Liner Conferences'. *Scottish Journal of Political Economy,* Vol. 10, 1963, pp. 322, 323.

3 See Chapter 3, Section 2.(c).

The nature of the market for freight shipping services is undoubtedly a very important factor in relative price making by shipping conferences. This is so because the market is very fragmented and compartmentalised. Buyers of freight shipping services for the movement of a particular class of goods, e.g., toys, have a common interest and in some cases act together through their trade association to bargain with a conference. But such buyers have practically no interest[1] in any other section of the market and are almost totally indifferent to the rates of freight charged for, say, biscuits, by the same conference on the same route. It is partly this lack of knowledge of or interest in the rates charged for shipping products not made by themselves or their competitors that makes possible the differential pricing policies of shipping conferences. The theoretical and practical implications of this situation are examined in Section 3 of this chapter.

Although the commodities transported are almost infinitely differentiated and heterogeneous, the freight shipping services offered by the conferences included in this study are fairly homogeneous, at least this was so until the container services were introduced into the UK-Australia conference in 1969. That this is a factor which is influential in conference price making is clear from the fact that a differential rate for container traffic has now been introduced. Leaving containers aside, there is some intra-conference competition in terms of quality of service (handling of cargo and documents), speed of transit and degree of promptness in settling claims for cargo lost or damaged. But these non-price differences do not appear to have been sufficiently great to have generated any serious difficulties for the conferences in their common price-making procedures. Any increase in output by an individual member due to non-price competition has usually been allowed to take place by some increase in the individual shares of members in one or other of the quantitative allocations of the conference. There are however some curbs on non-price competition. Advertising is undertaken, but free gifts and other 'handouts' to shippers are limited by conferences.[2]

Unit cost differences between member lines within a conference can arise from the non-price competitive differences just described, but largely they are due to differences in scale and in operating costs and efficiency, for example, differences in wage rates between members of different nationalities. These cost differences are a factor which is influential in the making of conference prices in common and an account of how they are handled is given in the next section of this chapter.

2. Static and dynamic price making

An examination is made first of what actually happens in the specified conferences when prices are formed.

---

1   In the post-war period and particularly since 1955 when it was founded, the British Shippers' Council has tried to bring together and represent the interests of buyers of all types of overseas freight shipping service, but the Council does not negotiate with conferences on freight rates on behalf of its members.

2   A circular notice to the members of one conference refers to a conference decision, taken a month earlier, which limited 'free trips, cruises and reduced fare passages to shippers' to £25 in value. Later the £25 limit was removed from the record, but members were advised to exercise restraint in the matter of gifts to shippers.

a. Price differentiation

Price making by shipping conferences is on a large scale. In the UK-Australia Conference, for example, some 7,125 commodities are priced in the outward tariff, but far fewer, about 1,170, in the homeward tariff. The reason for this is the obvious one that the homeward trade is quite largely in primary commodities (such as wool, meat, dairy products, fruit) of relatively few distinct types, whereas the outward trade is almost entirely of manufactured goods of very wide-ranging variety in terms of description. The trade homewards in this conference, and in some others studied here, is becoming more differentiated as the less developed countries served by these conferences diversify their output and export trade by investment in secondary industry.

For obvious practical reasons price differentiation is not complete. That is to say, there is not a separate rate of freight for each and every commodity shipped. In some conferences, typically the outward ones, there are a number of 'price classes' and all or most of the commodities in the tariff are allocated a class rate. In other conferences prices are more thoroughly differentiated and the number of separate and distinct prices is as much as a third or a half as great as the number of commodities listed in the tariff.

An illustration is given in Table 4.1. of the range and spread of price classification and of price differentiation in both outward and homeward conferences.

From the analysis shown in Table 4.1 some broad conclusions may be drawn.

There is some uniformity of pricing policy among the six outward conferences in that they all use a price class system of typically 20–30 price classes, with the UK-India/Pakistan Eastbound Conference using a few more classes at 34. Over 90 per cent of all rated commodities are allocated to a price class in these conferences. The remaining 10 per cent of commodities are separately priced, with some intra-conference overlap of prices, so that there are on average across the six outwards conferences 2.9. commodities per separate price. These conferences carry outwards manufactured products of the industrialised West European economies. The commodities are numerous and of great variety.

With the exception of the Japan-Europe and Hong Kong-Europe trades, the homeward trades are from less industrialised countries whose exports to Europe are quite largely of primary commodities. The lower unit value primary commodities, such as grains and copra, will usually be shipped by tramp vessels and other bulk carriers of various types which are not organised in conferences, but this will depend not only on the unit value of the consignment but also on its size. Small 'parcels' of relatively low unit value primary commodities often do travel by conference liner. The higher unit value primary commodities, such as wool, rubber and ore concentrates normally travel by conference liner, so also do the manufactured goods of these Indian, Far Eastern and Australasian areas. Exports of manufactures are growing in volume as these economies develop their primary and secondary industries. For the high unit value primary commodities the conferences homeward largely adopt the system of separate pricing. If the Japanese and Hong Kong export trades, which are chiefly in industrial goods, are omitted, then 2,711 out of a total of 2,887 separate commodities in the homeward tariffs of the remaining four conferences are separately priced (again with some intra-conference overlap in prices), and price classes are used only in the trade from Singapore and Malaya. Price classes are employed in the Japanese and Hong Kong trades and 2,041 commodities are fitted into 58 classes.

73

Table 4.1 *An analysis of liner conference freight tariffs*

	1. Number of separate price classes or prices (a)		2. Number of rated Commodities		3. Average Number of Commodities per price class and per separate price			4. Ratio of top: bottom price or price class (a)
	a Price Classes	b Separate Prices	a Price Classes	b Separate Prices	a Per Price Class	b Per Separate Price	c Per price class and per separate price	
UK – Australia Outward (Southbound)	20	130	6,830	295	341.1	2.3	47.5	18.20:1
UK – Australia Homeward (Northbound)	0	210	0	1,170	–	5.6	5.6	19.17:1
UK – India/Pakistan Outward (Eastbound)	34	42	2,130	50	62.6	1.2	28.7	12.86:1
UK – India/Pakistan Homeward (Westbound)	0	346	0	900	–	2.6	2.6	14.98:1
UK – Japan Eastbound (b)	23	59	2,845	209	123.7	3.5	37.2	7.29:1
UK – Japan Westbound	29	62	1,536	114	53.0	1.8	18.1	10.80:1
UK – Hong Kong Outward (b)	23	59	2,845	209	123.7	3.5	37.2	9.28:1
UK – Hong Kong Homeward	29	72	505	115	17.4	1.6	6.1	11.75:1
Europe – Philippines Outward (b)	23	59	2,845	209	123.7	3.5	37.2	9.28:1
Europe – Philippines Homeward	0	60	0	120	–	2.0	2.0	6.48:1
UK – Singapore/Malaya Outward (b)	23	59	2,845	209	123.7	3.5	37.2	10.80:1
UK – Singapore/Malaya Homeward	29	123	176	292	6.1	2.4	3.1	19.97:1
Totals and 1. Outward	146	408	20,340	1,181	139.3	2.9	38.8	11.29:1
Average ratios 2. Homeward	87	873	2,217	2,711	25.5	3.1	5.1	13.86:1

(a) Excluding 'ad valorem' rates and 'ad valorem' options.
(b) These conferences operate a common freight tariff with small rate differentials corresponding to different sea route distances.

74

A measure of price differentiation is shown in col. 3 of Table 4.1 This is the *average* number of commodities per price class or per separate price, together with an overall measure of the average number of commodities per price class *and* separate price (Col.3.c). These ratios may be compared with the extreme position of perfect price differentiation where each commodity is separately rated and the ratio is one. So the lower the average in this column the greater is the degree of price differentiation.

There are considerable differences in the degree of price differentiation between the conferences studied here. The highest degree of differentiation occurs in the Europe—Philippines Homewards Conference where the average is 2 commodities per price, and the lowest occurs in the United Kingdom—Australia Outwards conference where the average is 47.5 commodities per price. There can be no doubt that in part the degree of price differentiation is higher the fewer is the number of rated commodities in the tariff. In the last mentioned conference there are a total of 7,125 rated commodities. This fact alone must limit, on practical grounds, the extent to which separate prices can be made for each commodity. It is unlikely that a very fine differentiation of price for a body of goods this size would be worth doing to the extent of complete differentiation. From the point of view of a conference there will be an optimum degree of differentiation, which is not in practice determinable, at which the marginal cost of differentiation is equal to the marginal revenue gain which arises from the marginal act of price differentiation.

The fact remains that whatever the reason for the degree of price differentiation, be it the pursuit of revenue maximisation or the result of bargaining initiated by shippers in developing countries who are seeking to use the differential price system to their advantage by getting a price which is below cost, the system exists as shown here for the conferences named. It may be that occasionally the arrival for shipment of new products, which were not previously listed in the tariff, leads to a new entry being made almost automatically without any conscious decision to differentiate prices being taken; but in fact we know from attendance at conference meetings that new products are carefully examined in respect of their characteristics of unit value, weight/measurement ratio, stowage factor and degree, if any, of hazard involved in their shipment, and they are then either placed in an existing price class judged to be suitable in relation to the product's characteristics, or a separate, unique price is made for them. In both cases the new price is made with discrimination, but only in the latter case is the system of differentiated prices extended.

Further to this type of price differentiation it sometimes occurs that a conference will make a relatively undifferentiated (in respect of price) entry in the tariff, for example, 'other machinery' (see case history 3 in Chapter 6) and subject it later to a process of 'separate enumeration'. By this is meant price differentiation, usually based on ranges of unit value of the commodity group concerned.[1]

If these conferences are divided into two sections, the outward and the homeward conferences, there is a marked inter-sectoral difference in the degree of price differentiation. The outward group as a whole have an average of 38.8 commodities per price, and the homeward group an average of only 5.1 commodities per price. If the homeward conferences from the relatively industrialised economies of Japan and Hong Kong were to be omitted then an even greater degree of price differentiation

---

1 Examples of this process are quoted in Chapter 7.

would appear in this section which would then comprise only the developing economies served by the homeward group of conferences.

There are two principal reasons for this high level of price differentiation, and they appear from an inspection of the tariffs. One is that the relatively high value primary commodities, such as wool, jute, meat and dairy products are shipped in many different grades and forms and the conference gives a separate tariff rate for each one, and each is treated as a separate and distinct commodity. The other reason is that the developing countries which generate these liner cargoes are becoming industrialised and are shipping a wide range of manufactures. So the tariff must cover both the highly differentiated primary products as well as a wide range of industrial products where the degree of price differentiation is much greater than that which occurs in the outward tariffs. If the conferences listed in Table 4.1 were ranked in order of this measure of price differentiation, all the homeward conferences from developing countries would appear at the top as being those with the smaller average number of commodities per price quoted, and all the outward conferences would be at the bottom of the list.

b. Additional pricing

It has been shown that the basic pricing process consists of the allocation to a commodity of an individual or a class rate. There follows a further process which consists of additions to or subtractions from the basic rate of freight, the principal ones are given below.

Additions, commonly known in the conference shipping industry, as 'additionals'
  (a) *Outport additionals* — a charge for delivery to a port which is not on the schedule of regular calls made by the conference and published in advance. The 'additional' can apply to a loading or a discharging port, or both. It is also a charge for delivery to a port which is on a schedule of regular conference calls but for which the volume is too low to warrant what is known as 'base port' status.[1]
  (b) *Transhipment charges*. These are made for arranging and sub-contracting the onward shipment of goods from the regular port of discharge to another port or ports within or outside the conference sphere or area.
  (c) *Surcharges*. These are of various kinds and frequently arise due to special circumstances and events. For example, the closing of the Suez Canal in 1967 resulted in a surcharge of 10 per cent on tariff rates in the FEFC. Temporary surcharges are also applied in cases of port congestion where the waiting time for conference vessels is abnormally long.
  (d) *Premia*, and special rates of various kinds which arise from the nature of the commodity shipped. These are numerous; examples are:
      (i) Long length.
      (ii) Heavy lift.
      (iii) Tank cleaning (for liquids).
      (iv) Hazardous cargo (such as explosives, low flash point chemicals).
      (v) Refrigerated and 'cool chamber' stowage.
      (vi) Special stowage for fragile cargo, valuable cargo, cargo liable to taint other cargo.

1 See Chapter 3, Section 2(a), for a description of this term.

76

(vii) A large number of *ad hoc* premia or special rates for unusual cargo which cannot be weighed or measured in the usual way, e.g., livestock.

(viii) In some conferences an *ad valorem* rate (up to 3 per cent) is charged on cargo of high unit value.

The method of applying the basic rate of freight listed in the tariff is normally as follows. Against each tariff entry is written one of the symbols, W/M, W, M, lbs. W/M means that the freight to be charged will be assessed either per ton (of 20 cwts) weight or per ton measurement (40 cubic feet) at the option of the shipowner, and this option is exercised in such a way as to yield the largest amount of freight revenue. The symbols W and M used separately indicate that the commodity concerned will be freighted on the basis indicated, without option. Among the conferences we have examined this general procedure is common, but there are exceptions. The UK–India/Pakistan Westbound Conference quotes, in many instances, separate rates for W and M for the *same* commodity and also reserves the option to members as to which basis to charge on.

c. Discounts

It is well known that shipping conferences allow discounts on their standard tariff rates. These discounts are given under various conditions, and the most usual types allowed by the conferences included in this study are as follows:

(a). A contract rate of freight, which is, for example, 10 per cent below the tariff or gross rate of freight, is offered to shippers who sign an annual contract to ship *all their goods*[1] over specified routes in conference vessels. In some cases (see Appendix A) the tariff rate is the net contract rate and the non-contract rate is the tariff rate *plus* 10 per cent.

(b). Deferred rebates are granted to shippers for loyalty to conference services over a specified period, typically six months. The gross rate of freight is charged and the rebate, subject to continuous and complete loyalty, is paid to the shipper at the end of the specified 'rebate period' (see Appendix A for examples of various rebate terms).

(c). Sometimes the two methods are combined. In the UK–Australia Conference there is a net contract rate of freight which is the tariff rate, and a non-contract rate is also offered. This is the tariff rate *plus* 10 per cent, *less* 10 per cent six months deferred.

Some conferences, for example the Australia–Europe Conference, do not offer rebates at all. This is due in this case to legal prohibitions in Australia. It can also be a result of closely negotiated rates of freight between a conference and shippers organised as a group and covering a particular class or type of commodity. Such negotiations typically result in a contract at an agreed rate of freight with, in some instances, rebates for the volume of freight made ready for loading at specified ports within specified periods of time.

---

1 See Chapter 3, Section 2(c).(iii). for a fuller description

Dual rates, and loyalty rebates are alternative descriptions or variations on what has been described above. Secret rebates are a method by which an individual ship-owner can increase his share of a trade contrary to conference agreements, and this is a malpractice under conference rules.

d. Open rates

These are usually applied only to commodities transported in bulk. They are also usually, but not invariably, applied to commodities of relatively low unit value and therefore subject to competition from tramp shipping services. The conference leaves the rates of freight for such commodities 'open' to members to make as they judge best in the particular circumstances. There is no fixity about the number of these rates. Conferences can and do from time to time extend or contract the number of open rates in their tariffs. Examples of commodities subject to open rates are as follows:

> Potassium Bicarbonate, in bulk and unpacked.
> Crude Fluorspar, in bulk
> Rock, in bulk
> Salt, in bulk
> Maize, in bulk
> Granular Sodium Carbonate, in bulk
> Fertilisers, in consignments of 4,000 tons (W) minimum.

If the commodity concerned is not transported in bulk it is not usually given an open rate quotation in the tariff. On the other hand, not all commodities transported in bulk are given an open rate. In some cases there is agreement between conference members on a 'floor' for open rates of freight.

e. Dynamic processes in price-making

What has been described so far has been the static pattern or structure of prices, the methods of quoting prices, the relative degrees of price differentiation and the methods of dealing with the main differences in cargo type and with standard transits. We now turn to the conference practices in making *changes* in prices. These are of two general kinds. First, the 'across-the-board' changes of all, or most prices by a stated single common percentage. It should be made clear straight away that there are sometimes exemptions from these general rate changes, which are important in trade volume terms, and these can have a significant influence upon the level and trend of liner freight rates.[1] Such exemptions can, and do, also add to the stability of liner rates, making their comparison with tramp rates more favourable than an inspection of the unadjusted aggregate rate movements suggests. These effects are considered and, in respect of one conference, are estimated in Chapter 5.

United Kingdom—Australia Conference. 'Across-the-board' rate changes are essentially and almost completely 'cost based'. That is to say, changes (almost invariably[2] in an upwards direction in the post war period) are made after a consideration of

1 See comparative trends set out in Chapter 5.

2 But see note (e) to Table B1 in Appendix B.

78

changes in the various categories of cost which are involved in providing the services. As between the conferences considered here the practices in this type of rate change vary considerably.

In the UK—Australia conference an elaborate cost 'formula' was devised and introduced in 1956. In principle it is an analysis of the annual performance, in terms of revenue, cost, profit and physical resource utilisation, of members of the conference in respect of that conference. The basis was devised and comprehensively worked out by a British firm of Accountants and is comparable and consistent across member lines of various nationalities. The costs entering into the formula include all operating, repair and maintenance items, including major overhauls, together with a quite elaborate provision for depreciation at *replacement cost* — a matter of crucial importance in this heavily capital intensive industry. A 'profit allowance' is built into the formula.[1] In many of the years since 1956 the 'profit allowance' (confusingly named a 'capital allowance' in the formula accounts) has not been fully earned.[2] As the cover for this allowance sinks, the case for an upward, across-the-board rate change becomes stronger. The need to make a case for freight rate increases arises in this particular conference from the long established[3] bargaining procedure with representatives of Australian shippers of many of the principal groups of commodities exported to the UK and Europe.[4]

Before 1956 such bargaining was based on a very small amount of cost data from the shipowners' side and was prolonged for this reason among others. The establishment of the formula in that year gave a firmer factual basis for bargaining, and a further move to the same end was the appointment by the shippers' representatives of accountants to inspect the formula calculations and results.

In the outward conference in this trade less bargaining takes place. The conference members meet together to consider a general rate increase and the member lines are represented at a senior level. Consultations, rather than negotiations, are held with two main bodies representing British shippers of goods outwards to Australia. The more general body is the Australian and New Zealand Merchants' and Shippers' Association and the other body, having more specialised but nevertheless important interests in this trade, is the Society of Motor Manufacturers and Traders.

The relative general rate experience in each direction of this trade is set out in Appendix B, Tables B1 to B3 inclusive.

Based upon the general level of freight rates in this conference in 1948, we get an *unweighted* increase in gross freight rates from that year to the end of 1970 of 202 per cent in the outward trade. In the homeward trade the increase is rather less at 177 per cent over the same period. In both cases the surcharges, which were from time to time applied, had by 1970 either been incorporated in basic rates or removed altogether.

---

1 In recent years it has been eight per cent on the historic cost of employed ships, on major additions to such vessels and on investment in new ships in the course of construction.

2 See Chapter 8, Section 3.

3 See Chapter 3, Section 1a.

4 Federal Exporters Oversea Transport Committee (FEOC).

Shippers in the homeward trade were undoubtedly better orgainised and backed more strongly by their government than was the case in the outward direction, and undoubtedly this is one factor which goes towards accounting for this difference in the movements of the two rate levels. But only broad conclusions may be drawn, because the exemptions and exceptions from general rate changes and the changes, which may occur at any time, in individual rates of freight have not yet been examined.[1]

In the case of this conference our conclusion as to methods of making general, across-the-board price changes is that it is a process of costing allied to a process of collective bargaining with customers. Where relatively few large volume commodities are moving the bargaining is relatively tough, but where many thousand different commodities are moving in individual consignments of relatively small volume in each case the bargaining is less well organised, no doubt for obvious practical reasons. This conclusion is supported by documentary evidence of general rate bargaining in both directions in this trade which is given in Chapter 3, Section 1.a.

Far East Freight Conference. In this conference no 'formula' or similar apparatus exists for measuring conference revenue, cost and profit levels and movements in a way which is highly standardised and comparative over time and between member lines. The process for making general rate changes is largely consultative between members with, in very recent years, some quantitative assessment of the movement of certain main components of total cost. There is much less organisational separation in the FEFC of trades by direction than there is in the UK—Australia conference group. The outward and homeward trades are much less distinct, and in fact the FEFC covers the liner trades to and from the United Kingdom/Continent and Korea, Taiwan, Hong Kong, Thailand (Eastbound only), Malaysia and Singapore. Also Japan through the Europe/Japan and Japan/Europe Freight Conferences and the Philippines through Philippines/Europe. It is closely integrated with several other conferences[2] serving the large area of 'the Far East' and its sea links with the United Kingdom and Europe. It also covers the same Far Eastern areas to intermediate areas of the Gulf of Aden and the Red Sea.

The consultative process on rate making embraces not only the member lines but also the conference representatives, known as local chairmen, resident in the Far East, and they in particular give advice about the homeward, or westbound trade. The local chairmen are in touch with local bodies who represent the interests of shippers of particular commodities. There is consultation with these bodies but no negotiations with them on *general* rate changes. No single body exists to negotiate on behalf of shippers interested in either the homeward or the outward trade as a whole, but in certain areas there are shippers' councils and associations of exporters which have recently been active in consultations on general rate changes.

We have examined the consultative processes which are carried out before general rate increases are made in the FEFC. We started with documents relating to events in 1950 and worked forward. In the earlier years the process of consultation was chiefly the assembly of opinions about the size of the upward revision in

1 They are examined later in Chapter 5.

2 See **Appendix A**, where further data on conference area coverage and on membership are set out.

rates as a whole, with some reservations about particular class rates, or the rates for individual commodities, often coupled with recommendations for the exemption of these from the forthcoming increase or for the application to them of a lower rate of increase. In more recent years this process has continued with more emphasis upon exemptions and exceptions in the light of 'outsider' competition, and with the important addition of the collection of cost data in a more precise and systematic form. Previously, some cost data were added by a member in support of an opinion, but no framework existed for the collection, comparison and aggregation of such data. In 1969 an effort was made to collect data on movements in five categories of cost which in total were estimated to account (on average over the membership) for 80 per cent of all costs. Depreciation and capital costs were not collected. The main features of this new procedure for general price making are described below. Attention is given to it because we understand that it is likely to continue and to develop as a method of general price formation.

On January 1st, 1969, member lines were asked individually to submit cost figures according to the following rules:

'(a) Take the round voyages of all vessels which commenced voyages in January 1966, i.e., which benefited fully from the rate increase of 1st December, 1965;

(b) Convert the figure to (U.S.) Dollars at the I.M.F. parity rate then ruling.

(c) Repeat this exercise in respect of the same vessels on imaginary similar round voyages based on costs ruling in December 1968, at the I.M.F. rate now current, disregarding the effects of Suez closure;

(d) Resulting from the above, it should be possible accurately to assess increases in:

(i) Handling charges

(ii) Port dues (excluding Suez Canal Dues)

(iii) Wages and salaries (including Administration)

(iv) Fuel

(v) Ship repair costs.'

There were 21 full members of the FEFC at that time. One member was inactive and so did not take part. Two were relatively new members who were not members during the base period set for this exercise, and so were unable to supply figures. Of the remaining 18, 12 sent figures in the form requested. Of the others, some did not respond and some replied that they were unable to provide the data requested.

Cost experiences differed widely between the 12 members who made returns to the conference secretary.

The cost experiences of member lines over this two year period vary widely. It should be remembered that although members are operating vessels in the same trades and largely on the same routes they are of different nationalities and their different domestic cost trends are reflected in the above table. It is reasonable to expect that all of cost item 3 is incurred at home, while a proportion up to 50 per cent of items 1,2 and 5 will also be domestic expenditure. Wage rate changes differ between countries. Fuel is generally purchased internationally on a contract basis and the terms and time span of such contracts differ between member lines.

The final result in this case was a 9 per cent increase in basic rates which was applied generally to the tariffs outwards and homewards in the FEFC, and a

Table 4.2 *Percentage changes in various shipping costs incurred in round voyages in the Far Eastern Freight Conference. A December 1968 voyage compared with a January 1966 voyage*

Member Lines	Percentage changes				
	1 Handling charges	2 Port Dues (excluding Suez Canal dues)	3 Wages & Salaries (incl. Admin.)	4 Fuel	5 Ship Repairs
A	17.4	12.8	45.5	0.4	25.0
B	14.4	3.7	10.5	1.0	17.5
C	8.3	18.0	13.8	9.5	17.0
D	11.8	7.8	16.0	Nil	17.3
E	14.2	10.3	17.7	11.5	10.5
F[a]	6.0	10.3	−3.1	10.9	−7.9
G	4.8	0.1	24.6	11.3	2.9
H	24.0	11.0	33.0	Nil	13.0
I	19.1	−4.6	1.4	−5.1	−1.0
J	10.0	6.0	21.0	Nil	18.0
K[a]	7.7	10.8	−3.3	7.1	7.5
L	9.0	8.0	20.0	9.6	16.0
Unweighted Average	12.2	7.9	16.4	4.7	11.3
Conference Average	12.5	6.5	15.5	5.5	10.0

(a) These two lines reported that their decreases arose from the request (by the Secretariat) for cost movements to be calculated on the basis of U.S. dollar prices. In terms of Sterling, the two negative items in Line F's return would have read + 12.9 (Wages and Salaries) and + 7.4 (ship repairs). Similarly, the wages and salaries item for Line K would have read + 12.9 per cent in terms of Sterling reflecting the effect of the devaluation of Sterling in 1967. The return from Line I does not point out the devaluation effect, but it is reasonable to suppose that its negative items are due to this cause. The Member Lines are of course of various nationalities: British, Dutch, French, West German, and Japanese shipowners and operators are included here.

reduction in the Suez surcharge of 2½ percentage points to 7½ from the 10 per cent applied in June 1967.

In the trades covered by this conference, rate changes have tended to move together in each direction to a greater extent than in the UK–Australia Conference. The FEFC rate experience in the post war period is given in Appendix B, Tables B4–B6 inclusive.

The total, cumulative increase in the basic liner freight rates in the Far Eastern Freight Conference over the period 1948–70 were 133 per cent outwards and 127 per cent homewards, and the surcharged rate changes (after Suez and devaluation surcharges) were 150 per cent outwards and 144 per cent homewards). If these changes are compared with those in the United Kingdom–Australia Conference, it may be seen that in both cases the outward rates increased rather faster than the homeward rates, although the difference between the two series in the Far East trade was very small. From evidence already presented we know that general across-the-board rate changes are largely cost-based, and therefore it is reasonable to conclude that costs rose faster in the UK–Australia trade than they did in the Far East trade. One obvious difference between the two trades is that the Australian trade is very largely served by refrigerated vessels, which operate in both directions of trade.

United Kingdom—India/Pakistan Conference. The same difference between rate changes in each direction of the trade is found in the UK—India/Pakistan Conference Group, where over the period 1948—1970 the eastbound basic freight rates increased generally by 206 per cent and the westbound rates by 165 per cent. (After Suez and devaluation surcharges are taken into account, the changes were 247 per cent eastbound and 201 per cent westbound). Data on freight rate changes and on surcharges in this conference group are set out in Appendix B, Tables B7—B9 inclusive.

f. Comparative price changes, 1948—70

The general rate changes which have now been given for the three main conference groups under study are unweighted, that is to say no account has as yet been taken of individual exemptions from a general rate change, nor has weight been applied where individual freight rates have been changed (usually decreased) at times other than at a general change in all rates. A weighting exercise to take account of these individual rate changes is undertaken later and the results are presented in Chapter 5. A simple comparison of these general freight liner rate changes over the whole period from 1948—1970 is given in Table 4.3 and is associated with the concurrent changes in the time charter tramp shipping rates, in retail and wholesale prices in the United Kingdom and in other prices over the same period. It must be emphasised that the increase in conference freight rates is overstated for the reasons given above and also for the compounding effect of across-the-board rate increases based on the previously existing rates without any allowance being made for exceptions and exemptions in the previous period.

The average, unweighted increase in gross basic rates of freight in the three conferences in both directions of trade was substantially greater over the period (1948—1970) than the increase in any of the UK price series quoted here for the same period, although the UK retail prices rose by only a little less than the surcharged rates in one of the three conferences, the FEFC. World wide primary product prices rose not at all in this period and time-charter tramp rates increased by only 34 per cent.

The relative stability of liner and tramp rates is shown in Table 5.10., Chapter 5, and annual average rates of change of the various freight rate series are estimated (Table 5.4) by the method of least squares, which is chosen so as best to overcome the difficulties of trend measurement of variables having very large short run variations, as is the case with the tramp shipping rate, and further analysis is therefore deferred now until these calculations are presented and examined in Chapter 5.

g. Secondary pricing

We now consider the secondary but in some cases very important aspects of dynamic price-making by liner conferences.

The secondary pricing processes are of two kinds: exemptions from general, across-the-board rate changes in either direction; and changes in individual rates of freight which may take place at any time. Exemptions are themselves of two kinds. Some are made on the initiative of the conference at the time a general rate increase is made, others are made in response to requests received from shippers, acting either individually or collectively, at the time of a general rate increase or soon afterwards.

Table 4.3 *'Deep sea' liner and tramp freight rate changes, unweighted, compared with each other and with other price changes, 1948–1970*

| | | Percentages | | |
		Outwards from UK	Homewards to UK	Combined (average)
UK–Australia				
	a. Basic rates	202	177	190
	b. Surcharged rates	202	177	190
UK–Far East				
	a. Basic rates	133	127	130
	b. Surcharged rates	150	144	147
UK–India/Pakistan				
	a. Basic rates	206	165	186
	b. Surcharged rates	247	201	224
Unweighted average	a. Basic rates	180	156	169
for these Conferences	b. Surcharged rates	200	174	187
Time charter tramp rates[a]				34
UK wholesale prices[b]	(i) All manufactured products			103
	(ii) Materials and fuels used in manufacturing industry			83
UK prices of capital goods[b]				106
UK retail prices, all items[b]				137
World-wide primary product prices[b]				no change

(a) The change between average 1948 and average 1970 rates are given here. These rates are prone to violent fluctuations. The best measure of changes in them is the method of least squares, see Chapter 5.

(b) Source: *The British Economy Key Statistics, 1900–1970*. Table E. Published for the London and Cambridge Economic Service by Times Newspapers Ltd. London.

Consideration is given below to the secondary rate changes associated with a number of general rate increases in the UK–Australia conference.

In March 1951 a 15 per cent general rate increase was applied owing to 'heavy increases in operating costs'. The exemptions made at the time were not to specific commodities but the following special rates were left unchanged: heavy lifts, *ad valorem* rates and minimum freights. The yield of freight revenue from *ad valorem* rates (which are applied to cargo of exceptionally high value/weight ratios) would rise with the values of this class of cargo which may be expected to move in the same direction as shipowners' costs, if not always *pari passu*.

Later the conference becomes more aware of the sensitive commodities, i.e., those which can least well bear the general rate increase, and which are most likely to drive shippers to 'chartering'. i.e. the use of voyage or time chartered shipping. Later general rate increases with exemptions are given in Table 4.4.

In this conference, general rate changes and exemptions are agreed jointly with the Continent–Australia Outwards Conference, and meetings of representatives of all or nearly all[1] member lines of both conferences are held in London.

As has been shown earlier, rate changes of a general nature tend to move in step in both directions of the trade. This is generally known by shippers and it can enter

1 At the meeting held on 20 November, 1963, the representative of one member line was unable to be present. The agreement of this member to the March 1964 general rate increase of 7½ per cent, which was under discussion at this meeting, was obtained by telex to make the decision a unanimous one.

Table 4.4 *United Kingdom—Australia Conference, general rate increases. Reasons and Exemptions.*

Date of General Increase and percentage	Reasons Given [a]	Exceptions and Exemptions
March 1957 14%	'Continuing heavy increase in cost of maintaining services'.	Class 0.18 from 440/- to 450/- (2¼ per cent only), and class 0.20 increased by ¼ per cent only.
March 1964 7%	'Continuing increases in operating costs, i.e., port expenses, labour costs in UK and Australia, and in the running expenses of ships.'	'Special' increases for Machinery and Tools, and for Motor Vehicles. [b]
November 1965 5%	'Continuing increases in the cost of maintaining shipping services i.e., increasing costs in stevedoring and port charges in UK and Australia and in seamen's wages. Shipowners' return on capital employed is below that in industry generally.' [c]	Some types of Paper, Boards, Woodpulp and Timber. Motor Vehicles. No increase.
March 1967 4%	'Continuing increases in costs in the operation of the service'.	Motor Vehicles. No increase.

(a) And publicly announced.
(b) See Table 4.5. No increase was applied to this important commodity at this time because in the case of CKD motor vehicles a rate *decrease* of 6% in July 1963 was made firm for 18 months to January 1965 (when in fact it was raised by 6%). The 'unpacked' motor vehicle rate also followed an individual course, being exempted in March 1964 following an increase of 38% in January of the same year and remaining unchanged for more than three years, until April 1967 when the rate was raised by 10 per cent.
(c) This statement is doubtless based upon the 'formula' calculations of return of capital employed by the conference in the outward and homeward 'legs' of UK–Australia trade, which is referred to and briefly described earlier in this chapter.

the rate bargaining processes as is shown by the following extract from the minutes of a conference meeting.

'The Chairman said that as soon as possible after the percentage increase in homeward rates is known, which he understood would probably be towards the end of December, it is proposed to approach the Australian and New Zealand Merchants' and Shippers' Association in regard to outward rates. He added that whilst every effort would be made to obtain the same percentage increase outwards as that obtained homewards, it might be necessary to make some small concession in view of the criticism by the Merchants' Association on the last occasion when rates were raised by 10% in the outward trade, although only 7½% was obtained homewards.'[1]

In the event, an increase of 14 per cent was obtained homewards in February 1957, and this was followed in March by an increase of 14 per cent outwards.

It was about this time that a major exemption from a general rate increase occurred in the outward trade. In March 1957, unpacked and C.K.D. (completely

1 Meeting of 27 November, 1956. The changes referred to were +10% outwards in July 1955 and +7½% homewards in September of the same year.

'knocked down') motor vehicles took the 14 per cent general rate increase. Very soon this led German and also British motor manufacturers into chartering for their shipping needs to Australia and New Zealand. This breakaway and the consequent loss of freight revenue was very serious for the conference. Motor vehicles were estimated to account for between 25 and 30 per cent of total bill of lading tonnage at that time.[1] Special rates were quickly made by the conference and the course of the two motor vehicle rates of the general rate changes are shown below (Table 4.5.) for the period from January 1955 to May 1971. Over this period general (unweighted) freight rates increased by 148 per cent, CKD motor vehicle rates by 65 per cent — less than half this increase, and unpacked motor vehicle rates by only 53 per cent. The competitive pressure (from chartering outside the conference, particularly by Volkswagen) was strongest in the years 1958, 1959 and 1960 and its effect may be seen in terms of motor vehicle rate reductions in these years. From about 1965 onwards motor vehicle rates moved much more closely in step with general freight rate movements.

From September 1958 the two motor vehicle rates diverge markedly in a downwards direction from general rate movements. They also diverge from each other from November 1959 onwards, and they do not move in step again until January 1967 when the CKD rate was fixed for two years (until January 1969). In absolute money terms the CKD rate was lower (at 155/-) after the increase in April, 1967 (+ 10%) than it had been ten years earlier in March 1957 when it was 168/9. The 'unpacked' rate was also lower over the same period. Of the two, the CKD rate was by far the most important in terms of freight revenue in the later part of this period.

These special rates for motor vehicles are very important exemptions from general rate changes, and when conference freight rate indexes are compared with each other and with tramp rates over the post war period a weighted general freight rate index is needed to take account of the really significant departures from the general trend which such items as these represent.

In addition, there are some exemptions from a general rate increase (GRI) which arise from applications from shippers, acting either individually or collectively. In Table 4.6. is shown the results of an analysis of requests made for exemptions, requests refused and requests granted.

A breakdown of these figures as between the United Kingdom and the Continent is possible for the last four general rate increases given in Table 4.6., but not for the GRI of October 1960.

Only just over one in ten of the requests made over the period 1960 to 1967 were granted. Approximately 7,125 commodities were listed in the UK—Australia outward tariff in 1967, exemptions from general rate increases were granted on only 0.036 per cent of them over a seven year period. The rates which are candidates for exemption for one reason or another and which are known by the conference to be sensitive to a general rate increase, such as the two motor vehicle rates, are often dealt with by the conference at the time of the GRI and are not left until a request

1   The more important measure is the percentage of gross freight revenue, but this is not available for this period. Later more conference statistics were compiled and we know that for the year to 31 August, 1967 motor vehicles in packed (CKD) and unpacked form accounted for 12.1 per cent of total gross freight revenue outwards.

Table 4.5. *United Kingdom–Australia Conference, motor vehicle and general freight rate changes compared, 1955–1971*

Date of rate change	Motor vehicles C.K.D. (%)	Index	Motor vehicles unpacked (%)	Index	General freight rate changes and surcharges (%)	Surcharged Index
1955 Jan.	—	100.0	—	100.0	–	100.0
Jul.	10	110.0	10	110.0	10	110.0
57 Mar.	14	125.4	14	125.4	14	125.4
58 Sept.	− 10	112.9	− 10	112.9	–	125.4
59 Nov.	− 12½	98.8	–	112.9	–	125.4
60 Mar.	–	98.8	− 7½	104.4	–	125.4
Oct.	–	98.8	–	104.4	7½	134.8
61 Jan.	4	102.8	4	108.6	–	134.8
62 Feb.	5	107.9	–	108.6	–	134.8
Oct.	–	107.9	− 35	70.6	5	141.5
63 Jan.	− 2½	105.2	–	70.6	–	141.5
Jul.	− 6	98.9	–	70.6	–	141.5
64 Jan.	–	98.9	38	97.4	–	141.5
Mar.	–	98.9	–	97.4	7½	152.1
65 Jan.	6	104.8	–	97.4	–	152.1
Nov.	–	104.8	–	97.4	5	159.7
67 Mar.	–	104.8	–	97.4	4	166.1
Apr.	10	115.3	10	107.1	–	166.1
Jun.	–	115.3	–	107.1	5(a)	174.4
Nov.	12½(b)	129.7	12½(b)	120.5	12½(b)	196.2
69 Jun.	5	136.2	5	126.5	–	196.2
70 Jun.	10	149.8	10	139.2	–	196.2
Sept.	–	149.8	–	139.2	12½	220.7
71 Mar.	–	149.8	–	139.2	12½	248.3
May.	10	164.8	10	153.1	–	248.3

(a) Suez surcharge. Not applied to motor vehicle rates which had been raised by 10 per cent only two months earlier.

(b) Devaluation surcharge, immediately applied to all rates.

Table 4.6. *United Kingdom–Australia and Continent–Australia Outwards Conferences. An Analysis of Requests for Freight Rate Reductions*

1 Date and size of General Rate Increase (GRI)	2 Number of requests made	3 Number refused	4 Number granted	5 % Granted
Oct. 1960 (+ 7½)	52	49	3	5.8%
Sept. 1962 (+ 5)	35	35	0	0
Mar. 1964 (+ 7½)	76	61	15	19.7
Nov. 1965 (+ 5)	43	37	6	14.0
Jan. 1967 (+ 10)	23	21	2	8.7
	229	203	26	11.4

for exemption is received. This, in part, explains why nearly 90 per cent of GRI requests for exemption are turned down. Another reason is that many of the requests are for commodities which move in very small quantities.

Of the exemptions to a GRI made on the initiative of the conference (generally they are proposed by individual member lines) and noted in Table 4.4, only two, those relating to motor vehicles, were of importance in the post-war period to the

Table 4.7. *An analysis of requests from United Kingdom and Continental Shippers for freightʒht rate reductions*

Requests from shippers in:	Number of Requests made	(% share)	Refused	(% share)	Granted	(% share)	% Granted
United Kingdom	125	(71)	112	(73)	13	(57)	10.4
Continent	52	(29)	42	(27)	10	(43)	19.2
	177	(100)	154	(100)	23	(100)	13.0

UK—Australia conference. The exemptions granted to shippers of 'paper, boards, woodpulp and timber', in November 1965, were important in the Continent—Australia liner trade but not in the UK trade to Australia. The special increases in the rates for 'machinery and tools' (in March 1964) were increases *above* the general rate increase and were due to an increase in the value/weight ratios for these commodities. This pricing rule of higher rates for commodities of higher value is widely applied by conferences in setting *relative* prices, and its entry here is incidental to the dynamic process of making general price changes. Relative price-making in individual cases is examined in detail in Chapter 6.

In the Australia—Europe Conference exemptions also occur but the common pattern is for the rates for some commodities to move independently as a result of bargaining with individual Australian produce boards. General increases in rates also take place and these apply to general cargo and also quite widely, but separately negotiated rate changes frequently apply to wool, apples and pears, and canned fruit, for example. The negotiating machinery which has for many years been established in Australia virtually precludes applications from shippers for exemptions from general rate changes. This is of course because such changes are negotiated with shippers before they are announced and put into effect.

In the Far Eastern Freight Conference the pattern of exemptions is similar in that in the outward trade exemptions from a general rate increase were very rare in the early post war years. In September 1961, when there was a 10 per cent general rate increase, exemptions numbered four: motor vehicles, tinplate, asbestos cement sheets, and fertilisers; the first three being of importance to UK trade with the Far East, but motor vehicles are of proportionally less importance in this trade than they are in UK—Australia trade. Later, in March 1964, a longer list of exemptions appears, and this trend is apparent also in the UK—Australia outward trade, though to a lesser extent.

The homeward trade in liner commodities covered by the FEFC also has parallels with the UK—Australian trade homewards in that relatively high value primary commodities are also concerned. As to industrial products from Japan and Hong Kong, the conference policy on exemptions is similar to that adopted in the outward trade, but the trade homewards from Malyasia and Singapore exhibits the pattern shown in Table 4.8. In a way which is rather similar to the motor vehicle case in the outward trade, special consideration is given to the rates for rubber.

There has been a long history of special treatment of the freight rate for Malaysian rubber, and there are also other cases of similar action for the shipment of particular commodities in this trade (palm oil and timber are examples). Rubber is particularly interesting because of its importance to the conference in volume and

Table 4.8. *Carryings by FEFC full members homewards from Singapore, Port Swettenham and Penang, 1966.*

	('000 Bill of Lading Tons).
Rubber	320.7
Bulk Latex	86.8
Drummed Latex	26.3
Sawn.Timber	224.6
Bulk Palm Oil	92.6
Canned Pineapples	53.7
Tin	13.6
Coffee	10.7
Palm Kernels	9.1
Pepper	8.8
Plywood	5.3
Canes and Rattans	5.2
General Cargo	70.6
Total	928.0

freight revenue terms,[1] and the rate of freight charged for it is vital to growers because it is a considerable proportion of the landed price of rubber. As is well known, rubber is an important export trade of Singapore and Malaysia. It enters a highly competitive market in Europe where it competes not only with synthetic rubber but also with natural rubber from other sources. The price elasticity of demand for Malaysian rubber is high due to this competitive situation, and because the shipping freight per ton is a relatively large proportion[2] of the landed, cif, price of rubber and because the gross freight receipts from rubber are important to ship-owners the rate bargaining acquires great significance for both shippers and the conference. If other influential factors are assumed unchanged, a relatively small change in the rate of freight can have a relatively large effect upon the volume of rubber shipped.

The trend of freight rates for Malaysian rubber is given below in comparison with general rate changes in the Far East Freight Conference Homewards over the period 1957 to 1968.

Including the small favourable effect which stemmed from the devaluation of sterling, the conference freight rate for sheet rubber from this area rose by only 5 per cent over this ten year period. The rate for crepe rubber fell by $6\frac{2}{3}$ per cent, while the conference rate for general cargo from this area to Europe rose by approximately 23 per cent in terms of local currency, i.e., including allowances for the devaluation effect and for the devaluation surcharge effect.

It may be seen from Table 4.8. that rubber, in its various forms, accounts for a high proportion of the total carryings in this section of the FEFC trade homewards. The trend of unweighted conference rates as a whole clearly overstates the true position in this branch of this trade. The construction of a weighted conference freight rate index poses complex data assembly and statistical problems. An attempt to construct such an index for the homeward direction of the UK—Australia Conference is made in Chapter 5.

1   In terms of bill of lading tons rubber shipments accounted for 47 per cent of total conference shipments from Malaya and Singapore in 1966.

2   Typically between 6 and 8 per cent. See case history 8 in Chapter 6.

Table 4.9. *Conference liner freight rate movements for Singapore and Malaysian rubber, in comparison with general conference rate movements over the same routes and the same period.* [a]

	Rubber Rate		General Rates
	Sheet	Crepe	
1957 Jun.	100.0	100.0	100.0
1958	100.0	100.0	100.0
1959	100.0	100.0	100.0
1960	100.0	100.0	100.0
1961 Sept.	110.0	110.0	110.0
1962	110.0	110.0	110.0
1963 Apr.	108.0	108.0	110.0
Jly.	108.0	97.2	110.0
1964 Mar.	108.0	97.2	121.0
1965 Dec.	113.4	101.9	127.1
1966	113.4	101.9	127.1
1967 Nov.	110.1	98.9	123.2
1968 Mar.	105.4	94.1	123.2
Sept.	105.0	93.3	123.2

(a) The Suez surcharge of 10 per cent was applied in June 1967 to all rates quoted here, but it has not been included in any of the indexes. The devaluation surcharge of 12½ per cent left the rates for rubber lower by the change shown above for November 1967; the Singapore/Malaysian dollar was not devalued at this time, and the full devaluation effect was 16.67 per cent. The resulting difference on *these indexes* is reflected in this table.

Figure 2 *Theoretical cost structure of freight liner operation*

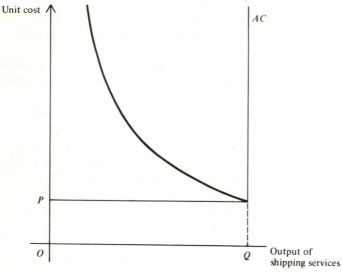

3. Theoretical aspects of price formation in the shipping industry

a. Conditions of Supply

In terms of cost characteristics the shipping industry has something in common with railways and air transport. A common feature is the large share of capital costs in total costs. In this respect the railways are a prime example because, unlike the other two, they have to provide the capital in the form of their tracks and terminals as well as their vehicles. In all three transport industries the high proportion of capital and other overhead costs, including organisational costs, which are fixed in the short run (and for the railways at least to some extent in the long run also), implies that average total costs per unit of output will decline as output increases from zero. Furthermore, marginal cost (MC) must be lower than average total cost (AC) at any level of output which occurs under conditions of falling AC.

It is most important to establish at an early stage the basic differences between the cost structure of the operations of a single ship, which will reflect the economics of ship size, and the cost structure of a shipping fleet serving a liner trade which may or may not be controlled by a conference. In the case of the single ship there are substantial economies to large scale in several types of vessel, particularly oil tankers, other bulk carriers and the new large container ships. The average cost curve of operating a single freight-carrying vessel is typically of the shape shown in Figure 2.

If the vessel is to be put into a condition to earn any revenue at all a very large proportion if its total costs are fixed regardless of the volume of output of shipping services it can produce. This implies that average cost per unit of output[1] (AC) falls steeply as output increases from zero until at an output of OQ units AC rises vertically.[2] At this point the capacity of the vessel has been reached and further freight shipping services can be produced only at the cost of providing another vessel, which may be expected to have cost characteristics which are similar to those illustrated in Figure 2. In the *short run*, therefore, the costs which have to be met before *any* output can be achieved account for a very large proportion of total costs, and are in fact total costs less only selling, cargo handling, and a proportion of ship's time costs; and these are the only costs which will vary with output in the short run. So once the vessel has been put 'on the berth' a large proportion of total cost is fixed and inescapable in the short run. Average total costs will therefore fall steeply as the large proportion of fixed costs is spread over an increasing output. This characteristic of a ship's cost structure puts a premium on a high level of utilisation of the ship's capacity at any level of price, for an assumed homogeneous cargo unit, [1] above OP. At any price below OP the vessel could not be continued in operation beyond a short term regardless of the proportion of capacity utilised, but the cost of laying-up the vessel has to be compared with the cost of continuing it in operation before a decision of this kind can be reached.

For the specialised bulk carriers and for the container types of vessel referred to earlier, scale economies can be very large as deadweight tonnages rise to 50,000, 100,000 and well beyond in the case of oil tankers. The cost characteristics which have been described change with greater size of vessel only in that variable costs then constitute an even lower proportion of total costs in the short run situation. Average total costs will therefore fall further the greater is the size of vessel and therefore, in order to gain the full economies of scale, it becomes even more

1   It is assumed that the cargo and the costs of handling it are respectively homogeneous and constant per unit of output.

2   In practice, for a freight liner but not for a bulk carrier, AC will start to rise before OQ is reached as loading and stowage becomes more difficult as the final 10 per cent or so of cargo is fitted into, and taken out of, the vessel.

necessary than it is with the smaller vessel to utilise it at or near its full capacity: because as output increases total costs increase proportionately less until full capacity is reached.

It has already been noticed that marginal cost will be lower than average cost when average cost is falling, and so $MC < AC$ will hold for all outputs below OQ. Therefore the application of a 'marginal cost pricing' rule to ship operation under short run conditions will lead to the obvious loss-making problem at any output below OQ. This result is of course a common one which invariably arises when this pricing rule is considered for activities which are highly capital intensive, as is ship operation, and which also have a large proportion of fixed costs and which accordingly experience declining total costs per unit of output in the short run. So, whatever may be the wider economic and social virtues[1] of this rule in terms of optimum resource allocation, its application to ship economics in the short run would create a need for subsidies from public funds which would be exceeded only by railway operations where short run marginal cost can approach zero under some quite common operating conditions; so great is the proportion of fixed to variable cost in railways.

The above discussion on ship costs has been related to the short run. It may be noticed before going on to consider long run cost structures, that the larger the ship the longer is the short run.

We must now turn to consider the cost characteristics of a liner trade in the long run. Others[2] have shown that in this context much more constant costs per unit of output may be expected over the *long term*.

Unlike the railways, sea freight transport has no track costs and very little long run fixity in terminal costs. The output of freight shipping services, the flow of cargo and the total costs of sea transport will therefore vary directly with each other and by approximately the same proportion over an extended range of output in the long run. In other words a liner trade is likely to experience approximately constant marginal and average real costs in the long run. This may be illustrated in the way set out in Figure 3. On the same assumptions as have already been made, namely that the cargo is composed of homogeneous units, a flow of trade over a deep sea route constitutes a long run demand for freight liner shipping services which may be supplied by a large number of individual 'sailings' of cargo liners. As noticed above, there are no long term fixed costs in the form of track or terminal costs, and what is an even more important distinction, the costs of adding or subtracting a unit of production, i.e. a 'sailing'. are all variable costs to the 'shipping industry' supplying the 'trade' concerned. This is so because vessels may be switched between 'trades', and alternative uses are available over a wide range due to the essential flexibility in the employment of freight vessels.

1 These virtues, and some associated vices, occupy extensive territory in the literature, and no attempt is made here to provide references beyond one to a well known article which provides an admirable summary and critique of the many versions and variations of the theory of marginal cost pricing. This article is by Nancy Ruggles, 'Recent Developments in the Theory of Marginal Cost Pricing' *Review of Economic Studies*, Vol. 17 (1949–50), pp. 107–26.

2 Ferguson. Lerner, McGee, Oi, Rapping & Sobotka: *'The Economic Value of the United States Merchant Marine'*. Northwestern University, USA, 1961. Also: J.O. Jansson *'Rate-making in Liner Shipping: some puzzling features'*. Paper published by the International Cargo Handling Co-ordination Association. London, 1970.

Vessels sail successively to supply the trade, and given efficient organisation of supply and reasonably well-balanced trade flows in each direction, short run discontinuities involving sharply rising marginal costs do not arise. Evidence given later[1] shows that under 'closed' conference organisation vessels sail with a high (80–90 per cent) level of capacity utilisation, and so under such conditions it is reasonable to postulate a smooth 'envelope' long run cost curve representing both long run average total cost and long run marginal cost (the dotted line in Figure 3). Under conditions of less buoyant demand a conflict does arise between capacity utilisation and frequency of sailings. If capacity utilisation levels fall, average unit costs rise, and if sailings become less frequent the quality of service to shippers declines and competitive pressures from outside the conference increase.

Figure 3 *Theoretical cost structure of freight conference fleet operation*

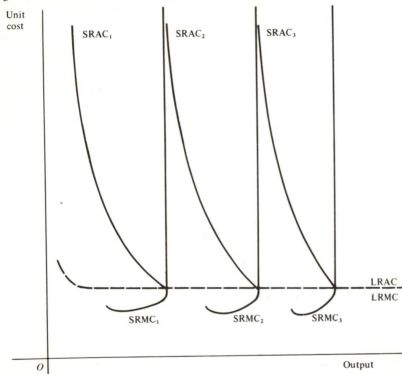

This assumes that there are no economies or diseconomies of scale to the shipping industry serving this trade. The operation of ships in a conference, or collective monopoly, will generally avoid the discontinuities which arise due to a sequence of sailings which does not match the flow of trade, but other discontinuities due to the operation of vessels of widely different efficiencies are more likely to arise. Scale economies from organisational sources are not likely to be great, unless the conference is composed of a small number of large shipowning companies which in

1   See Chapter 8, Section 1

themselves are capable of realising scale economies relating to their *fleets* which then appear as scale economies in the operation of the shipping services serving the trade concerned.

In the case of large container consortia serving a trade, the vessels are more likely to be of similar performance to one another and if discontinuities in sailings are avoided, scale economies are likely to arise from organisational sources, as distinct from scale economies due to ship size which will also be present in this case.

There is considerable homogeneity in the supply of shipping services offered to customers of shipping conferences. In terms of regularity of sailings and times of transit there are only small variations between conference members. In terms of care of handling goods throughout their transit and in the degree of promptness in handling claims there are some fairly small differences between shipowners and between types of goods in the shipping service supplied to customers by conference lines. Tramp shipping services do not aim to supply a complete range of services to a trade. Where their services are substitutes for liner services, whether controlled by a conference or not, they are less homogeneous in the terms described above. The evidence set out earlier[1] suggests that liner services provided independently, i.e., outside a conference, provide services which are less homogeneous than conference liner services in terms of regularity and speed. But by and large the service product of liners is fairly homogeneous and this makes for the unity of the market in shipping services of this general type.

b. Conditions of demand

If we look now at the demand side and the state of buyers' knowledge about this market we find many imperfections. So many in fact that they break up the market demand curve for liner shipping services into many relatively small sections. Although shippers sometimes have quite complete intra-sectional market knowledge about the terms on which their competitors' goods are shipped, they do not have much knowledge of the terms on which other goods in other sections of the market are shipped over the same trade route. So the market for *liner* shipping services is a fragmented one, and the demand curve is broken and disjointed. Not so the market for tramp shipping services, where whole vessels are hired on a voyage or time charter basis. Charter rates, largely subject to violent fluctuations, are often made in a single market (the Baltic Exchange) and are generally applicable to an extensive range of different cargoes, and buyers (the charterers) are knowledgeable about prices over a wide area of the market, and often the entire market. These characteristics of the liner freight market and of the consequent nature of the demand for liner shipping services have important consequences for price formation, and these are examined next.

c. Differential pricing

It has already been pointed out that the demand for liner freight shipping services is sectionalised and fragmented by lack of buyers' knowledge. In economic terms the demand curve for shipping space for the carriage of liner cargo in a specified

---

1 See Chapter 3.

trade is not smooth and continuous. There are likely to be many discontinuities in it and, what is even more important, there will be sections of market demand where the coefficient of price elasticity of demand will be very low. These characteristics of demand for this type of freight shipping service lead to the making of differential prices by sellers. The conditions for successful price differentiation in the longer term are that entry to the industry be restricted and that the product is not resaleable. Both these chief conditions are met by shipping conferences.

The economics of differential pricing or, in non-economic terms, 'charging what the market will bear', has received considerable attention from academic economists.[1] Two major points stand out. The first is that if perfect price differentiation were to be practiced, that is to say, if a separate, single price were charged for each and every separate consignment of goods over a specified trade route; and if, further, the market demand or average revenue (AR) curve were downward–sloping, then the marginal revenue (MR) curve would co-incide with the average revenue curve, and buyers would lose all their consumers' surplus. By contrast, if we assume again a straight-line downward sloping demand curve, but this time a homogeneous product sold by an industry in a *single* market, i.e., without any price differentiation, we get the well-known relationship[2] between MR and AR, with MR declining twice as fast as price (AR) as sales increase.

The second main point, which follows from the first, is that given the long run cost structure in freight liner shipping which has been described earlier in this chapter, output may be expanded up to the point at which the average revenue curve meets the horizontal long run average cost curve. For all units of output up to this point, marginal revenue (equivalent under perfect price differentiation to average revenue, i.e., price) will exceed long run marginal and average (since costs are constant) cost. Many differential prices will be far above their corresponding long run marginal costs, and this situation is open to some well-known objections of welfare economics. On the other hand, output is not restricted because of rapidly falling marginal revenue as output increases; as it would be if price differentiation were not practiced. There is a point here which needs looking at in further detail and it requires another slightly deeper, excursion into economic theory. In concerns the importance of 'satisfying marginal conditions' (which is explained below) and the extent to which price differentiation does this.

d. Marginal conditions

One of the chief proponents of the case for marginal cost pricing, Harold Hotelling,[3]

1 Especially from A.C. Pigou, *The Economics of Welfare,* 4th Ed. Part II, Ch. XVII. which deals with discriminating monopoly, including cartels. Pigou goes on (in Ch. XVIII. of Part II) to consider the more practical aspects of price differentiation in the setting of railway rates.

2 Joan Robinson, *The Economics of Imperfect Competition,* Ch. 2.

3 This is a major landmark in statements of the case for marginal cost pricing. Harold Hotelling, 'The General Welfare in relation to problems of taxation and of railway and utility rates.' *Econometrica,* Vol. 6 (1938), pp. 242–69.

Figure 4 *Illustration of J. Dupuit's price and utility theory*

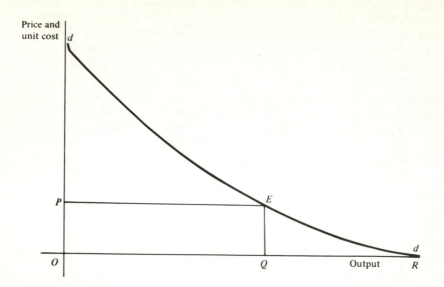

has based himself upon Jules Dupuit's example of the bridge toll.[1] The salient point made by Dupuit is that the consumers' surplus, which he uses as a measure of utility, is greatest when no tolls are charged for the use of a bridge.

In Figure 4, if dd represents the demand for 'crossings' of the bridge, a toll of OP will result in the loss of utility to potential consumers of EQR (which, for *small* tolls, Dupuit showed to be proportional to the square of the rate of toll or tax). If we assume that the marginal cost of crossing the bridge is nil, then a policy of marginal cost pricing will involve setting price equal to zero for maximum consumer benefit and for *the fulfilment of marginal conditions*. The cost of maintaining a bridge and providing for its depreciation is best met from sources of tax which in their incidence involve less loss of welfare (utility) than the charging of a toll. So, it is concluded, marginal cost pricing is a desirable aim of public economic policy and ought to be applied to public utilities such as gas supplies and railways. Price differentiation such as is practiced by railways and shipping conferences involves loss of utility by raising *some* prices far above their corresponding marginal cost.

We now turn to consider some arguments which are more favourable to price differentiation as an economic pricing policy. Nancy Ruggles, in her survey article on marginal cost pricing,[2] examines the situation of industries, similar to liner shipping (the actual example she considers is electricity supply) in that there are discontinuities and inelasticities in the demand for their products. She is worth quoting in full on this point.

1 J. Dupuit was a French engineer. He lived in the first half of the nineteenth century and held a senior post in the Department des Pont et Chaussées of the French Government. The aspect of his work in economics which we are concerned with here is contained in a paper 'On the measurement of the utility of public works', *Annales des Ponts et Chaussées*, second series, Vol. 8, 1844; translated by R.H. Barback for *International Economic Papers*, 1952, no. 2, pp. 83–110.

2 Nancy Ruggles (1950) op. cit.

'It is quite likely that in certain sectors of the economy, price discrimination which would meet the marginal conditions would not be difficult to arrive at, despite protestations to the contrary of the proponents of marginal cost pricing. Demand curves are not smooth and continuous and single-valued; they contain many discontinuities, and there are many products for which demand is almost perfectly inelastic within the relevant range. Taking advantage of such discontinuities and inelasticities, the construction of workable systems of price discrimination which *will not violate marginal conditions*[1] is quite feasible. For example, it is probably true that the use of block systems of rates for electricity does not appreciably interfere with the meeting of the marginal conditions, since it is to be doubted whether householders greatly reduce their consumption of electricity because they cannot obtain additional amounts at the industrial rate.'

If we now turn back to consider the freight liner shipping industry serving a trade, we find price differentiation on a large scale. What are the class rates in, for example, the UK–Hong Kong Outwards Conference, but a 'block system'[2]? Here we find 23 class rates into which are fitted **2,845 se**parate commodities, together with 59 special rates covering a total of 209 commodities. This is a long way from perfect price discrimination, and like, the electricity case cited by Nancy Ruggles, it is to be doubted whether shippers greatly reduce their consumption of shipping services because they cannot obtain additional amounts at a lower class rate. This at least may be claimed for commodities to which the higher class rates apply. Price is well above marginal cost but, unlike Dupuit's bridge where more would cross if the toll were reduced or abolished, no more cargo would travel if the higher class rates were reduced. But it is important to notice that a distinguishing feature of the liner shipping situation is the considerable sectionalisation and inelasticity of demand within each section. This holds true for commodities with a high value/weight[3] ratio which also have low coefficients of price elasticity of demand.[4] When, lower down the price scale of the demand schedule, we meet commodities with a much lower value/weight ratio, the price elasticity of demand for shipping space for them tends to be higher and so in these sections of the market *marginal conditions are much more difficult to fulfil*, and we begin to approach the Dupuit case, particularly when we come to consider the sea transport of primary commodities which have value/weight ratios which are relatively low in relation to those of manufactured goods, but relatively rather higher than those of goods which generally travel in bulk in specialised vessels or in large consignments in tramp vessels.

4. Price theory and conference pricing practice

The precise position and the shape of a demand curve for freight liner shipping services over a particular trade route cannot of course be determined, but in general

---

1   Our italics.

2   See Table 4.1. earlier in this chapter.

3   See the results of the application of a price model to liner shipping data and the accompanying analysis of the relative importance of component factors in Chapter 7.

4   See later studies of the price elasticity of demand in Chapter 6.

terms it is known that competition from air freight transport at the top end of the price scale, and from tramp vessels at the bottom end of the scale, impart greater elasticity to demand in these extremes of the price range. In between these there is likely to be a wide band of price where less elasticity will prevail for reasons which have been given in the previous section. In Figure 5 a curve representing an approximate demand schedule with these characteristics is shown in relation to *long run* cost 'curves' which are based on empirical data.[1] From the same set of observations some prices have also been assembled. So it is possible to relate costs to prices and to indicate, subject to two assumptions, some broad conclusions. First the assumptions.

a. That costs are homogeneous per unit of cargo. We know that they are not, and some empirical evidence can be assembled, but it cannot be represented diagrammatically in a way which is useful.

b. That price differentiation is perfect; that is to say that a separate price is charged for each consignment of cargo. Some shipping conferences nearly reach this degree of 'perfection', but the one from which the data are drawn here does not. It employs a 'block' system of class rates in association with some 'special' and *ad valorem* rates. In economic terms this means that the AR and MR are not, in fact, conterminous as drawn in Figure 5. Some relaxation of this assumption will be made later in this analysis.

Bearing in mind these assumptions, the broad conclusions which may be drawn are as follows.

a. That the profit, represented in Figure 5 by the area ABC, just about balanced the loss, represented by CEF, at the output OQ_2. The results of three conference voyages are shown here in respect of prices and costs. A very small profit was in fact earned after depreciation.[2] Average revenue per B/L ton was £15.20 and long run average total cost per B/L ton was £15.07. The gross margin on freight receipts was 13.3 per cent, and the net, pre-tax margin (after depreciation) was 0.8 per cent.

b. Following from a. above it is clear that cross-subsidisation of shipping services occurred. The 'higher-priced' consignments, defined as those priced above LRAC, were carried at profitable rates, while those priced below LRAC were carried at a loss in the *long run* terms illustrated here.

c. That the lowest price charged,[3] £5.04 per B/L ton, was only just above average incremental cost, i.e. only just higher than the average extra cost of putting an additional unit of cargo into a vessel and taking it out again, *plus* the associated selling costs (commissions and rebates), but without an allowance for the ship's time cost invoived.

d. It follows from c. above that, in this example, price has not been set lower than AIC which is the best proxy we have for *short run* marginal cost

1 The cost figures are derived from the cost data of three voyages of vessels of similar size which sailed outwards from the United Kingdom in one of the conferences included in this study and covering one specific 'trade'.

2 At current replacement cost.

3 We have price data in detail for only one of the three voyages concerned.

Figure 5 *Conference price and cost structure in a particular freight liner trade*

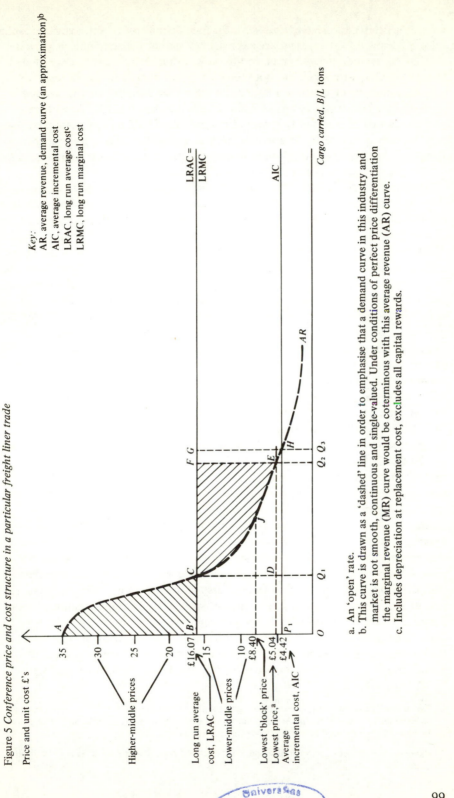

Price and unit cost £'s

Key:
AR, average revenue, demand curve (an approximation)[b]
AIC, average incremental cost
LRAC, long run average cost[c]
LRMC, long run marginal cost

Cargo carried, B/L tons

a. An 'open' rate.
b. This curve is drawn as a 'dashed' line in order to emphasise that a demand curve in this industry and market is not smooth, continuous and single-valued. Under conditions of perfect price differentiation the marginal revenue (MR) curve would be coterminous with this average revenue (AR) curve.
c. Includes depreciation at replacement cost, excludes all capital rewards.

99

(SRMC). In the *long run*, MC must include the cost of extra voyages as the demand for shipping space expands beyond the capacity of a single vessel. So we may conclude that, in this case, output could have been expanded to OQ_3 with some, but not much, *short run* benefit to the shipowner. Some, small, contribution to costs other than incremental costs would have been made by an extra output equal to $OQ_3 - OQ_2$. Any cargo carried in excess of OQ_3 would not even have paid its incremental costs as measured by AIC. In practice AIC was greater by the average unit cost of extra ship's time involved in loading and unloading the extra units of cargo carried. It has not been possible to measure these extra costs.

The three voyages used as a basis for this exercise are all in the direction outwards from the United Kingdom, and their cargoes consist almost entirely of manufactured goods, although in the one sailing for which we have cargo details the lower-rated commodities do include some semi-manufactured plastic and other chemical products which are of low value per B/L ton in relation to the other cargo carried. It is permitted in conference rules to charge an 'open' rate, subject to a minimum level, for cargo which is not 'liner cargo' as defined by the freight tariff.[1] This has been done in the case of some consignments in these cargoes and, as has been shown in one case, it has come very close to *average* incremental cost.[2] It follows that the 'block' system of class rates is abandoned at the lower end of the schedule of freight rates and price differentiation gives way to conditions under which marginal revenue will decline faster than average revenue as output (cargo carried) expands. The consequence of this is to relax assumption b. (see above) in respect of prices (freight rates) below £8.40, which is the lowest 'block' rate in this tariff. It follows from this that for the range of the AR curve from J to E and beyond, MR will not be conterminous with AR but will fall away from it in a downwards direction. This will mean that the loss on cargo carried at rates per B/L ton which are less than long run average cost will be greater than is represented on Figure 5 by the area CEF. Further, circumstances *could* arise in which marginal revenue becomes negative as the MR curve falls below the x-axis and, since marginal cost must always be positive in this industry, losses will become inevitable on marginal cargo.

We have seen earlier that there is a strong motivation by operators toward a high degree of utilisation of ship capacity, due in most part to *short run* factors governing ship economics. There is also a desire on the part of shipowners to attract some bulk or 'base' cargo, as it is called, to each voyage for technical reasons associated with the handling of the vessel at sea, and also in order to deny such cargo to actual or potential competitors who wish to attract such cargo for similar reasons. From conversations we have had with shipowners and operators within conference, we understand that base cargo is so called for both physical and financial reasons. It is loaded into the hold first and so is the base upon which the smaller 'parcels' of manufactured goods are then loaded. The freight revenue from base cargo is also

---

1 Either specifically by description, or by general classification under an 'n.o.e.' clause. Additionally, some liner cargoes are given 'open' rates when they travel 'in bulk' (which in some cases is defined in the tariff but in other cases is not).

2 Probably below AIC if extra ship's time cost could be included in AIC, as conceptually it should be.

deemed to cover a substantial part of the basic cost of the voyage, and therefore it is regarded as the basis upon which the, usually small, individual consignments of higher-valued and higher-rated cargo then provide the profit. The shipowner is therefore regarding economically marginal cargo as being non-marginal, in fact as 'base' cargo, and this may lead to financial loss on the voyage concerned, but if the competition is warded off by these pricing tactics then there is some commercial advantage to the individual conference member and to all conference members. On wider economic grounds the conclusion must be different in that in so far as the actual cost of carrying this 'base' cargo is higher by conference liner than by other means, for example, specialised bulk carriers, then the least use of scarce resources per unit of this output would be achieved by the alternative means.[1]

The above is the *short run* situation. In the *long run* marginal cost is equal to average cost in the constant cost case which applies in a conference liner trade.

In the example studied[2] and analysed above much cargo was carried at prices which were far below long run average and marginal cost, and cross-subsidisation by cargo carried at prices above LRAC was clearly substantial.

In welfare economic terms the loss of welfare due to some prices being far above long run marginal cost is to a greater or lesser extent (varying in individual cases) offset by the subsidy given to cargo which is freighted at prices below long run marginal cost. The incidence of the cross-subsidies, from high to low unit value cargo are an arbitrary re-distribution of welfare without economic justification. In so far as conference prices are directly related to the unit value of the commodities to which they apply, and it is shown in Chapter 7 that there is a strong association between these two variables, the conference is in effect taxing shippers of relatively high unit value goods and subsidising shippers of goods of relatively low unit value. The satisfaction of marginal conditions by differential pricing processes (as described in Section 3 above) provides some mitigation of the bad features of cross-subsidisation, but the welfare argument remains. The satisfaction of marginal conditions ensures no more than that the level of freight charged in such cases does not hinder trade by preventing goods from being shipped which would otherwise be shipped if freight rates were lower.

Even if the net loss of welfare due to cross-subsidisation is small, and we have no means of measuring the gains and losses, the arbitrary re-distribution of it is to be deplored. However, in general terms it may be argued that a re-distribution of welfare by cross-subsidisation is largely to be preferred to the action of a unitary monopolist who raises his prices far above long run marginal cost without re-distribution by cross-subsidy to other buyers of his products.

Summary

This chapter has been concerned with both static and dynamic price formation by shipping conferences, and with a theoretical analysis of cost characteristics of firms operating in highly capital intensive industries generally and in shipping in particular. The results of the theoretical analysis were then applied to a practical example of

1 Some further economic investigation of this question may be found *in The Economics of Bulking Cargoes*, Institute for Shipping Research, Bergen, Norway.

2 Comprising the cargoes of three conference liners.

price formation related to an actual cost structure in conference freight shipping. The conclusions of this analysis are given below.

1. Shipping conferences can charge differential prices for their services for three main reasons.
   a. The service they produce is not re-saleable.
   b. Entry to closed shipping conferences is very restricted.
   c. Buyers' knowledge of market prices is generally limited to the section which is concerned with the shipping of their own and their competitors' products.
2. In relative terms conference prices (freight rates) are found to be highly differentiated from one another and more so in trades from developing countries than in those from developed, industrialised countries.
3. There is no doubt that price differentiation in the trade from developed countries is less complete than that from developing countries, partly because of the simple practical difficulty of differentiating with respect to price several thousand commodities rather than several hundred. The greater use of price classes, or block pricing, rather than separate pricing, for the conference trade of developed countries reflects this problem.
4. Price differentiation is practised in order to put into effect a policy of 'charging what the market will bear'. The market demand for conference services is very fragmented and buyers (the shippers) often have little or no knowledge of prices beyond the sector of the market which offers transport services for their own and their competitors' products. The supply of conference services, on the other hand, is relatively homogeneous.
5. 'Across-the-board' general price (freight rate) changes are found to be largely cost based, but with exemptions from increases and exceptional rate changes which respect the greater elasticity of demand for the service of shipping some products. Demand-based elements are thereby introduced into the pricing process.
6. Over the period 1948—70 conference freight rates, after additions for surcharges, but before allowances for exemptions from general rate increases and for exception to them, rose considerably more rapidly than British retail prices, prices of capital goods and of all manufactured goods. Comparison between changes in an index of time-charter tramp rates and in a weighted index of conference freight rates is described in Chapter 5.
7. The process of 'secondary pricing'. i.e. exemptions from general freight rate increases and price changes which result from individual freight rate bargaining, are explained. From the evidence examined it is clear that the unadjusted index of conference freight rates, given in this chapter and in Appendix B, overstates the effective rise in conference freight rates in the period 1948—70, and there is some evidence to support the view that this overstatement of rate rise is more important in the more recent years of this period.
8. The first part of the theoretical analysis links price differentiation in the fragmented market situation, which is common in conference shipping services, with demand inelasticity, lack of market knowledge by buyers and the 'satisfaction of marginal conditions'. This applies to the 'higher middle'

range of the conference price structure — the top range being actually and potentially more price elastic due to competition from air freight transport services. In this 'higher middle' price range marginal conditions are more likely to be satisfied. That is to say no further shipping services for the commodity types concerned would be purchased at lower prices. This cannot be proved *a priori*, but it is reflected in the very low price elasticity of demand in the clearly very sectionalised market for conference shipping services over this range of price, and we believe that price discrimination which would meet these marginal conditions would not be difficult to arrive at in practice.

9. The second part of the theoretical analysis deals with the 'lower middle' and lower price ranges. In the first of these the marginal conditions are less easy to satisfy. This is so because price differentiation is based largely, but not completely, on the unit value of the commodity shipped, and in this 'lower middle' range the rate of freight constitutes a much higher proportion of the total c.i.f. price of the commodity. This makes for higher price elasticity in the lower part of the price range, and this elasticity also increases markedly for a second reason, which is the competition from tramp vessels and specialised bulk carriers which enters this section of the market.

10. An empirical analysis of conference prices in relation to short and long run costs is linked with the results of theoretical work on the likely behaviour of *long run* average and marginal real costs in a *conference liner trade*. It is concluded that these costs are generally constant. From the usual welfare arguments associated with marginal cost pricing it follows, and it is shown, that the profit from carryings freighted at prices above long run average and marginal cost is very nearly completely offset by losses on cargo carried at prices below this cost level. So in aggregate terms the welfare losses in the upper price section tend to offset welfare gains in the lower section. The 'taxing' and re-distribution aspects of this cross-subsidisation remain open to substantial criticism, although the welfare losses which arise from monopoly pricing without cross-subsidisation are even more deplorable.

11. It is further shown that in the short run some 'open' rated and other very low rated cargo is carried at prices which are very close to 'average incremental cost', that is, the 'escapable' average unit cost of loading, stowage, unloading and selling (commissions and rebates). These average incremental costs (AIC) are calculated here. Conceptually they should include the incremental cost of the time the ship spends loading and discharging this extra cargo. If this extra cost were to be added to AIC some cargo in our example would almost certainly have been shown to have been carried at prices below full AIC. This involves losses on every unit of such cargo carried, and no revenue contribution is in these circumstances made to the inescapable costs of the voyage.

5   An Analysis of Price Movements

In this chapter an analysis is made first of the movements in freight rates in each of the three conference groups included in this study.

1. Conference freight rate movements

In Table 5.1 below are set out the cumulative annual average movements in the rates of freight for each of three conference groups in each direction of trade. These rate movements are unweighted, and therefore the effects of exemptions from the general, across-the-board rate changes are not registered here, nor are the effects of the normally downward changes in individual rates of freight which we know do occur from time to time when bargaining takes place between a conference and individual shippers.[1] Later in this chapter are set out the results of a weighting exercise which has been carried out for one conference. This enables some appreciation to be made of the differences to general rate movements which arise from the changes to individual rates of freight which take place from time to time.

It may be seen from Table 5.1 that the period covered is lengthy, it is the 22 years from 1948–70, virtually the whole post-war period. It is divided into two sub-periods, 1948–60 and 1960–70. The movements of both basic and surcharged rates are shown. The surcharges are explained in the notes to the table, and details about the incorporation of certain surcharges in basic rates are explained in Chapter 4 and in Appendix B.

Two conclusions may be drawn from the results set out in Table 5.1. The first is the general one that movements in basic freight rates over the whole period (1948–70) are very similar in all three conferences and with the exception of the Far Eastern Freight Conference the increases in general freight rates have been rather slower in the more recent period (1960–70) than they were in the earlier period (1948–60).[2] The surcharges are due chiefly to Suez closures (in 1956/57 and 1967 onwards) and they are at different rates for each conference (see Appendix B).

The second and more significant and interesting finding is that, with only one exception, freight rates (whether basic or surcharged) have risen faster in the outward than they have in the homeward direction (see Figure 6). The exception is also interesting. It is the Far Eastern Freight Conference in the period 1948–60, and there is also a very small difference between outward and homeward rate movements in these trades in the 1960–70 period. The other two conference groups

---

1   See Chapter 6.

2   But see Statistical Note to Table 5.1.

'Table 5.1. *Movements in Conference Liner Freight Rates (as measured by the gradient of the least squares regression line). Unweighted, 1948–70, 1948–60 and 1960–70*

	Annual average percentages		
Outwards from the United Kingdom	1948–70	1948–60	1960–70
UK–Australia Conference			
a. Basic rates	7.64	6.91	5.86
b. Surcharged rates[a]	7.84	6.91	6.15
Far East Freight Conference			
a. Basic rates	6.06	4.40	5.45
b. Surcharged rates[b]	6.75	4.50	7.02
India/Pakistan Conference			
a. Basic rates	8.15	9.04	4.49
b. Surcharged rates[b]	9.58	9.47	7.13
Homewards to the United Kingdom			
UK–Australia Conference			
a. Basic rates	6.93	6.35	5.39
b. Surcharged rates[c]	7.13	6.35	5.69
Far East Freight Conference			
a. Basic rates	5.63	4.44	5.47
b. Surcharged rates[b]	6.30	4.55	7.04
India/Pakistan Conference			
a. Basic rates	6.13	7.85	4.39
b. Surcharged rates[b]	7.39	8.26	7.01

(a) Includes Suez surcharges in 1967 and a surcharge for loading in Antwerp, rather than Tilbury (closed by a strike) in 1969 and 1970.
(b) Includes the Suez surcharges applied in 1956 and 1967.
(c) Includes Suez surcharge in 1967 only, none applied in 1956.

Statistical Note to Table 5.1
The trends in the freight rate series shown here, and also in various different combinations in Tables 5.2, 5.3, and 5.4, have been estimated, as noted above, by the 'method of least squares'. The linear trend has been fitted to each freight rate time series by calculating the regression line of each time series from the equation $y = a + bx$. The linear trend which results from this calculation has the sum of the squares of deviations of the value of the time series from the trend as small as possible. The rate of change of each time series is the gradient of the trend line and this has been calculated separately by this method from an index of each series based upon a value of 100 in year one. Rates of change for sub-periods of any period are therefore independent of the rate of change for the whole period.

serve trades which link predominantly developed economies on one side with predominantly under-developed, or developing, economies on the other. In these cases it is the developed economies which have faced the faster increases in both basic and surcharged rates of freight. The Far Eastern Freight Conference is different in that it links West European, developed economies with Japan, Hong Kong and Malaysia and Singapore, a group of countries which include much advanced economic development along with a relatively small proportion which may be described as developing. So we get an interesting association between fast rising freight rates and developed economies, and slower rising freight rates and developing economies. This is shown more precisely in Table 5.2.

When all three conferences are taken together the difference between movements in outward and homeward freight rates is narrower in both periods than it is when the Far Eastern Freight Conference is dropped out. It is also apparent that the outward and homeward freight rates move more closely in step with each other in the

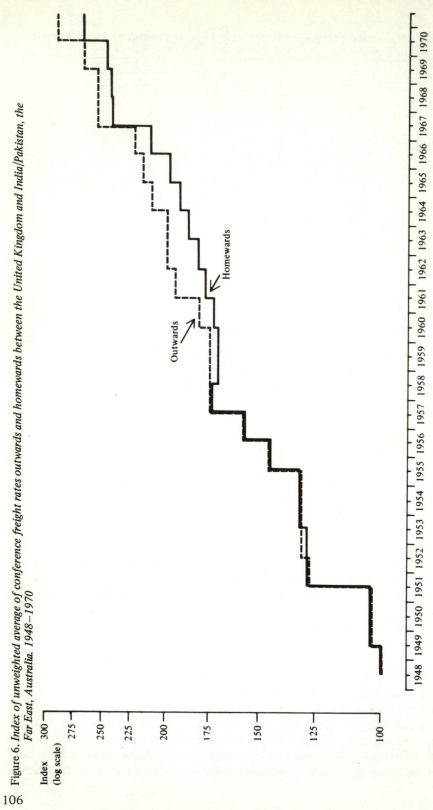

Figure 6. *Index of unweighted average of conference freight rates outwards and homewards between the United Kingdom and India/Pakistan, the Far East, Australia, 1948–1970*

106

Table 5.2   *Combined Conference Freight Rate Movements, with Comparisons between Outward and Homeward Basic Rate Changes (unweighted)*

	(Annual average percentages[a] rows 1,2,4,5 and proportions (%) rows 3 and 6)	
All three conference groups (unweighted[b] average of basic rate changes)	1948–60	1960–70
1. Outward	6.78	5.27
2. Homeward	6.21	5.08
3. Rate movement Homeward as a proportion of Outward	91.6	96.3
United Kingdom–Australia and the UK–India/ Pakistan Conferences only, (unweighted average of basic rate changes in each conference group)		
4. Outward	7.98	5.18
5. Homeward	6.53	4.89
6. Rate movement Homeward as a proportion of Outward	81.8	94.4

(a) Calculated from the gradient of a fitted linear least squares regression line.
(b) If the constituent conference rate movements are weighted by the freight tonnage of goods which each conference group transported in 1965, we get for the period 1960–70 a combined movement of 5.46 per cent p.a. outwards and 5.24 per cent p.a. homewards. For rows 4 and 5 respectively the corresponding rates of annual increase for the same period are 5.50 and 4.94.

period 1960–70 than they do in the period 1948–60, and this is so whether all three or only two conferences are considered together.

The same conclusion emerges if the total increase in basic rates of freight (unweighted) are examined for the whole of the period 1948–70. From Table 4.3 in Chapter 4 it may be seen that outward basic freight rates increased, on the basis of a comparison of rates in the terminal years only, by 202, 133 and 206 per cent respectively in each of the three conferences, and homeward rates by 177, 127 and 165 per cent. The middle figure in each series represents the rate movement in the Far Eastern Freight Conference and here it is seen that there is only a relatively small difference between outward and homeward rate movements, which confirms the conclusion already drawn from the analysis shown in Table 5.2.

2. Weighted conference freight rate movements

It has been shown in Section 2g. of Chapter 4 that the rates of freight for the various different commodities shipped by a conference do not always move uniformly in step with each other. Individual rate changes do take place, both at times of general rate changes and at other times, and a description is given below of an exercise to weight an index of freight rates in order to bring into account all rate changes which have occurred over the period 1948–70.

In the UK–Australia conference outwards one important exemption from general freight rate increases occurs in motor vehicle shipments. The special rates for CKD and unpacked motor vehicles in the UK–Australia conference outwards have been shown (Table 4.7) and discussed earlier. For the year to August 1967 it is known that all motor vehicle shipments from the UK to Australia in conference vessels yielded gross freight revenue which accounted for 12.1 per cent of total freight revenue; for CKD 9.9 per cent and unpacked 2.2 per cent. Using these proportions as weights, and finding the gradient of the least squares regression line for the two motor vehicle rate indexes for the period 1960—70 by the method of least squares, we get a rate movement weighted for the special motor vehicle rates only, of 5.64 per cent for this period in basic freight rates. This may be compared with a movement of 5.86 per cent per annum unweighted. This conclusion rests on the assumption that the rates of freight for all other cargo moved *pari passu* with the general across-the-board rate changes. In fact, as we know from the data given in Tables 4.4, 4.6 and 4.7, there were other exemptions from general rate increases and some individual commodity rates were altered, most usually in a downward direction, at times other than the times of general rate increases. So the rate of change of 5.64 per cent per annum in basic rates over the period 1960—70 must be regarded as an upper bound. If it had been possible to weight correctly all rate changes, the index of weighted changes would undoubtedly be lower than 5.64 per cent per annum, but it is not possible to calculate how much lower because data on every individual rate change and on its relative weight in this trade in this long period are not available.

In one trade however, the United Kingdom—Australia Homeward trade, we have been able to weight the various rate changes to the extent of 31 individual commodities for which separate rates have at some time in this period been made. The weights used are the freight revenues received in the year 1967 for each commodity or class of commodity. The weighted and unweighted freight rate movements in this trade and in the outward trade are set out below in Table 5.3 and the related trends in (index form) are shown in Figures 7 and 8.

Table 5.3   *Unweighted and weighted freight rate movements[a] in both directions of the United Kingdom—Australia trade, 1948—1970, 1948—1960 and 1960—1970*

	Annual average percentages		
	1948—70	1948—60	1960—70
Outward			
Unweighted	7.64	6.91	5.86
Weighted only for motor vehicle rate changes	n.a.	n.a.	5.64
Homeward			
Unweighted	6.93	6.35	5.39
Weighted for 31 individual commodities	6.49	5.85	5.17
Weighted rate change as a proportion of unweighted rate change	93.7	92.1	95.9

(a) The movements in basic rates are taken throughout. These include the devaluation surcharge of 1967 (which was immediately incorporated in basic rates), and also the Suez surcharge of 1967 after it was incorporated in basic rates homewards in 1968 and outwards in 1969.

Although motor vehicles are an important part of the UK—Australia outward conference liner trade, the weighting here is less than complete and little significance can be attached to the partly-weighted rate of increase of 5.64 per cent per

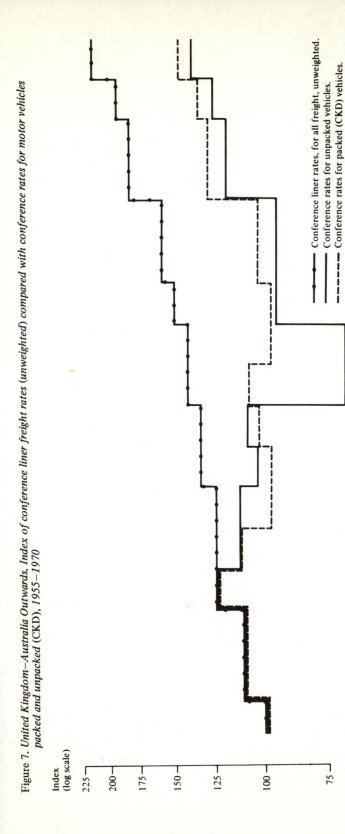

Figure 7. *United Kingdom–Australia Outwards. Index of conference liner freight rates (unweighted) compared with conference rates for motor vehicles packed and unpacked (CKD), 1955–1970*

Index
(log scale)

——•—— Conference liner rates, for all freight, unweighted.
———— Conference rates for unpacked vehicles.
– – – – Conference rates for packed (CKD) vehicles.

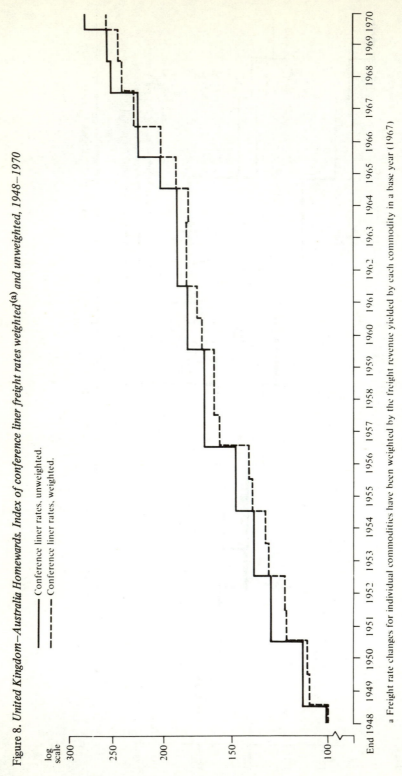

Figure 8. *United Kingdom–Australia Homewards. Index of conference liner freight rates weighted*[a] *and unweighted, 1948–1970*

——— Conference liner rates, unweighted.
- - - - - Conference liner rates, weighted.

log
scale

300

250

200

150

100

End 1948 1949 1950 1951 1952 1953 1954 1955 1956 1957 1958 1959 1960 1961 1962 1963 1964 1965 1966 1967 1968 1969 1970

a Freight rate changes for individual commodities have been weighted by the freight revenue yielded by each commodity in a base year (1967)

annum beyond the observation that the shippers of motor vehicles from the United Kingdom to Australia were able by bargaining to lower quite substantially the speed of increase in the freight rates payable by them in comparison with the trend of freight rates measured by the general rate changes in this period (1960–70).[1]

Firmer ground for a conclusion is reached when the homeward direction of the UK–Australia trade is subjected to a much more wide-ranging exercise in weighting. There are 210 separate rates which are quoted in the tariff for this trade (see Table 4.1), but nearly all individual rate changes (i.e. changes in rates of freight which are not general changes) which have occurred at any time in the period 1948–70 have been confined to the 31 commodities and commodity classes for which separate weights have been assembled and applied here. The results, given in Table 5.3, show that over the whole period the weighted index of freight rates rose at a rate per annum which was about one sixteenth slower than the unweighted index of freight rates. This is not a dramatic difference, but it does of course indicate that the un-weighted index overstates the true rise in rates of freight. How far this conclusion, which relates to only one direction of trade and one conference, can be extended to other conferences must depend on other evidence.

3. Movements in conference liner freight rates and in time-chartered shipping rates compared

A test is now made of hypothesis A:

'That conference freight rates in three specified "deep sea" trades have risen faster than time-chartered shipping rates over the period 1948–70'.

Trends in conference liner freight rates and time-chartered shipping rates are shown in Table 5.4.

The movement of conference freight rates by conference and by direction of trade are shown in Figures 9 and 10. From the results shown in these Figures and in Table 5.4, it may be seen that over the period 1948–1970 conference liner freight rates examined here rose on average by 6.76 per cent per annum, while the rates for time-chartered shipping barely changed at all on balance. The difference between the average annual movements in these two sets of rates was approximately 7.3 per cent per annum over the period 1948–1970.

When this long period of 22 years is divided into two sub-periods, 1948–60 and 1960–70, it is found that the time-charter rate declined at an annual rate of 1.35 per cent in the first period, which included the very high peaks and subsequent troughs associated first with the Korean war and with the Suez Canal closure of 1956/57, and rose by 6.81 per cent per annum in the more recent period, 1960–70. This latter rate of increase is higher by 1.63 per cent per annum than the increase in the combined conference rates examined here.

In the first period (1948–60) the evidence suggests that the time-charter rate is demand-based. This is also the conclusion of D.L. McLachlan.[2] The evidence presented in Chapter 4 shows the cost-based nature of across-the-board rate changes by

1 During this period the rate of freight for CKD motor vehicles increased by only 4.29 per cent, and 'unpacked' motor vehicle rates by 2.92 per cent per annum.

2 D.L. McLachlan 'Index Numbers of Liner Freight Rates in the United Kingdom, 1946–1957'. *Yorkshire Bulletin of Economic and Social Research,* Vol. 10, No. 1. June 1958.

112

Figure 9. *Trends in conference liner freight rates*(a) *and in time-charter tramp rates. Outward trades, 1948–1970*

Index
(log scale)

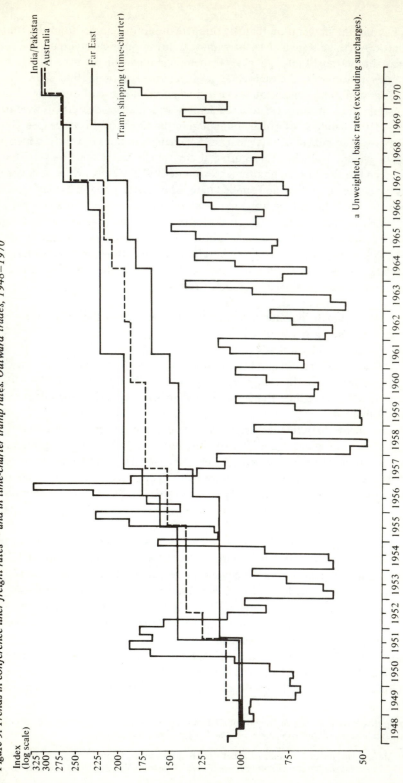

India/Pakistan
Australia
Far East
Tramp shipping (time-charter)

a Unweighted, basic rates (excluding surcharges).

1948 1949 1950 1951 1952 1953 1954 1955 1956 1957 1958 1959 1960 1961 1962 1963 1964 1965 1966 1967 1968 1969 1970

325
300
275
250
225
200
175
150
125
100
75
50

Figure 10. *Trends in conference liner freight rates*[a] *and in time-charter tramp rates. Homeward trades, 1948–1970*

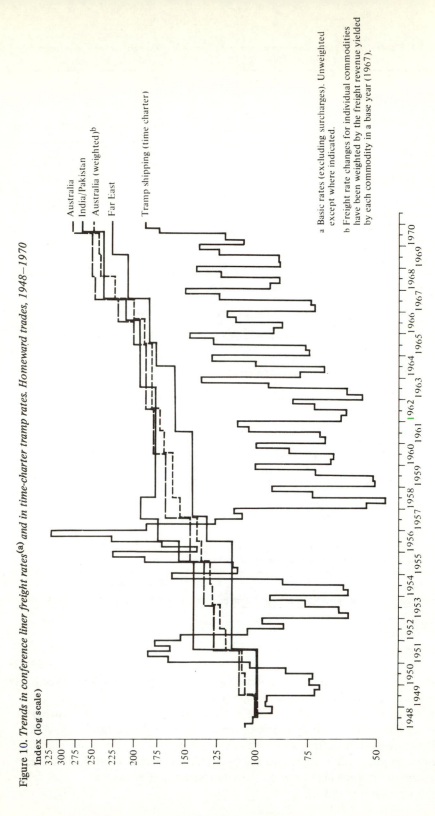

Index (log scale)

Australia
India/Pakistan
Australia (weighted)[b]
Far East
Tramp shipping (time charter)

a Basic rates (excluding surcharges). Unweighted except where indicated.

b Freight rate changes for individual commodities have been weighted by the freight revenue yielded by each commodity in a base year (1967).

113

Table 5.4. *Movements in some Conference Liner Freight Rates Compared with Movements in Time-Chartered Shipping Rates, 1948–1970 (Average annual percentages[a])*

Movements in previously specified[c] combined general conference liner freight rates	Basic rates, unweighted[b]		
	1948–1970	1948–1960	1960–1970
1. Outward	7.28	6.78	5.27
2. Homeward	6.23	6.21	5.08
3. Both directions of trade	6.76	6.50	5.18
4. Movements in Time-charter rate index[d] (*annual average data*)	−0.56	−1.35	6.81
5. Liner rate movements *minus* time charter rate movements (Row 3 − Row 4)	7.32	7.85	−1.63

(a) As measured by the gradient of the least squares regression line.
(b) General freight rate changes only, and a simple unweighted average of movements in the rate indexes of each of the three specified conferences.
(c) See Tables 5.2 and 5.3.
(d) Source of basic data: The Chamber of Shipping of the United Kingdom, London.

Explanatory notes to Table 5.4
1. Basic rather than surcharged conference liner rates have been used in this comparison because the surcharges (which are for Suez closures and for loading at Antwerp rather than at Tilbury due to a dockside strike) will not appear in corresponding form in the index of time-charter rates. These obstacles to shipping, which are what the surcharges are charged for, will be met equally by conference and chartered vessels; they are excluded from both services in this table in the interest of comparability.
2. The time-charter tramp rate index is for vessels which fall within the size range 9,000–16,000 d.w.t. for the period 1968 to 1970. This size-class of vessel is the one which in these terms is most closely comparable with conference freight liners. In the years before 1968 the time charter tramp rate index is not divided by its compilers, the Chamber of Shipping of the United Kingdom, into size classes, but the chartering of very large bulk carriers, which are clearly not comparable with conference liners, was much less frequent in the years 1948 to 1967 than it has been since 1967.

Table 5.5. *Changes in Conference Liner Freight Rates and in Time-Charter Rates over the whole of each period 1960–65 and 1965–70*

Average change for the three specified conferences	(Percentages)	
	1965–65	1965–70
Outward direction	+20.2	+33.3
Homeward direction	+16.4	+32.3
Time-charters	+34.0	+38.7

conferences, and these are largely independent of the large market forces which have influenced the time-charter rate in this period.

In the second period (1960–70) the two rate series move much more closely in step with one another. A further breakdown of this period is given in Table 5.5.

The movement of conference rates in these sub-periods appears to lag that of time-charter rates. This is also suggested by McLachlan's analysis. If this is so, then the comparisons made here between these two series over coincident periods will include a measure of this lag.

It is most important now to qualify this rate differential further by showing first that the conference rate movement is a general one and is unweighted for the individual commodity rate exemptions from general rate increases, and for the most usually downward adjustments to individual rates of freight which take place from time to time as a result of bargaining between shippers and a conference. From the results of an exercise of weighting individual commodity freight rates, which we have carried out in the Australian trade (see Table 5.3 and Figure 8) it is apparent that the difference between the two rate series for the period 1948–70, which is shown in Table 5.4, is overstated. In Tables 4.8 and 6.1 evidence is given of the rate decreases which are from time to time granted to shippers of particular commodities during this period.

If ΔCLR_{uw} represents the *unweighted* movement over time of conference liner freight rates; and if $\Delta TCTR_{ua}$ represents the *unadjusted* movement of the time-charter rate, then it is clear from the evidence assembled in the course of this study that $\Delta CLR_{uw} > \Delta TCTR_{ua}$ for the period 1948–1970.

It is also true that if ΔCLR is weighted in the way just described, then $\Delta CLR_{uw} > \Delta CLR_w$, where subscript w represents the weighted movement in rates of freight.

To set against this, a conference may sometimes raise an individual rate of freight either at a time of a general rate increase or at another time, (see Chapter 6, case history 3, for an example of this). We have studied a large number of cases of individual conference rate bargaining in the course of this research and cases of *individual* rate increases are rare. The only ones discovered are cases where the commodity has been altered over time and has become more sophisticated and of a higher unit value than previously, and the rate for it is increased largely for this reason. Arguably it is not the rate which has increased but rather it is the commodity that has changed and this has led to a new and higher rate being made. The same is sometimes true of rate reductions. The conference freight rate index does therefore change due to changes in the character of the commodities shipped as well as for reasons associated with the cost of the shipping service provided.

Individual rate reductions, and exemptions from general rate increases, greatly exceed individual rate increases, so if it were possible to compile completely weighted conference freight rate indexes, then the difference $\Delta CLR_w - \Delta TCTR_{ua}$ would be less than $\Delta CLR_{uw} - \Delta TCTR_{ua}$.

This comparison of trends could also be improved if certain practical difficulties relating to the measurement of a charterer's costs could be overcome. A time-chartered tramp vessel comes equipped with crew and all costs other than those set out below are a charge upon the vessel's owners and, subject to the forces of supply and demand which operate in the free market conditions which govern the Baltic Exchange, are reflected in the time-charter rate. Before the chartered vessel can earn revenue the charterer has to meet the following additional costs:

> Port dues
> Loading and unloading expenses
> Rebates and commissions
> Transhipment freight and expenses
> Claims
> Bunkers
> Canal dues

A proportion of total administrative expenses and sundries, (the remainder are borne by the owners of the chartered vessel).

These additional costs are reflected in the weighted and unweighted indexes of conference liner rates, but they are not reflected in any measure in the time-charter index. So the comparability of movements in the two indexes is thereby diminished. In order to improve the degree of comparability it would be necessary to determine the costs named above on a unit basis, to add them to the unit price of time-chartering over the period 1948 to 1970 and thereby to form the basis for an index of time-charter tramp rates adjusted ($\Delta TCTR_a$).

Research has not been pursued here in detail in this direction, and so it is not possible to determine the extent by which $\Delta CLR_{uw} - \Delta TCTR_{ua}$ differs from $\Delta CLR_{uw} - \Delta TCTR_a$. But it is possible to demonstrate that loading and unloading costs, a large proportion of the total costs (see note (a) to Table 5.6 for definition) of conference liners have risen substantially over the period 1958 to 1968. Another cost which is relevant to this comparison is the cost of time spent in port, and it is shown in Table 5.6 that this too has risen as a proportion of total conference liner time.

Table 5.6. *Stevedoring costs and Ships' time in port as proportions of Total Cost and Total Ships' Time. Europe–Australia Conference Group. Average of both Directions of Trade, 1958, 1961, 1965 and 1968*

	(Percentages)	
	Total stevedoring costs as a percentage of total costs[a]	Ships' time in port as a percentage of total ships' time
1958	25.9	43.7
1961	26.6	45.2
1965	31.7	51.2
1968	32.6	51.2

(a) Total current expenditure, cost of idle time and of overhauls and depreciation at replacement values.

Both the stevedoring costs and the time in port costs affect both conference and time-chartered vessels. Changes in these cost elements are not included in changes in the time-charter rate index given in Table 5.4, but they should be included for a complete comparison of movements in the operating costs of conference liners with those of time-chartered vessels of approximately equivalent performance.

From the evidence given in Table 5.6 it may be concluded that

$$(\Delta CLR_{uw} - \Delta TCTR_{ua}) > (\Delta CLR_{uw} - \Delta TCTR_a) \quad \dots \quad (1)$$

From earlier considerations it was shown that

$$(\Delta CLR_{uw} - \Delta TCTR_a) > (\Delta CLR_w - \Delta TCTR_a) \quad \dots \quad (2)$$

therefore

$$(\Delta CLR_{uw} - \Delta TCTR_{ua}) > (\Delta CLR_w - \Delta TCTR_a) \quad \dots \quad (3)$$

The two sets of qualifications which have been considered above both work in the same direction, that of closing the gap between movements in conference liner rates and movements in comparable time charter tramp rates over the period 1948–70.

What can certainly be concluded is that the unweighted and unadjusted rate differential is greater than the weighted and adjusted differential, expression (3) above, but it cannot be shown conclusively, without further research, whether or not weighted conference liner freight rates, as defined, rose faster than time-charter rates adjusted for changes in associated operating costs.

The results of the research so far carried out do validate hypothesis A. viz:

'That conference freight rates in three specified "deep sea" conferences have risen faster than time chartered shipping rates over the period 1948–1970'.

Further research is needed to show whether or not the very wide difference between these two rate movements is closed when the trends are adjusted to a more closely comparable basis which reflects reality more accurately. The evidence examined strongly suggests that the adjustments defined work in the direction of reducing the differential.

In the shorter and more recent period (1960–70) the movements of the unweighted and unadjusted freight rate series suggest that the time-charter rate rises faster. There appears to be a lag effect in these data, with liner rates lagging the time-charter rate (Table 5.5), which, if substantiated, would bring the two movements very close together. In general, though this period is too short to serve as a basis for conclusion, and such provisional and qualified conclusions as have been stated above must rest as they do on the results of examining movements in the longer period, 1948–70.

Some further understanding of the alternative to conference freight shipping service may be gained by examining the comparative cost *levels*, rather than the price *trends*, of these two modes of freight transport by sea. This is attempted in the next section.

4. Comparative voyage costs for a representative conference liner and for a chartered vessel of similar size and performance

Shipping conferences do charter vessels on a time cost basis on the Baltic Exchange and employ them in their trades for such purposes as meeting seasonal peaks of demand, or replacing a conference vessel under repair.

The aim of this exercise is to show, in respect of a particular time and trade, the cost categories involved, the comparative total costs of operating a conference vessel and a chartered vessel under closely similar conditions, and an analysis of total costs into (a) costs in common and (b) additional costs for conference vessel operation, and for chartered vessel operation.

The actual cases described here are of round voyages between the United Kingdom and the Far East. The voyage took place in June and July 1971. The conference liner involved was operated by a member of the Far Eastern Freight Conference. It was a modern vessel of 560,000 cubic feet capacity, loading approximately 9,000 B/L tons eastbound and the same quantity westbound. The chartered vessel was of closely comparable performance and was also of 560,000 cu.ft. capacity and carried the same quantity of cargo as the conference liner in each direction. The round voyage took 143 days for both vessels. Costs are actual at mid-1971 levels; they are divided into three sections in Table 5.7.

Table 5.7 *Comparative Cost Levels of Conference and Chartered Vessels at mid-1971*

Section A   Costs in common, the same for both vessels

		(£'s)
Stevedoring and other cargo expenses	77,243	
Agency and commissions	13,349	
Transhipment freight and expenses	5,100	
Claims	2,475	
Bunkers	36,680	
Port expenses	17,900	
	£152,747	

Section B   Conference liner costs in addition to those in Section A

Crew wages	48,048
Victualling	5,005
Insurance	1,359
Lubricating oil	1,550
Sundries	5,434
Administration	26,741
Repairs and stores	24,596
Depreciation of vessel	12,298
	£125,031

Section C   Charter hire and extra costs incurred by the chartered liner

Time-charter hire at the rate of £550 per day for 143 days.	78,650
Less 2½% discount	1,966
	76,684
Extra insurance	2,000
Crew overtime at £200 per month	954
	£79,638

Total round voyage costs for:

a. The conference liner = A + B = £277,778, or £9.92 per bale ton.

b. The chartered liner = A + C = £232,385, or £8.30 per bale ton.

During 1970–71 the time-charter hire rate for vessels of the type considered here fluctuated downwards to £500 per day and upwards to £1,150 per day. The highest and lowest rates have been included in the exercise set out below as an indication of the range of fluctuation of charter-hire prices in the free market for shipping capacity.

Although some profit may be assumed in the charter-hiring rate none is allowed in the above figures for the conference liner. However, when the hiring rate is as low as £500 per day, and it was nearly down to this point in the actual hiring period in mid-1971, the profit element to the owner in the rate cannot be large. Depreciation has been accounted in respect of both vessels.

Fluctuations in time charter rates are very considerable. An analysis of them will be given in the next section of this chapter. They are reflected in these results which also include the extra 'on costs' of operating time-chartered vessels. On average over this period the cost per 'bale ton' of space available on a representative chartered liner was £9.67. This compares closely with the cost per bale ton of a conference

118

Table 5.8 *The range of comparative costs, 1970–1971*

	1. Cost of Round Voyage (£'s)	2. Cost per Day (£'s)	3. Single voyage cost per bale ton.[a] of space available (£'s)
a. Conference liner	277,778	1,943	9.92
b. Chartered liner on the basis of a hire charge of £500 per day net after discount (2½%).	225,513	1,577	8.05
c. Chartered liner on the basis of a hire charge of £1,150 per day net after discount (2½%).	316,040	2,210	11.29
d. Average of b and c.	270,777	1,894	9.67

(a) Of 40 cubic feet.

liner of £9.92. But at the peak of the charter market the rate for a charter rises to £11.29 and falls in the trough as low as £8.05.

Subject to the narrowness and specificity of the base provided by this example of practice, the level of conference liner costs is not widely different from the *average* annual level of costs of hiring and operating a chartered vessel in a conference trade under conference conditions.

5. A comparative study of freight rate stability
We now consider hypothesis B:
'That liner freight rates in three specified conference groups have been more stable than time-chartered shipping rates over the period 1948–70'.

It is necessary first to define what is meant by stability in this context. It is useful to distinguish two aspects. First, frequency of rate change per given period of time; and, second, the extent by which over a given period of time, a rate series departs from its mean value for the same time period, i.e. the extent of variation from the mean, usually known as the *coefficient of variation.*

Table 5.9 *Number of general, basic rate changes in individual conference groups, 1948–1970*
1948–1970

United Kingdom–Australia	Number of general rate changes
Outward	13
Homeward	12
Far Eastern Freight Conference	
Outward	9
Homeward	8
United Kingdom–India/Pakistan	
Outward	9
Homeward	10

As to *frequency of change,* the time-charter rate can and does change day by day. Monthly averages are compiled and quarterly averages are plotted on Figures 9 and 10. The basic conference rates change very much less frequently. The range of frequency of change for the six (three outward and three homeward) conference groups is from 8 to 13 general freight rate changes over the 22 years of the whole

119

Table 5.10 *Standard deviation and coefficient of variation for conference liner and time-charter rate indexes, 1948—70*

Conference Liners (basic rate indexes).	1 Mean	2 Standard Deviation	3 Coefficient of variation (%)
United Kingdom—Australia			
1. Outward	189.1	54.3	28.7
2. Homeward	179.3	49.8	27.8
Far Eastern Freight Conference			
3. Outward	152.9	40.8	26.7
4. Homeward	151.8	37.9	25.0
United Kingdom—India/Pakistan			
5. Outward	190.4	53.9	28.3
6. Homeward	175.9	41.6	23.6
7. Time-chartered shipping (quarterly rate index)[a]	107.0	45.8	42.8

(a) The period covered by this index is Qtr.1 1948 to Qtr.4 1970.

period 1948—1970. Some individual conference freight rates change at different *intervals,* but not necessarily at a greater *frequency*; the frequency of change for some individual rates is less than the frequency of general rate changes because in some cases individual rates are exempted from increase at a time of a general rate increase.

The time-chartered shipping index changed very much more frequently than any of these conference rate indexes over this period.

As to stability in the sense of the extent of variation of any rate index from its mean, it is apparent from an inspection of Figures 9 and 10 that on the basis of quarterly average data for the time-charter tramp rate this rate is less stable than the conference liner rates. A statistical exercise confirms this impression.

As would be expected from what is already known about the trends[1] of these conference and time-charter rates, the means for the conferences are much higher than that for the time-charter rate. Stability in the sense now being examined is best measured by the coefficient of variation (col. 3 in Table 5.10), which is no more than the standard deviation (col. 2) expressed as a percentage of the mean (col. 1). On this measure the conference rates are very much more stable, even on a comparison with average quarterly data of tramp rate changes.

During the early part of the post-war period, defined as 1948—1960, the time-charter (and voyage-charter) tramp rate was very much influenced by the high level of demand for shipping of this type which was generated by the Korean war. This occurred chiefly in 1950 and 1951. The first closure of the Suez canal in 1956 also created a very high level of demand for tramp shipping capacity and led to a large departure from the mean of the rate index concerned. After 1958 the market in tramp shipping settled down, and no fluctuations of a violence similar to those just referred to have since occurred and the time-charter index became more stable after 1960 than it had been before that year.

1　All the trends involved are based on 1948 = 100.

120

Table 5.11 *Coefficient of variation for conference liner and time-charter rate indexes, 1948–60 and 1960–70*

Conference Liners (basic rate indexes)	1948–60	1960–1970
United Kingdom–Australia		
1. Outward	18.5	15.0
2. Homeward	17.2	14.8
Far Eastern Freight Conference		
3. Outward	14.0	13.9
4. Homeward	14.0	13.9
United Kingdom–India/Pakistan		
5. Outward	21.7	12.5
6. Homeward	20.3	13.1
7. Time-chartered shipping (quarterly[a] rate index)	48.7	31.3

(a) The periods covered by this index are Qtr.1 1948–Qtr. 4 1960, and Qtr.1 1960 – Qtr.4 1970.

The conference rates were also more stable in the more recent period, 1960–1970, particularly the United Kingdom–India/Pakistan conference.

The evidence presented here (mainly in Tables 5.9, 5.10 and 5.11) supports hypothesis B, which is validated. The basic[1] conference liner rates examined were considerably more stable, as defined in terms of both frequency of change and extent of deviation from the mean, than the time-charter rate index over the periods 1948–1970, 1948–1960 and 1960–1970.

Summary

1. The movements in conference freight rates in the period 1948–70 have been of broadly similar magnitude in all the three conference groups examined. The average gradient of the three least squares regression lines drawn through each of the series representing each direction of trade is 6.76 per cent per annum.

2. A more interesting and significant finding is that, with one exception, conference freight rates (whether basic or surcharged) have risen faster in the period 1948–60 in the outward direction, 6.78 per cent per annum on average, than in the homeward direction, 6.21 per cent per annum on average for basic rates. In the period 1960–70 the respective movements were 5.27 per cent per annum outwards and 5.08 homewards. The exception is also interesting. It is in the Far Eastern Freight Conference where very small differences are found between rate movements in each direction of trade. This conference links European countries with Japan, Hong Kong

---

1 The coefficients of variation for the *surcharged* conference liner freight rate indexes are a little higher than those for the basic freight rate indexes, but in all cases they are well below the values of the coefficients for the time-charter rate index in all the periods examined. For example, this coefficient for the surcharged rate index of the UK–Australia Outward Conference for the period 1960–70 takes a value of 16.4. This may be compared with a value of 15.0 for the basic rate index for the same conference over the same period.

121

and Malaysia and Singapore — countries which include much advanced economic development. The other conference groups studied here serve trades which link developed economies with developing economies, and it is the developed industrialised countries at the European end of this link which have faced the faster rise in conference freight rates in this period (1948–70). When sub-periods of this period are examined the difference between outward and homeward rates narrows in the most recent period (1960–70).

3. General, across-the-board percentage changes in conference freight rates overstate the amount of increase because of exemptions and exceptions to such increases and because of the individual rate bargaining (almost invariably resulting in a downward change) which takes place at other times. When all the freight rate changes in one conference (UK–Australia Homewards) are considered separately and weighted by the revenue yield of each commodity involved, then this truer measure of conference freight rate movement shows an increase of 6.49 per cent per annum weighted compared with 6.93 per cent unweighted, in the trade covered by this one conference in the period 1948–70.

4. Time-chartered shipping rates are seen to be subject to wide fluctuations, some of which are clearly due to strong and abrupt changes in the forces of demand. This is no more than confirmation of the findings of D.L. McLachlan whose work is cited. On a least squares regression analysis, particularly needed for this fluctuating series, there was on balance practically no change in rates over the whole period from 1948 to 1970. So the gap between movements of conference freight rates and time-charter rates is a wide one in terms of a simple comparison of these basic trends.

5. A truer comparison of movements in these rates would require conference rate changes to be weighted in the way referred to at paragraph 3 above, and time-charter rates to be adjusted to a basis comparable with the conference freight rates. This adjustment would need to take the form of adding the 'on cost' elements of stevedoring costs, port charges and other cost elements. These 'on cost' elements are shown to have increased faster than the rate of increase in total costs. So the movement of time-charter rates adjusted for changes in the 'on costs' described would rise faster than the unadjusted time-charter rate, and the difference between movements in weighted conference rates and an adjusted time-charter rate must be narrower than the difference between movements in unweighted conference rates and the unadjusted time-charter rate in the period 1948–70.

6. From an analysis of the period 1960–70 there is a suggestion, but no more, that conference rate movements lag time-charter rate movements.

7. A comparison of the costs of operating a conference liner on a particular route and a time-chartered vessel of similar size and quality at the same time on the same route and loading a similar amount of cargo reveals that, subject to the qualifications inherent in the narrowness of the data base, the cost (in terms of £s per bale ton) of the conference liner is not widely different from the *average* level of cost of hiring and operating a chartered vessel under conference conditions. The average here being that of hiring

rates over the year in which the compared voyages took place.
8. Rates of freight in three specified conference groups are found to have been more stable than time-chartered shipping rates over the period 1948—70. The measure of stability used is the coefficient of variation, which was found to be between 23.6 and 28.7 per cent for conferences, and 42.8 per cent for time-chartered shipping rates as measured by the quarterly index.

6   Pricing and Price Elasticity in Individual Cases

In earlier chapters (particularly Chapter 4) attempts have been made to explain and illustrate the pricing processes of conferences in so far as the broad, across-the-board rate changes are concerned, and also the way in which important exemptions from these general rate changes are agreed with shippers who in these cases often act collectively. In addition to these two types of pricing there is a third type, which is named individual rate-making, and this is described next. The description is illustrated by a number of case histories and an attempt is made to draw conclusions from these as to the importance of the price elasticity of demand in this aspect of conference pricing policy and the means by which some account is taken of this elasticity when individual prices are made.

It has been shown in Chapter 4 that individual commodities are sometimes exempted, or otherwise given special consideration and treatment, at the time of a general rate change. The fact that a general increase in rates has occurred spurs individual shippers to protest and to seek alleviation. There are also some individual commodity rates which are known by the conference to be particularly sensitive, and in some such cases rather less than the full rate increase will be applied to them. Again, some commodity rates are the subject of special bargaining procedures and are exempted from a general rate change on these grounds. As to the requests made by individual shippers at the time of a general rate change, it has been indicated in Chapter 4, Table 4.6, that for the UK–Australia and Continent–Australia Outward Conferences 229 requests were made between October 1960 and January 1967. Of these 203 were refused and 26 (11.4 per cent) were granted. This result is repeated here in order to aid comparison with the analysis set out below (Table 6.1) of requests made at all times other than at the time of general rate increases.

The number of requests made declined quite markedly from a peak in 1963. The figures of the percentage of requests granted each year do show some erratic movements from year to year, but there is no marked trend to a harder line being taken by the conferences in the more recent years. Compared with the requests made at the time of general rate increases in the same conferences over the same period of time, the results in the table below show that in these cases the number of requests made was just over six times as great and the rate of granting requests was nearly three times as great. Here are two reasons why greater attention is given in this study to the rate changes which are made at times other than at the time of a general rate increase.

Further analysis of these data are given in Table 6.2.

A closer examination of the circumstances and reasons behind conference pricing in the case of individual commodities means going into some detail in a number of instances. This is done in the following eight cases chosen at random from the records of the Far East Freight Conference and the United Kingdom—Australia Conference. In some of these cases the request for a rate reduction was granted, in others it was not.

Table 6.1 *United Kingdom—Australia and Continent—Australia Outward Conferences. An analysis of requests for freight rate reductions at times other than at a general freight rate increase*

	1	2	3	4
Year	Number of Requests made	Number refused	Number granted	% Granted
1960	208	163	45	21.6
1961	181	104	77	42.5
1962	209	147	62	29.7
1963	244	154	90	36.9
1964	171	114	57	33.3
1965	154	117	37	24.0
1966	146	94	52	35.6
1967[a]	117	78	39	33.3
Total	1,430	971	459	32.1

(a) Up to 6 December 1967.

Table 6.2 *United Kingdom—Australia and Continent—Australia Outward Conferences. Proportion of Requests for freight rate reductions granted, 1960—1967*

Requests from Shippers in:	Number of Requests made		Requests Granted		% Granted	
	At a GRI[a]	At other times[b]	At a GRI	At other times	At a GRI	At other times
United Kingdom	125	898	13	265	10.4	29.5
Continent	52	532	10	194	19.2	36.5

(a) General Rate Increase. The GRIs included are those of 1 Oct., 1962; 1 Mar., 1964; 1 Nov., 1965; and 1 Mar., 1967. No breakdown as between the UK and Continent is available for the GRI of 1 Oct., 1960 when, in total, 52 requests were received and three were granted.
(b) The period covered is from the beginning of 1960 to 6 December, 1967.

A. Case histories
These case histories are followed by a consideration of theoretical relationships between some characteristics of the market for the product shipped and some aspects of the market for freight shipping services.

1. The case of synthetic resins from the United Kingdom to Australia
This is an interesting and important case of freight rate bargaining between a large shipper and the United Kingdom—Australia Conference Outward. It began in March 1968 and ended in December of the same year.

The initiative, as commonly occurs in this type of bargaining over individual conference freight rates, was taken by the shipper, who wrote to the Conference Secretary quoting the then (March 1968) current tariff rates for various types of synthetic resin as follows:

125

	Rate of Freight (shillings)
1. Polythene, polypropylene, polystyrene and polyvinyl chloride:	360/- W/M
2. Other synthetic resins in lump, chip or powder form *with* fillers:	315/- W/M
3. Other synthetic resins in lump, chip or powder form *without* fillers:	403/- W/M

The shipper pointed out that this distinction between resins containing filler (low value 'woodfiller') dated from the late 1940's, and that the higher rate for the higher value resin without filler was justified at that time when the main traffic was in thermosetting powders. The growth of the plastics industry since that period had been almost entirely in the thermoplastics group, that is, in polythene, polypropylene, and similar types, and the suggestion was put that the first category be extended to cover the thermoplastics, such as polycarbonate, polyoxymethylene, polyamide and others which at that time were rated 315/- or 403/- depending on whether or not they contained fillers.

The technical aspects of this argument, which have been considerably condensed in this description, were not readily appreciated by the conference and the upshot was a visit by four conference representatives to the shipper's factory for 'instruction as to the characteristics, both technical and commercial, of different plastic materials.' The visit took place in June 1968 and occupied a whole day. On the shipper's side emphasis was given to the low profitability of plastics in international markets and the large and growing volumes being traded. The conference countered this argument by asking for f.o.b. values and measurement data on all plastics likely to come forward for shipment. The shipper responded in detail, but added: 'It is possible that a value-based scale could adversely affect individual products whose profitability has already suffered severe erosion as a result of competitive pressure, and this could harm our business considerably'. This seems to be an important point. The shipper, while acknowledging earlier that value-based pricing was 'justified' is now arguing that it is his profitability which really counts, and value as such is an inadequate basis for pricing policy. This points towards a conclusion that the conference uses value as a proxy indicator for the shipper's profit when they are pricing for 'what the market will bear'; but this proxy is not always a reliable indicator, as this example shows.

After studying the unit values of the various products despatched to Australia by this shipper, the conference came back with a revised tariff which took account of the newer products shipped, but was firmly based upon the value principle, with higher rates for higher values. This led to a senior representative of the shipper calling on the Conference Secretary for a discussion of the rates for the various synthetic resins shipped. This point was reached by mid-December after nearly nine months of negotiation. It took only two more weeks to reach a compromise. The conference proposed to revise the tariff yet again. This time all references to fillers, and lumps and chips were done away with, and a simple value-based scale was introduced as follows:

Synthetic Resins	Rate of Freight (shillings)
FOB value not exceeding US $550 per 20 cwt.	315/- W/M
Exceeding $550, not exceeding $720 per 20 cwt.	360/- W/M
Exceeding $720, not exceeding $960 per 20 cwt.	380/- W/M
Exceeding $960 per 20 cwt.	403/- W/M

The following conclusions may be drawn from this example. The result of the negotiations was a compromise, on the whole a favourable one for the shipper. In more general terms the case is illustrative of the problems which arise when a system of administered prices is coupled with price bargaining, and when some rather complex technical products are also involved. The resources, in terms of manpower, devoted to the resolution of the price of a very few out of several thousand prices set in this market were large. Senior management staff were engaged on both sides. Representatives of the twenty-three lines who were members of the conference met and discussed the matter several times. The shipper gave information and instruction to four representatives of the conference on recent developments in the technology of the plastics industry, and arranged a day-long visit to one of his factories for this purpose.

On the credit side it should be noticed that the tariff was brought up to date by the elimination of the distinction (no longer reflective of reality) drawn between plastics containing 'fillers' and other plastics. The principle of charging a freight rate which varies with the value of the product was further established and enshrined in the rate structure and accepted by both parties. Changes in the price elasticity of demand for the product are reflected in the price elasticity of demand for the shipping service, as one would expect from theoretical consideration, and a relatively high elasticity of demand does appear as a factor in the negotiations in terms of arguments put forward by the shipper on grounds of competition in the markets of destination and consequently low profit rates on these shipments. It is, however, notable that although such arguments may have influenced the final outcome – we have in fact no way of knowing whether or not they did – such considerations are not directly reflected in the revised freight rates for these commodities. The unit value of the commodity shipped was once again applied as a proxy for the shipper's unit profit, and no allowance is made in the revised tariff for products where competition has reduced profit rates and increased the elasticity of demand for them in the markets in the areas of destination.

The volume of commodities involved in these negotiations was considerable. In 1967, before negotiations began, the volume moving from this shipper was approximately 15,000 freight tons; in 1968 13,000 and in 1969 19,000 tons. Factors other than the freight rate will have operated over these three years to influence the tonnage moving, but the United Kingdom shipper concerned expanded his sales to this market in the year following these negotiations and the conference did more business as a direct result of this.

2. The case of liquid asphalt from the United Kingdom to various destinations in the Far East

The product involved in this case is liquid asphalt shipped in steel drums. The unit value at the time the request was made in 1961 was £34 per ton weight, and the M/W relationship 45 cu.ft. per ton weight. Although slightly disadvantageous to the shipowner, the product was rated in the tariff and charged in practice as 'weight cargo'.

The shipper requested a reduction in the rates from the United Kingdom to destinations in the Philippines, Hong Kong, Japan, Malaya and Thailand. The rate to Hong Kong, for example, which was current at the time of the request was £7.7.1 per weight ton net (i.e. the net contract rate, which is the gross tariff rate less 9½ per cent discount subject to contract). This is approximately 18 per cent of the landed value of the product in Hong Kong. This is a case of a relatively low unit value commodity shipped over long distances in quantities amounting to several hundred tons a year ex-UK in FEFC trades.

The case for a rate reduction which was put up by the shipper was based very largely upon competitive pressures in the various Far Eastern markets named above. Increased competition from American suppliers, who included the shipper's own subsidiary on the West Coast of the United States, was cited and so also was the likelihood of the early establishment of local production in some of the named markets. The narrowness of the profit margin was repeatedly stressed, and so was the keeness of the competition. For Hong Kong the shipper estimated that at existing rates the c.i.f. cost of the product ex-UK was 7/5d per gallon compared with a competitive product at 7/3d ex-US West Coast. The shipper had notice of a shortly forthcoming general rate increase in the FEFC of 10 per cent, and estimated that it would be impossible to absorb this increase by a reduction in profit margin or in any other way because of the relatively high proportion of the freight charge in the total landed price of the product in these markets. The shipper concluded, 'we consider that the proposed increase (of 10 per cent in the rate of freight on liquid asphalt) will be sufficient possibly to kill future business in this area'.

The first response of the conference was to check up on the comparative freight rates to the various market areas concerned from the UK and from the Pacific West Coast of the USA. Their findings were as follows.

The rates from the Pacific West Coast of the USA to:

Manila ⎫	
Japan ⎬	$28.15 per 2,240 lbs.
Hong Kong ⎭	
Bangkok	$27.50 per 2,240 lbs.
Singapore	$25.75 per 2,240 lbs.

To the above rates, they stated, must be added a Wharfage and Handling charge of $2.15 per short ton or 40 cu.ft.

A comparison of these combined rates with the new, higher rates ex-UK revealed differentials in favour of the UK shipper as follows:

To Manila	£3.11.2 per 20 cwts.
Japan	£3. 2.1 per 20 cwts.
Bangkok	£2.12.11 per 20 cwts.
Hong Kong	£3.11.2 per 20 cwts.
Singapore	£2.18.7 per 20 cwts.

The conference then drew the conclusion that as the case for a rate reduction was based upon competition from the United States it has little validity in view of the higher rates ex-US West Coast.

The shipper came back to claim that although 'we agree that the United States rates given by you are current and quoted by certain Shipping Lines, we equally know that more favourable rates can be negotiated'. They cited a rate 'in the region of' $20.00 per 2,240 lbs to Manila (from the Pacific West Coast), and this would cut the competitive advantage of the UK shipper almost to nil. The shipper also then shifted the emphasis of his case away from competition from United States' sources towards competition from local manufacture.

The conference then went further into the question of the rates from the Pacific West Coast and they found out, from their American Agents, that a rate to Manila of $20.00 was not in fact realistic. As to competition from local sources of supply, the conference did not see how they could assist shippers.

The final resolution of the request was founded by the conference on the unit value of the commodity shipped by this applicant. At £34 per ton weight it was found to be considerably more valuable than ordinary road-making asphalt, valued at £15 per ton weight, which was charged the same rate of freight and had continued to move after the rate increase without complaint from its shippers. The conference therefore decided that if the lower unit value commodity can bear the rate increase so *a fortiori,* can the commodity of higher unit value. At this stage it became known to the conference that the higher valued commodity served a different market, in fact it was used for water-proofing roofs and for damp courses, but this difference was ignored. This is tantamount to a rejection of the market competition argument put up by the shipper. The conference finally fell back on the principle of 'rating according to value'.

3. The case of other machinery from the United Kingdom to Australia
This is a case of an individual rate change being initiated by the conference, with reactions from shippers.

For many years in this conference Machinery other than Agricultural machinery was rated at class 0.13 (formerly class 0.9) which in 1962 carried the rate of 305/- per freight ton, with the exception of a list of 'small high-valued machines' which were classed 0.16 (formerly 0.10) and in 1962 carried a rate of 384/-. At the time of the general rate increase (G.R.I.) of 1964 (+7½%) the conference members agreed among themselves that 'owing to changes in types of machinery shipped to Australia, and to the many high-valued types now moving, there should be a scale of rates increasing with value'.

Before this change took place there had been a great deal of discussion by members of the conference about freight rates for machinery. This began in May, 1962, when the Freight Committee considered the possibility of charging a higher rate for machinery of greater unit value.
Two suggestions were put forward.
1. Rating according to value
2. Rating all machinery at 0.16 (384/-) with a list of exceptions of *low* value machinery, which would continue at 0.13 (305/-).

A comparison was made at this time with the freight rates for machinery in the Far Eastern Freight Conference, (i.e., it is a question to some extent of what others do). The FEFC rates at that time were as follows:

Ordinary machinery	
n.o.e. (not otherwise enumerated).	262/6 W/M
Normal, a list of 4 types.	325/- W/M
Higher value, a list of 10 types.	325/- or ad valorem.

The application of ad valorem rates was discussed but abandoned because there 'might have been an incentive to some shippers to undervalue to obtain lower rates which would have been prejudicial to the interests of the great majority of shippers'.

The records were examined for data on lower valued types of machinery and it was decided that it would be difficult to obtain a representative list until protests had been received from shippers.

The Freight Committee of the conference decided to take no further action at that time.

In 1964 the matter was brought up again. The following factors were brought into discussions of the Freight Committee of the conference.

'1. The United Kingdom is the largest supplier of general machinery to Australia, with the USA increasing last year to about two-thirds of the UK total.

2. There is very little at present coming from Japan (rate 254/6), but an increase in the UK rate might stimulate Australian interest in the growing Japanese industry making general machinery.

3. The main USA rate is 392/10 W/M with a list of higher valued machines at 471/6 W/M.

4. Ad valorem rates would increase the landed costs of goods ex-UK, and would probably benefit the USA.

5. If it is considered preferable to increase only the general rate of 0.13(305/-), then a step up of 2 classes would still maintain an advantage over USA. The result would be: 0.14 (334/-)
0.15 (370/-)

It may however be considered desirable to maintain current rates at present but to adopt the principle of varying the degree of rate increase for different categories of cargo, instead of an overall increase, when the next General Rate increase is contemplated. This is done at present with Motor Cars.

6. In the South African Trade, they have on one occasion increased their upper class rates only and left the low rated cargo alone.'

The general rate increase in March 1964 was agreed at 7½ per cent and at the time, following the discussions of the Freight Committee on the lines indicated above, the rates for Machinery were re-cast and the principle of 'rating according to value' was more specifically applied as follows

Machinery (General), at March 1964

Value less than £500 per freight ton	328/-[a]
Value £500–£750 per freight ton	360/-
Value £750–£1,000 per freight ton	414/-
Value Over £1,000 per freight ton	478/-

(a) That is, the old pre-1964 class 0.13 rate of 305/- plus the GRI of 7½ per cent.

There were some fairly quick reactions from shippers of machinery and some interesting replies to them from the conference.

One manufacturer and shipper of machinery raised objections on the grounds that the increases for him ranged upwards from 18 per cent *above* the standard 7½ per cent increase and for one item the increase in the rate of freight charged was 56.7 per cent. This shipper's objection was backed by his forwarding agent.

The conference replied in the following terms.

> 'The Lines have for some years been aware that Machinery has changed in character and value from the types for which the class rate (now 328/-, formerly 305/-) was designed. For some time they (i.e. the Lines) endeavoured to find a method of rating which would be more in line with the value of the cargo, and attempts were made to achieve this by separate enumeration of types of Machine. When this failed[1] the Lines were forced to adopt rating according to value.[2]
>
> Freight on the machinery referred to, value £505 to £1,021 per freight ton, represents only 2.3% to 3.6% of value. This percentage is still well below the average, and the Lines cannot agree to make any concession in the new scale of rates for machinery'.

In a reply to a second shipper who raised objections, the Secretary wrote as follows:

> 'In calculating rates of freight to Australia it is a general principle, as in most Liner Trades, that low-valued cargo should pay lower rates. If it were otherwise it would be quite impossible for shippers to export cheap items as the application of a general cargo rate would make the landed price in Australia uncompetitive'.[3]

When this argument was put to a third shipper he came back with the following view.

> 'It is deplorable to fix rates of freight in relation to value. Are exporters of expensive items of machinery being called upon to subsidise the transport of inexpensive cargo'? (In the margin of this letter the Conference Secretary has written, 'yes').

A fourth objector is the Secretary of a machinery manufacturers association. He produces the following table in support of his case.

Shipment value (£s per freight ton)	Previous freight rate (305/-) as % of value of consignment	New freight rates (shillings)	New freight rates as % of F.O.B. value of cargo shipped	Increase in freight per freight ton of cargo shipped
500	3.05	328/-	3.28	+ 7.54
750	2.03	360/-	2.40	+18.0
1,000	1.525	414/-	2.07	+35.7
1,200	1.27	478/-	1.99	+56.7

1 Due to classification difficulties.

2 This paragraph recurrs in many letters from the Conference Secretary replying to shippers' objections to increases in the rates for machinery.

3 See the results of the summary analysis of cross-subsidisation given at the end of Chapter 4.

'These figures', he writes, 'speak for themselves, and it is quite evident that the machinery industry will be contributing more than the 7½ per cent general increase which it was claimed was necessary in the general rate..... The character and value of machinery produced in this industry has not changed basically over the past 10–15 years. .....members already encounter considerable difficulty when quoting 3 or 4 years ahead for the sale and delivery of heavy machinery against international competition. When rate changes of this size occur these difficulties are magnified..... heavy lift charges are not related to the value of what is lifted, so why are the charges for shipment treated differently?'

The Conference Secretary's reply was on lines very similar to that given to the first shipper (see above).

This case as a whole emphasises the problem of all who attempt price differentiation in a market sector containing very diverse goods. There is a large class of products in the category 'other machinery'. The task of differentiation by 'separate enumeration' is regarded by the conference as too great to be attempted. What alternative is open? Only 'rating according to value'. This is a relatively painless (to the conference) method of market and price differentiation. It has advantages to the conference in that it incorporates the principle of 'charging what the traffic will bear' and freight charges as a proportion of f.o.b., or better still c.i.f. values, are still relatively small even when the new freight rate rises some 50 per cent over the previous class rate which is undifferentiated by value sub-sections.[1] Furthermore, it meets the case a conference always has to face of having to adjust some freight rates upwards at a speed greater than that of the general rate increase because the unit value of some goods rises faster than the general rise in costs and freight rates, and because some rates are reduced or exempted from general rate increases. If changes of this kind were not made, the general principle of value-based, demand-based rating would gradually disappear. The system of rating by value classes does of course keep itself up to date, with the occasional addition of an extra scale at the top end.

As to the drawbacks, from the conference point of view the collection of the correct values is not always an easy and straight forward process. Apart from any others, there are competitive reasons for shippers' reluctance to disclose the individual consignment values of their shipments.

4. The case of agricultural machinery from the United Kingdom to Australia and New Zealand

This case illustrates the importance of both the stowage factor and the strength of competition as influences upon the making of individual freight rates.

An association of manufacturers in this field took up with the conference in this trade the rate of freight on side-rakes, asking for a reduction on the following grounds.

'Australia is one of our main markets'. Attached to this request was a schedule showing items of agricultural machinery, their f.o.b. values, weights, cubic measurements and the current conference liner freight rates from the United Kingdom to Australia and New Zealand. For side-rakes the then current rate to New Zealand was 175/- per freight ton, and to Australia 198/9. A complaint was also made that

---

1 See above the case put forward by the Secretary of a machinery manufacturers association.

132

the Australian tariff is 'omnibus' i.e., one rate for agricultural implements, while the New Zealand tariff is more differentiated. The request was turned down.

Two months later the industry association and the Freight Committe of the conference met over lunch (given by the association). This time the discussion revolved round the difference in the UK–Australia rate for tractors, 168/9, and for agricultural implements, 198/9. The association pointed out that tractors have a higher unit value than implements. This could be a case for raising the tractor rate, rather than lowering the implement rate, but the conference gave attention to the request from the association that 'the rate for implements be fixed having regard for the W/M ratio'. Broken down and packed implements did travel at lower rates at that time, but some packing and unpacking costs were necessarily involved for the shipper at both ends of the journey. The conference now acceded to this request and fixed new rates for agricultural implements as follows

Not exceeding 120 cu.ft. per weight ton	198/9 W/M
Over 120 cu.ft. per weight ton	181/3 W/M
Over 200 cu.ft. per weight ton	158/9 W/M

The sign W/M against the rate of freight means that the conference gives to its members individually the option to charge on either a weight or a measurment basis, given that the rate for one weight ton shall be the same as the rate for one measurement ton of 40 cu.ft. The shipowner is required to choose a measurement basis of charging for any cargo which exceeds 40 cu.ft. per weight ton and a weight basis for cargo which has a M/W ratio of less than 40 cu.ft. The above revised rates gave some incentive to shippers to pack their implements for shipment, as well as some rate reduction for implements which have a very high M/W ratio, that is, are very bulky in relation to their weight. For example, an agricultural implement measuring 205 cu.ft. per weight ton and weighing 1.5 tons would be charged £61.02 under the revised scale (£76.38 under the immediately preceding scale). If, by packing, its cubic measurment can be reduced to 110 cu.ft. per weight ton, then the implement will now travel for only £40.98, a saving of £20.04, which may or may not fully offset the cost to the shipper of packing and of unpacking and assembly.

The association accepted this result, but noted in passing that its members exporting ploughs and harrows, which fall into the highest rated category, did not benefit at all.

A little later the association, assuming (incorrectly) that the new rates apply only to unpacked implements, asked for a lower rate for packed implements. But the conference refused to make further reductions. The new rates, they explained, apply to both packed and unpacked implements, but 'it is usual for implements to be packed'. They went on to explain that a packed motor car or tractor did not carry a lower rate than an unpacked one because it is packed, but rather the unpacked vehicle bore a higher rate than the normal or packed one in order to compensate the shipowner for loss of stowage. It may be noticed here that the stowage factor is a measure of the space which a particular consignment occupies in the ship, allowing for any loss of stowage due to the consignment's awkward shape, or fragility which would prevent 'stacking' or otherwise impede stowing. The M/W ratio measures bulkiness in terms of cubic feet per ton weight, but the stowage factor could well be a greater number of cubic feet per weight ton for the same consignment if the cargo is of awkward shape or fragile.

Two months later Australia reduced Imperial Preference on agricultural machinery imports from the United Kingdom. The association asked for the freight rate of 158/9 to apply to all packed implements, and quoted figures to show that the export trade of their members to Australia was declining. The conference declined the request, pointing out that 'other machinery' (q.v.) is currently rated at 270/- W/M, well above even the top rate in the scale for agricultural machinery.

This example shows that a conference is sometimes prepared, when approached, to give away some of the considerable advantage it derives from its option to charge on either a weight (W) or a measurement (M) basis for cargo which has a high W/M ratio, that is, its 'measurement tonnage' is several times as great at its 'weight tonnage'. But the scale of rates adopted for this purpose, which decline as W/M increases, does not come anywhere near to declining in the same proportion as W/M increases. That is to say, as W/M rises from 40 cu.ft. per weight ton (equivalent to one 'freight ton') to 120 cu.ft. per weight ton (i.e. three freight tons) the rate of freight does decline, but it must be noted that an additional loss of stowage would certainly be suffered by the shipowner when bulky cargo, such as side-rakes, are shipped unpacked. Not only is more space occupied, to the extent of the W/M ratio, but often it is impossible to load other cargo on top of cargo of this type, and further loss to the shipowner due to loss of stowage occurs for this reason. It is not possible to determine whether in this, or any other, instance of relatively bulky cargo whether the conference has retained for the shipowner a sufficient or a more than sufficient 'loss of stowage' premium.[1]

5. The case of toys from the United Kingdom to Australia

This case is similar to the preceding one on agricultural machinery in that it is concerned with the M/W ratio and the stowage factor.

In 1957 a United Kingdom manufacturer, and exporter of toys to Australia, approached the conference to seek a concessionary rate of freight for toys of high measurement in relation to weight. The case for a rate reduction was in this case a positive one. The shipper in effect said; 'If you give us a rate reduction on toys of high stowage factor we shall be able to increase our sales to Australia and therefore our business with you'. A further point which was made was that plastic of various kinds was becoming a more usual material for toys and that this led to toys becoming lighter and bulkier.

The conference agreed to change the rate for toys from 212/6 per ton W/M for all toys to the following scale:

Not exceeding 240 cu.ft. per 20 cwts.	212/6 W/M
exceeding 240 cu.ft. per 20 cwts.	181/3 W/M

Four years later the shipper put in another request supported by a similar argument. It was granted. In the meantime there had been a general rate increase of 7½ per cent and the new scale for toys according to M/W ratio was as follows:

Not exceeding 240 cu.ft. per 20 cwts.	228/9 W/M
240 to 360 cu.ft. per 20 cwts.	195/- W/M
over 360 cu.ft. per 20 cwts.	182/6 W/M

Except for general rate increases this scale remained unaltered for six years.

1 This aspect of conference pricing is investigated further in Chapter 7, where it enters a price model as one of the several factors influencing the structure of relative freight rates.

By way of conclusion this scale may be translated into the following form if we assume, as is nearly always so, that the shipowner chooses a measurement basis for calculating the freight to be charged.

Freight charged for shipping one weight ton of cargo at the following weight/measurement relationships:

240 cu.ft. per 20 cwt.	1,372/6
300 cu.ft. per 20 cwt.	1,462/6
400 cu.ft. per 20 cwt.	1,825/-

The cost per weight ton of shipping this cargo rises with the M/W ratio. To counter this the conference gives its members the option of charging on a measurement ton (40 cubic feet) basis, and this is the method by which shipowners reimburse themselves for the loss of stowage which is involved in shipping cargo which either very bulky or particularly awkward to stow, or both. But the conference gives away some of the advantage it gets from its W or M option when it judges that the demand for the product shipped is sufficiently price elastic to more than repay the conference in volume terms what it gives away in freight rate terms. The conference does not use this terminology but it argues along these general lines.

6. The case of motor vehicles from the United Kingdom to Australia

This is a case of severe outside competition in shipping services.

Before the second world war Australia obtained the bulk of her motor vehicle imports from the United States, but with the foreign exchange restrictions of the early post-war period there was a substantial changeover to the United Kingdom as the main source of vehicles. In the years 1945/49 a large quantity of unpacked motor vehicles were shipped over this route at first at 129/- W/M and then in 1948 at 150/- W/M. Thereafter some special and general rate increases brought the rates for motor vehicles to 200/- for unpacked and 157/6 for packed and KD (knocked down) vehicles by 1953.

In 1953, under threat of chartering by the Society of Motor Manufacturers and Traders (SMMT) these rates were abruptly reduced to 170/- and 135/- respectively. By March 1957, after two general rate increases, they had become 212/6 unpacked and 168/- packed.

From 1955 Volkswagen started to express dissatisfaction with the conference rates and from time to time they threatened to charter and claimed that they had a better offer from an outside Line. In the period from 1955 to 1958 the conference resisted and no reductions in the rates for motor vehicles were offered. In fact in March 1957 both vehicle rates took the 14 per cent general rate increase.

In June 1958 Volkswagen finally broke away from the conference and started to ship all its vehicles to Australia by an outside Line. The SMMT then requested a 15 per cent reduction on motor vehicle rates in order to enable them to meet the competition from Volkswagen in the Australian market which arose from the lower freight rates Volkswagen were now paying. The conference felt that they had to agree to the extent of a 10 per cent reduction and the motor vehicle rates were reduced in September 1958 to 191/3 unpacked and 152/- packed.

By the autumn of 1959 Volkswagen had obtained a substantial share of the Australian motor car market, but were becoming less than satisfied with their new shipping arrangements. They therefore offered to come back to the conference if the rate for packed, KD vehicles was reduced by 12½ per cent to 133/-. The conference agreed and this rate came into force in November 1959. The rate for unpacked vehicles was left at 191/3 until March 1960 when a further threat by shippers to charter for the shipment of unpacked vehicles led the conference to a reduction of 7½ per cent to 177/-.

From March 1960 the two motor vehicle rates lagged behind the advance of general rates in the Australian trade. In October 1960 general rates advanced by 7½ per cent, but neither motor rate was altered. In January 1961 both motor vehicle rates were increased by 4 per cent, and in February 1962 the rate for packed vehicles was raised by 5 per cent. In October of the same year general rates were increased by 5 per cent but both the motor vehicles rates were again exempted.

Late in 1962 and in January 1963 the conference held negotiations with Volkswagen on the rate for unpacked vehicles and with the SMMT and Simca on the rate for packed vehicles. The result was a very large 35 per cent reduction in the rate for unpacked vehicles to 119/-, (but this did not last very long, see below), and a comparatively minor 2½ per cent reduction in the rate for packed vehicles to 141/6.

With a confidence born of success, Volkswagen came back to the conference in May 1963 and managed to get another 6 per cent off the rate for packed vehicles, bringing it down to 133/-. It was further agreed at that time to hold this rate firm until December 1964.

In January 1964 the rate for unpacked vehicles was increased to 165/-.

Further negotiations were held with the SMMT and Volkswagen in October 1964. It was agreed to raise the rate for packed vehicles by 6 per cent to 141/- with effect from January 1, 1965 and, continuing the stable rate policy begun in 1963, it was agreed to keep this rate unchanged for two years, to the end of 1966. In the event the rate was not altered until April 1967 when both rates were increased by 10 per cent to 181/6 unpacked, and to 155/- packed.

A few months later, in June 1967, the Suez surcharge was applied generally to all rates except the two motor vehicle rates. They were exempted on the grounds that they had just been increased by 10 per cent.

Thereafter the rates for motor vehicles have moved more closely in step with general rates. Between July 1967 and May 1971, the two motor vehicles rates were increased by 12½ per cent (the devaluation surcharge of November 1967 which was immediately incorporated in all rates), by 5 per cent (June 1969), 10 per cent (June 1970) and 10 per cent (May 1971). General rates were raised by the 12½ per cent devaluation surcharge, by 12½ per cent in September 1970 and again by 12½ per cent in March 1971.

The movements of the two motor vehicle rates compared with the movement of general rates are shown in Table 4.5 in Chapter 4, and in Figure 7 in Chapter 5. The main conclusion to be drawn from this case study is that competition can force a marked downwards departure of particular commodity rates from the trend of general rates, provided the shipper or shippers acting in combination are large enough in terms of freight tonnage to be able to fill a whole specialised vessel, which is able to carry a homogeneous cargo at lower rates of freight than a conference liner, which can only carry smaller amounts of the same cargo at each sailing.

136

One measure of the success of the motor vehicle shippers, particularly Volkswagen, is that over the sixteen year period from 1955 to 1971 general freight rates in this trade rose by 148 per cent, while the rate for unpacked motor vehicles increased by only 53 per cent, and the rate for packed vehicles by only 65 per cent.

Not only were the motor vehicle makers acting together large enough, in terms of tonnage, to fill a chartered vessel for one or more voyages outward per year, they were also, for a similar reason, important to the conference. In 1967, for example, packed motor vehicles accounted for 12.1 per cent, and unpacked vehicles for 3.7 per cent of total conference[1] freight revenue. Loss of cargo on this scale is clearly a matter of great importance to the conference, both in terms of the revenue itself and also in terms of costs associated with the balance of outward and homeward trade on this route.[2]

7. *The case of synthetic fibres from the continent of Europe to Australia*
This is a case which includes considerations of supply from alternative sources. This involves the conference in inter-conference competition and in competition from 'outsiders' on an alternative route.

The shipper is a large international company with plants in various parts of the world, including the United States, Britain and the Continent of Europe.

In 1963 one of the shipper's subsidiaries in Continental Europe approached the UK/Continent—Australia Conference with a request for a freight rate reduction. His case was that due to the attainment of scale economies, amongst other factors, there was now little difference in total unit manufacturing cost of his product (a synthetic fibre) between one, particularly large, European plant and his group's large United States plants, and both sources were supplying the Australian market. The group also had interests in a trade from Australia to the United States, and they had recently chartered shipping capacity to run in both directions in this trade. In the US—Australia leg of this run the freight rates they were paying were, he claimed, a good deal lower than the conference freight rate on the product moving from the Continent to Australia. The applicant added that their charter in the US—Australia trade was making as many as 7 or 8 round voyages per year.

This is a tough problem for the conference. Very few shippers have such a volume of cargo moving as this, and it must be even rarer for a customer to have a large volume of cargo moving in *both* directions of a trade which, although not on the conference route, was on one which involved competition with the conference trade. A direct comparison of freight rates in 1963 shows that the conference was charging 384/- W/M per freight ton from the Continent to Australia, while the charter rate from USA to Australia was only 268/- W/M per freight ton.

The conference pointed out that the shipper was getting the advantage of a charter rate and could do so because of the size of his shipments *both to and from* the United States and Australia. The shipper replied that really it was a question of whether his firm increased its shipments by conference vessels to 700 measurement tons per month or left them at their then current level of 190 M. tons per month.

1   UK/Continent—Australia Conference Outwards. In the UK—Australia Conference Outwards the corresponding percentage shares were 9.9 per cent for packed and 2.2 per cent for unpacked vehicles.

2   See Chapter 8, Section 1.

The conference examined this request very fully. In particular it realised that if a reduction were given on the rate for the particular type of synthetic fibre concerned, then the same reduction would have to be extended to other synthetic fibres, which had similar values per 40 cu.ft., and which were currently moving from the United Kingdom to Australia in very considerable quantities.[1] The member lines were known to be most reluctant to lose freight revenue on this cargo, which they expected to move in even larger quantities in future. So the decision was finally taken not to reduce the rate of freight on the request of this shipper.

Later this decision was reversed and the rate for this commodity was reduced from 384/- to 334/-.

In 1967 another application, this time from a United Kingdom shipper of this commodity, was rejected. The conference had found that the shipper had increased the volume of his shipments in 1967 and his plea of increased competition in the Australian market was felt by the conference to be unsubstantiated, but in 1968 another UK shipper was successful in getting a reduction from 412/- (general rate increases had raised the tariff to this figure from 334/- in 1963/64) to 369/- by pleading 'intense difficulties in meeting United States and Japanese competition in the Australian market'. The shipper had made price reductions amounting in total to 50 per cent over the past nine years to meet this competition. The shipper's volume was approximately 10,000 measurement tons per year and the conference decided that: 'The British lines feel that in order to assist shippers to maintain and increase their exports of this product a reduction to class 0.12 (369/-) should be made'.

It may be concluded from this case that the conference is rather less sensitive to competition in the direct sense of shipment by an 'outsider' (on an alternative but competing route), than it is to competition in the product market in the area of destination. When the competition in such markets is recognised as strong, and the Australian trade statistics of imports of synthetic fibres of various types were examined in considerable detail by the conference when they were considering this case, a rate reduction is withheld if the volume moving in conference vessels is increasing. It appears that no account is taken of a falling share of the market held by the customer of the conference so long as the market is expanding faster than the customer's share of it is declining, so that shipments increase.

8. The case of rubber from Malaysia and Singapore to Europe

This is a case of collective bargaining.

In 1967 the Singapore Chinese Chamber of Commerce formed a special committee 'to break the monopolistic manipulations of Conference freight rates'. Later another special committee was set up 'to break the shipping conference system'. An anti-conference campaign was mounted in the press and support was obtained from the Associated Chinese Chambers of Commerce of Malaysia.

Later in 1967 Sterling was devalued, and the Far East Freight Conference applied a surcharge[2] of 12½ per cent to all rates quoted in sterling from Malaysia and

1 Although the United Kingdom—Australia Conference and the United Kingdom/Continent—Australia Conference have different, though to some extent overlapping memberships, they operate a common freight tariff.

2 It was later incorporated in the structure of basic rates. The surcharge procedure was used because it was not possible to recalculate all tariff rates overnight.

Singapore to Europe. For freights paid in terms of currencies such as the Singapore or Malaysian dollar which had not been devalued there was an effective rate reduction of about 4 per cent.[1]

Shippers of rubber protested that the normal 'current and the two following months' notice of this rate increase had not been given, but the conference pointed out that in certain clearly defined circumstances, including a change in exchange rates as published by the I.M.F., such notice was not required by the terms of their freight tariff.

A further problem arose when some rubber dealers, who had done business on a c.i.f. basis, claimed half of the devaluation surcharge from their buyers in Europe. But the Rubber Trade Association of London (whose c.i.f. contract No. 3 is used as a basis for European business as a whole) were not willing to agree to this, claiming that it was not a surcharge but a freight rate increase and as such payable by the seller.

In February 1968 the conference acceded to a request for a rate reduction which came from the Rubber Association of Singapore. Singapore cents 0.17 per lb., were taken off the rate for sheet rubber bringing it down to $S.3.82, its lowest level since September 1961 when it was raised from $S.3.62 to 3.98, despite cost increases over this seven year period which had led to two general freight rate increases.[2]

Some rubber dealers in Malaysia and Singapore continued their attack on the conference, turning their attention now to the contract discount system, which favours those shippers who contract to remain loyal to conference shipping services over a specified period of time, normally a year. In March 1968 62 contract shippers of rubber and latex in Malaysia and Singapore gave notice that they wished to terminate their contracts at the end of 1968. Although these 62 were the great majority of the Chinese shippers, they represented no more than about 25 per cent of the tonnage shipped. Foreign estate owners and dealers linked with European buyers were not included in this number. The conference then increased its efforts to win back the departing shippers, pointing out that their 23 member Lines from 11 European and Eastern countries (including the state-owned Singapore Line) provided 100 sailings per month from Singapore/Port Swettenham/Penang to some 46 European ports. It then became apparent that most of the defecting shippers believed that these services would remain in operation and that they could in future either use them, on gross freight rate terms, or 'outsiders' as they might find advantageous from time to time.

Rubber buyers in Europe then began to show concern because of the possible curtailment of regular conference services. One buyer wrote 'no adequate deliveries to West European ports at least can be assured without the conference system'. The group of 62 shippers nevertheless moved further with their plan to break away from the conference and they set up a 'Freight Booking Centre' which offered space by assorted non-conference vessels. This group found, after a while, that a service adequate for their needs could not be obtained at rates lower than the conference *net* contract rates. In subsequent negotiation with the conference the group tried

1 To compensate member Lines whose currencies had not been devalued would have required a sterling rate increase of 16.67 per cent.

2 See Chapter 4, Table 4.9.

hard to get a new form of contract which allowed them to use non-conference vessels from time to time without loss of discount. They wanted, in fact, the lowest rated form of both types of shipping service. The conference refused and the ex-contractors continued shipping a proportion of their total exports by outsiders during 1970, and the remainder they sent by conference vessels without benefit of discount.

It was shown in Chapter 4 that natural rubber from Malaysia and Singapore entered highly competitive markets in Western Europe and elsewhere. The c.i.f. price of natural rubber from these sources was in the neighbourhood of 55 cents per lb. in November 1968, and at that time the rate of freight was 3.82 cents (local currency in both cases). Therefore the freight rate accounted for 6.9 per cent of the c.i.f. price of natural rubber, but was subject to fluctuation as the price of rubber and the freight rate changed. Relatively this is a high proportion when it is compared with, say, machinery moving outwards from the United Kingdom (see case history number 3). The 9½ per cent contract discount reduces this proportion to 6.3. Even a fairly large rate cut, say, 10 per cent, would reduce the landed price in Europe by less than one per cent. Nevertheless, it may be concluded that the higher is the proportion which the rate of freight bears to the landed price per freight ton the greater is the responsiveness (or elasticity) of the volume of goods shipped to changes in the rate of freight, and hence in the landed prices, of commodities which enter a market which is as highly competitive as is the market for natural rubber. Such competition arises not only from shipments of natural rubber from other souces of supply, but also from supplies of synthetic rubber from local European sources.

In such competitive situations, bargaining, and particularly collective bargaining by well organised shippers appears from this case to be effective in reducing the freight rate per ton of rubber shipped. The rate level in 1969 was in fact below the average cost of shipment. This must be the conclusion drawn from this case.

B. Theoretical considerations

We turn now to consider some theoretical relationships between certain characteristics of the product market and those of the transport service market. These relationships are based on the work of Alfred Marshall[1] and have been developed by A.A. Walters,[2] and by E. Bennathan and A.A. Walters.[3]

The service of freight transport may be regarded as a factor of production which is employed by manufacturers to enable them to meet the demand for their product in markets which are distant from the place of manufacture. Looked at in another

1 Alfred Marshall *Principles of Economics* Book V, particularly chapter VI. 8th Ed. Also 'Trade and Industry' pp. 436 et seq.

2 A.A. Walters 'A Development Model of Transport' *American Economic Review.* Papers and Proceedings, May 1968. pp. 341–377.

3 E. Bennathan and A.A. Walters, *The Economics of Ocean Freight Rates.* Praeger, New York, 1970 pp. 19–22 and Technical Appendix.

way,[1] freight transport services may be seen as the means by which time and place utilities are added to form utilities. By these means the 'dis-utilities of distance' are overcome and the utilities of time and place become interleaved with those of form to produce the composite delivered utility in the markets in the areas of destination. These utilities do not necessarily add up to the utility satisfying *final* demands since goods satisfying various kinds of intermediate demand are also shipped.

Whether the role of freight transport is regarded as one of adding to form utilities or as a factor of production of goods delivered to the market they supply, it is highly probable that some interactions between the product market and the transport service market will occur. The demand for a factor of production is a derived demand, derived from the demand for the product of the factor. Equally the demand for freight transport services is a derived demand. How are the product and factor markets related?

From Book V of the Principles we get the relationship that the elasticity of the derived demand for a factor of production is equal to the cost of the factor expressed as a proportion of the price of the product multiplied by the elasticity of demand for the product. In this relationship we may substitute the elasticity of demand for transport service (ϵ_{trans}) for the elasticity of the derived demand for a factor of production, and likewise the transport cost (tc) for the cost of the factor of production. So we get

$$\epsilon_{trans} = \frac{tc}{p} \cdot \epsilon_d$$

where ϵ_d is the elasticity of demand for the product, and
p is the landed price of the commodity in the area of destination.

The conference must always be interested in ϵ_{trans}, the elasticity of demand for its services. Where ϵ_{trans} is relatively small, the transport service price may be set relatively high without much risk of losing the traffic; conversely, when the value of ϵ_{trans} is relatively high, traffic is very liable to be lost if the rate of freight is raised. This simple relationship has two main implications for pricing by shipping conferences. It is important to conference pricing policy in individual commodity cases because, *first,* it shows that the higher is the elasticity of demand in the product market (due e.g. to a higher degree of competition in this market) the higher will be the elasticity of demand for the transport service to that market, *ceteris paribus,* (most notably tc/p). *Second,* the relationship is important to pricing because it shows that the higher is tc/p — the cost of transport expressed as a proportion of the c.i.f. (landed) price — the higher is the elasticity of demand for the transport service to the point of landing.

Referring back to the case histories of individual rate changes given earlier in this chapter it may be noticed that cases 1 (synthetic resins), 2 (liquid asphalt), 3 (other machinery) and 8 (natural rubber) illustrate the second principle.

Theoretical considerations must be taken a step further and, working forward from Marshall, A.A. Walters has done so by incorporating supply elasticities in the

1 B.M. Deakin 'Towards a Freight Transport Function.' Department of Applied Economics, Cambridge. Reprint Series No. 312, 1971. This paper first appeared in *Programming for Europe's Collective Needs,* Edited by J.H.P. Paelinck pp. 244–284. North-Holland Publishing Company, Amsterdam, 1970.

product market into the simple expression $\epsilon_{\text{trans}} = tc/p \cdot \epsilon_d$ and he has arrived at the following:[1]

$$\epsilon_{\text{trans}} = T\left[\frac{\epsilon_s \cdot \epsilon_d}{\epsilon_s - (1 - T)\epsilon_d}\right]$$

where in addition to ϵ_{trans} and ϵ_d which have already been explained,

T is tc/p, the transport cost of the individual commodity expressed as a proportion of its c.i.f. price,

ϵ_s is the elasticity of supply of the commodity shipped, and has a value between zero and some number less than infinity.

In practical terms it may be understood that where, in the short run, the supply of any commodity is inelastic, i.e. supply is relatively unresponsive to changes in the price of the product, then ϵ_s takes a low value and the value of ϵ_{trans} will also be low.[2] In other words, on a *ceteris paribus* assumption, the lower is ϵ_s the lower is ϵ_{trans}, and the conference is in a position to raise its rate of freight without losing traffic. Conversely, when ϵ_s takes a relatively high value, so does ϵ_{trans}. This last condition is illustrated by case history 7 (synthetic fibres). Here, it will be recalled, the supply of the commodity to the Australian market was highly elastic due to alternative markets and alternative sources of supply under the control of one large, internationally-based shipper. Conversely, in case 8 (natural rubber) the elasticity of supply to the large European market may be expected to be relatively low because although there are alternative markets they could not readily absorb large quantities of rubber which had been priced out of Europe, neither can the total supply of natural rubber be reduced or increased in the short period, and furthermore the alternative supplies of natural rubber are not under the control of Malaysian shippers.

From the evidence we have examined, conferences do not seem to be aware of the importance of supply elasticities to their pricing policy, and it is unlikely that a conference can ever know very much about the range of different foreign markets served by a particular shipper, nor can it know in detail all the sources of supply to a particular market via other routes. Therefore in its policy of relative pricing in individual commodity cases, a conference acts on the basis of what it knows about (a) the physical characteristics of the product, see case histories 4 (agricultural machinery) and 5 (toys), and (b) the value of tc/p, which it can calculate, and (c) some kind of feeling about ϵ_d which cannot of course be precise, but at least the conference knows that ϵ_d will be large when there is a high degree of competition in the product market. Little is known, and probably for practical reasons little can be known, about the value of ϵ_s.

So, in practice, differential conference prices (rates of freight) are made on the principle of 'what the market will bear', and this in turn is judged from what is known of the values of tc/p and ϵ_d. We have not found any evidence that the elasticity of supply is brought into the reckoning when differential prices are made by conferences.

1 The steps by which this stage is reached are explained in the works to which reference is made at the beginning of this section.

2 It is necessary, when using Walters' expression quoted earlier, to bear in mind that ϵ_d is of negative, and ϵ_s of positive sign.

Summary

Eight case histories of individual freight rate bargaining between shipping conference and shippers acting individually or, in some instances, collectively are described
in this chapter. They provide some evidence of the way in which differential freight
rates are made. Certain features of this process stand out, and are given below.

1. The administrative resources involved in negotiating freight rates for individual
commodities can be considerable, particularly where the technical factors relating
to the commodity shipped are complex and when negotiations are protracted for
this and other reasons. Cases 1 (synthetic resins) and 3 (other machinery) show this
process.

2. Competition in the product market in the area of destination is a shipper's argument which clearly carries weight with the conferences. A high degree of competition in the product market implies a high coefficient of price elasticity of demand
for the product shipped and this reflected in the price elasticity of demand for the
shipping service concerned. Cases 1 (synthetic resins), 2 (liquid asphalt) and 7 (synthetic fibres).

3. When the rate of freight forms a high proportion of the total landed (c.i.f.) value
of any commodity, then the elasticity of demand for the shipping service also tends
to be high. In case 3 (other machinery) the obverse of this argument is used by the
conference to defend a rate increase, and it is pointed out by the conference that
the rate of freight forms only a very small proportion, less than 4 per cent, of the,
f.o.b. value (in this case) of the commodity. In cases 2 (liquid asphalt) and 8 (natural rubber) the rate of freight rises as a proportion of the landed value to 18 per cent
(asphalt) and 7 per cent (rubber). It is therefore true that for any given increase in
the rate of freight the consequent increase in the landed c.i.f. price will be greater
the higher is the rate of freight *as a proportion* of the landed price, other factors,
such as tariffs, being unchanged.

4. Competition in the market for shipping services, see cases 6 (motor vehicles) and
7 (synthetic fibres), whether such services are on the same route (case 6) or on a
different but competing route (case 7). In case 7 the competition takes the form of
an alternative geographical source of supply of the product under the control of the
same shipper. The alternative supplies are competitive principally because the shipping services are cheaper on their route to the market in the area of destination of
the conference route. More competition and therefore higher price elasticities are
thereby introduced into the market for liner shipping services.

5. 'Charging what the market will bear,' in other words pricing higher in those
sections of the market for shipping services where the price elasticity of demand is
low and pricing lower where the elasticity is higher, is apparent in all these cases as
in other evidence of differential pricing given in Chapters 4, 5, and 6.

6. The physical relationship between the weight of individual commodities and
their cubic measurement leads in the first instance to the pricing rule, noticed in

Chapter 4, that the shipowner must charge on a weight (W) or measurement (M) basis according to whichever yields the higher freight, except where commodities are rated by the conference specifically on a weight or a measurement basis. In two cases described here, case 4 (agricultural machinery) and case 5 (toys), the exercise by the shipowner of his measurement option leads to a violation of other pricing principles, such as that of 'charging what the traffic will bear'. In cases where the M/W ratio is very high (e.g. toys) the shipowner's option to charge on a measurement basis is one of powerful effect upon the freight charged per weight unit of the commodity. As the M/W ratio rises, the unit value of the same commodity will decline. Some compromise is therefore needed whereby the shipowner gives up some of his advantage from this option. The solution adopted is a scale of freight rates declining as M/W rises, and this is shown in the cases 4 (agricultrual machinery) and 5 (toys).

7. A consideration of some theoretical relationships between certain characteristics of the product market and those of the market for transport services involved in supplying the product market leads to the following conclusions.

- a. The higher is the cost of transport as a proportion of the total landed c.i.f. price of the commodity shipped the higher is the elasticity of demand for the transport service concerned and *vice versa.*
- b. The price elasticity of demand for the transport service varies directly, but not proportionately, with the price elasticity of demand for the commodities shipped by such service into markets in the area of destination.
- c. The greater the competition in the product market the higher is the price elasticity of demand in that market and, following from b. above, the higher is the price elasticity of demand in the transport service market, and *vice versa.*
- d. The elasticity of demand for the service of transport varies directly, but not proportionately, with the elasticity of supply of the product shipped.
- e. From the evidence of differential pricing practices of shipping conferences which we have examined, attention appears to be paid to relationships a, b and c above, but the evidence about relationship d. is inconclusive.

7 A Computable Model of Relative Prices in Conference Trades

In Chapters 4, 5 and 6 prices have been studied in absolute terms over time, in association with costs and in context with various market situations. In the present chapter an attempt is made to construct a model of *relative* prices.

The structure of prices in a number of different freight liner conferences is examined, at a particular moment in time, for relationships which may exist between the rate of freight and various determining factors. Broadly such factors may be divided *a priori* into two groups: the demand-based factors and the supply or cost-based factors. In most cases, in both groups, the determining factors arise from various characteristics of individual items of cargo carried. In the case of the cost-based factors, it is one or more physical characteristics of the cargo which cause differential costs to fall on the shipowner; examples are cargo requiring refrigerated stowage, secure and safe stowage (for very valuable cargo), and hazardous cargo requiring special care in both handling and stowage as well as special insurance cover of particular risks. In the case of the demand-based factors the characteristics of the individual items of cargo which are important are such qualities as unit value, size of consignment and magnitude of the flow of trade in a particular type of cargo, and certain qualities of the market or markets supplied in the areas of destination of the shipping service. Obviously it is not possible to quantify all factors which are influential in the formation of the structure and pattern of relative prices made by shipping conferences. What we have done is to examine trades served by particular conferences, to take cross-sectional samples of cargoes actually moving in a number of specified liner trades and to apply a computable price model which takes the form which is now described.

1. The form of the price model employed

The relative rate of freight was found, by experiment, to be a function of a number of identifiable factors, together with others which cannot be identified. In functional form:

$$FR\, f\,(\beta,\, V,\, T,\, M/W,\, H,\, R,\, C)$$

and in computable terms:

$$FR(P) = b_1 + b_2 \log_e V + b_3 T > 50 + b_4 (M/W) > 2 + b_5 H + b_6 R + b_7 C.$$

Where

$FR(P)$ is the predicted rate of freight in terms of decimalised £s.

b_1 is a constant, and b_2, b_3, b_4, b_5, b_6 and b_7 are coefficients.

V is the unit value of each consignment in terms of £'s per bill of lading ton.

T is the weight or measurement tonnage, (according to whichever is used as a basis for rating), of each consignment. This term enters the model only when T has a value in excess of 50.

M/W is the ratio of measurement tons to weight tons of each consignment. A measurement ton is 40 cubic feet and is regarded as requiring transport services which are equal to those needed for a weight ton of 2,240 lbs. This term enters the model only when M/W exceeds 2.

H, R are dummy variables representing consignments which are respec-
and C tively hazardous, require refrigeration or cool chamber stowage. Their values are given by their coefficients when the model is applied to data of actual freight rates $(FR(A))$ and of V, T and M/W.

The special characteristics of cargo, such as the requirement of refrigeration, which are included in the price model are among those for which no specific additional freight charge is made in the tariff. In many other such cases, such as extra charges for tank cleaning and for heavy lift and long length, the additional charge is specified in the tariff, and so it is not necessary to put it into the model. Rates of freight are therefore entered net of these specified items of extra charge.

In sections 3 and 4 of Chapter 4, conference pricing practices were examined in relation to theories of pricing. There it was shown that price differentiation was practised over a wide range of price, but that where demand became more elastic, due especially to competition from tramp vessels at the lower end of the price range, a more open and less definitive pricing policy was followed. It seems necessary now to try to discover the main basis or principle upon which the policy of price differentiation is founded, and then to go on to estimate by means of the price model the relative importance of this and other factors in the making of relative prices.

a. Value

We have made an examination of the freight tariffs of a number of shipping conferences. One result of this study has been the estimates of the degree of price differentiation which is set out in Chapter 4, Section 2. Further study has shown that in a number of commodity classes of a residual nature, for example, 'Iron and steel products, n.o.e. (not otherwise enumerated)'; 'glassware, hollow or otherwise n.o.e.', and 'asphalt and bitumen', are further differentiated with respect to unit value. So we get the following tariff entry which is representative of pricing according to this principle.

146

Iron and steel (not scrap), n.o.e. (including angles, bars, channels, plates, rods, sheets and tees)

	Rate of Freight
Not exceeding US $168 per 20 cwts.	20.60W [a](US$)
Exceeding $168, not exceeding $204 per 20 cwts	24.05W
Exceeding $204 not exceeding $276 per 20 cwts	31.05W
Exceeding $276 not exceeding $348 per 20 cwts	37.25W
Exceeding $348 not exceeding $420 per 20 cwts	40.35W
Exceeding $420 not exceeding $492 per 20 cwts	44.95W
Exceeding $492 not exceeding $564 per 20 cwts	48.05W
Exceeding $564 not exceeding $696 per 20 cwts	55.50W
Exceeding $696 not exceeding $840 per 20 cwts	58.60W
Exceeding $840 not exceeding $1,116 per 20 cwts	62.85W
Exceeding $1,116 not exceeding $2,100 per 20 cwts	69.80W
Exceeding $2,100 per 20 cwts.	69.80W *or* *3% ad. val.*

(a) W indicates that this cargo *must* be charged on a weight basis. There is no option to charge on a measurement basis.

This is closely graded pricing according to unit value, with provision in the highest unit value sub-class (exceeding $2,100 per 20 cwts) for a further extension of this principle. This extension is provided for by the addition of an *ad valorem* option to the rate of freight quoted for this sub-class of the commodity class of 'Iron and Steel (not scrap), n.o.e.'

Many other examples of rating according to unit value may be found in conference tariffs, as well as some variations on the same practice, such as a stated rate of freight, with or without a W or M option and with the addition of an *ad valorem* option which the shipowner must exercise, according to conference rules, in his own favour. Some conferences set a limit upon the maximum rates which may be charged under some *ad valorem* options.

Some rates of freight fixed by conferences are clearly related to the unit value of the commodity shipped, and this is *one* method adopted by conferences to differentiate prices and to attempt to 'charge what the market will bear' or, in economic terms, to charge a higher price the lower is thought to be the elasticity of demand for the shipping service in a particular section of the market.[1] Conferences do not of course know the price elasticity of demand for their services.[2] In some cases they use unit value as a proxy for the coefficient of price elasticity of demand in an inverse sense — the higher the unit value the lower the coefficient of price elasticity.

1 See Chapter 6 for a fuller investigation of this aspect of conference pricing.

2 We have been told by conference officials 'that conferences usually investigate and confirm from other factors any competitive f.o.b. or c.i.f. prices, either from other supplying sources or from indigenous supplies at the place of reception of cargo. They usually have in mind also any competitive rates offered by "outsiders" operating against their own services and to some extent therefore they have some idea of the elasticity of demand for their own shipping services in respect of the goods concerned'.

The next matter which seems to require examination is the relationship between unit values and freight rates, other influential factors being assumed neutral. A number of examples of pricing according to unit value, similar to the one quoted above for iron and steel (n.o.e.), were examined and we have calculated the ratios of change in unit value to change in freight rate. In 25 examples of corresponding change in these two variables we get a range in the ratios of percentage change from $1:1.0$ to $1:6.9$ rate of freight to unit value of the rated commodity, and a mean ratio of these examples of $1:2.9$ and a median of $1:2.5$. This suggests that in the sample the distribution is biassed in favour of the higher ratios, and from the iron and steel example quoted earlier it can be seen (from Table 7.1) that the ratios tend to rise with unit value.

Table 7.1   *Ratios of Successive Changes in Freight Rates (FR) to Corresponding Changes in Unit Values (V) for a particular sub-class of commodities, viz. Iron and steel (n.o.e.)*

$\Delta FR : \Delta V$	
$1:1.0$	First change in *FR* and corresponding change in *V*.
$1:1.5$	
$1:2.8$	
$1:1.7$	
$1:2.3$	
$1:1.2$	
$1:3.9$	
$1:3.7$	
$1:5.8$	

This is what might be expected. Freight rates begin by moving in step with unit value changes. From this example, an actual 29 per cent increase in unit value is matched by a 29 per cent increase in freight rate at the first step up. Thereafter freight rate changes lag behind unit value changes, and at the upper end of the scale of unit values and freight rates a 64 per cent increase in unit value is matched by an 11 per cent increase in the rate of freight.[1]

From this preliminary exercise in sampling the range of relative prices, it may provisionally be concluded, subject to confirmation by application of the comput-able price model, that relative prices may *in part* be explained by reference to the unit value of each consignment, and further that the *relative* association between the rate of freight and the unit value of consignments is logarithmic rather than arithmetic or geometric. Some of the evidence assembled from the tariff, and the last quoted example is a case in point, suggest that the rate of freight varies directly as the square root of the unit value of the rated commodity. In the example quoted $\Delta FR : \Delta V$ was $11:64$, and $\Delta FR : \sqrt{\Delta V}$ would be $11:8$. But this example appears to be an extreme case, not because it is at the upper end of the scale of a particular sub-class of commodities rated by unit value, but because it is well above the mean of the sample of ratios of this type. The second term in the computable price model was accordingly set as $b_2 \log_e V$. The form $b_2 \sqrt{V}$ was in fact tested on the computer

---

1   In some cases, though not in this one, the ratio changes radically because at certain points the scale of freight rates brings the product shipped close to the threshold of customs charges and, in order to maintain the flow of shipments, the conference ensures that its freight charges do not imply landed prices which are above certain threshold levels.

and found to be of less explanatory value. Two examples may help to illustrate the point made here.

Table 7.2 *Comparative Ratios of Freight Rates to Unit Values expressed in natural logarithms and as square roots*

1	2	3	4	5
Commodity	Freight rate charged (£'s)	Unit value, V, £s per B/L ton	$\log_e V$	$\sqrt{V}$
1. Ammonium chloride	9.00	25	3.22	5
2. Raincoats	24.90	1,250	7.12	35.4
Ratio of Row 1 : Row 2	1 : 2.76	1 : 50	1 : 2.21	1 : 7.1
3. Sodium Silicate	9.42	14	2.64	3.7
4. Golfshafts	34.00	2,214	7.70	47.0
Ratio of Row 3 : Row 4	1 : 3.61	1 : 158	1 : 2.92	1 : 12.7

In both examples the $\Delta FR : \Delta V$ ratio between the pairs of consignments, which differ widely in unit value, is much closer when ΔV is expressed in natural logarithms than when the change is measured by the difference between the square root of each unit value.

The above reasoning explains why the first terms in our price model are as follows:

$$FR(P) = b_1(\text{a constant}) + b_2 \log_e V$$

b. Tonnage

Next we consider the likely influence upon the rate of freight of tonnage in terms of consignment size.

In Chapter 4, Section 2d. the usual conference system of charging 'open rates' for certain cargoes was explained. In brief, cargo listed in the tariff as subject to an 'open rate' is rated at the discretion of the individual member of the conference. Such rates are commonly applied to consignments described as 'in bulk', and in these cases the conference liner is in direct competition with tramp shipping services. In some cases the description 'in bulk' is defined, e.g. 'Fertilisers, in consignments of 4,000 tons (W) minimum: *Open*'. In other cases it is not and an entry of the brevity illustrated by the following examples appears to be adequate for all practical purposes.

'Rock, in bulk, open

Maize, in bulk, open

Crude fluorspar, in bulk, open.'

If a commodity is not transported in bulk it is not usually given an open rate in the tariff. On the other hand, not all commodities transported in bulk are given an open rate. Further, an examination of tariff books and of liner cargoes has suggested that in some cases freight rates appear to be lower for those commodities which *tend* to move in large consignments but do not invariably do so. We have therefore attempted to test the hypothesis that 'commodities which are moved by conference

149

liners in consignments greater than 50 tons M or W, are for this reason rated lower than other cargoes which are in all other respects comparable with the large consignment cargoes as defined'. Hence the inclusion of the third term in the price model which now becomes

$$FR(P) = b_1 + b_2 \log_e V + b_3 T > 50$$

C. Stowage Factor

Consignments coming forward for shipment by conference liners are rated in the way described in Chapter 4, Section 2. In the tariff books commodities are generally designated 'W', 'M', or 'M or W' (also sometimes shown as 'O', optional). W means that the commodity is shipped as 'weight cargo' and the rate of freight shown against it in the tariff is applied to its weight in tons. Likewise M means that the commodity is shipped as 'measurement cargo' and the rate of freight is applied to its cubic measurement on the basis of 40 cubic feet equals one measurement ton.

A liner's cargo is therefore almost invariably a mixture of weight and measurement tons, and this mixture is designated 'bill of lading tons', (also referred to in other works as 'freight tons'). The reference to 'M or W' (or 'O') means that the shipowner (conference member) is obliged under conference rules to charge on either a 'W' or an 'M' basis, whichever yields him (the shipowner) the greater rate of freight.

Some consignments, such as unpacked motor vehicles and some kinds of toys, have a very high ratio of weight to measurement. An unpacked motor car, for example, typically has a ratio of $W:M$ of $1:8$, weight tons to measurement tons of 40 cu.ft. This ratio may also be expressed in terms of cubic feet per ton weight, in the case of the unpacked motor car this would be 320 cu.ft. per ton. A typical private motor car weighs a ton. The freight rate for motor vehicles from the United Kingdom to Australia in 1962, for example, was 'unpacked, 184/- W/M'. This gives the shipowner the option to charge on a measurement basis which means that the vehicle is shipped for 184/- $\times$ 8 = £73.6. The incentive to the shipper to reduce the vehicle's dimensions by packing are great (see Chapter 6, for examples), and in 1962 the freight rate for KD (knocked down) vehicles was 145/- W/M. This provided an *additional* incentive to knock down. If, for example, the weight : measurement ratio could be reduced by 'knocking down' to $1:4$ (160 cu.ft. per ton), then the vehicle would be shipped for £29.0. Behind these different rates lie cost differentials which arise from wide differences in stowage factor.

The stowage factor must first be distinguished from the $W:M$ ratio. The ratio relates to weight and measurement characteristics of each individual consignment as they exist immediately prior to loading. The stowage factor is a measure of the cubic space occupied by the consignment when it has been loaded into the ship, and it includes an allowance for any *loss of stowage* which may arise from the shape or nature of the consignment. To consider again private motor vehicles; the KD vehicles are packed in boxes and these may be stacked on top of each other, but it is not practical to load any cargo on top of unpacked cars. So the unpacked vehicles involve greater loss of stowage than do KD vehicles and this aspect is reflected in the lower freight rate (W or M, but in practice, M) for KD vehicles.

It is of course likely that the stowage factor, measured in cubic feet per ton weight, will always be greater than the M/W ratio measured in the same terms.

150

A simple example can illustrate that in cases where the weight:measurement ratio cannot readily be calculated, rates appear to reflect the stowage factor (S) directly.

	Rate of Freight U.S.$'s
Bears (under 6 months in age)	56.70
Bears (over 12 months in age)	190.35
Lions (full grown)	190.35
Elephants (over 5 ft. high)	378.00
Giraffes (over 18 months in age)	527.85

In more precise terms it may be shown that $S > (M/W)$ [1] and, further, that the greater is M/W the greater is the 'loss of stowage', defined as $S - (M/W)$. This is shown in Table 7.3, where the loss of stowage *per measurement ton* is also shown.

Table 7.3 *Ranking Order of Loss of Stowage Related to Weight and Measurement of Consignments*

1 A random sample of consignments actually shipped, ordered by loss of stowage per M ton, (Col. 5)	2 M/W, cubic feet per ton weight	3 Stowage factor, in cubic feet per ton weight	4 Loss of stowage; cu.ft. per ton W (20 cwts) shipped. (Col. 3 − Col. 2)	5 Loss of stowage; cu.ft. per ton M (40 cu.ft.) shipped. (40 × Col. 4 ÷ Col. 2)
Footwear	200	380	180	36
Toys	200	330	130	26
Transistor radios	188	300	112	24
Tobacco	115	172	57	20
Electrical goods	200	300	100	20
Graphite electrodes	40	56	16	16
Sewing machines	80	110	30	15
Plywood	64	85	21	13
Glassware	76	100	24	13
Cotton goods	104	135	31	12
Plastic/PVC goods	108	135	27	10
Canned goods	52	65	13	10
China clay (in bags)	66	80	14	8

There does appear to be a prima facie case supporting the hypothesis that 'the greater the M/W ratio (in cubic feet per W ton) the greater the loss of stowage *per measurement ton*'. The consignments listed in Table 7.3 are ordered by loss of stowage per measurement ton. It may be seen that the loss of stowage (measured per weight ton) can be as high as 90 per cent of the volume of the consignment, and as low as 20 per cent. With some exceptions, col. 2 data rank with col. 5 data. This suggests that the greater the M/W ratio the greater the loss of stowage per measurement ton. Consignments with a M/W ratio greater than 40 are almost invariably rated by conferences on a measurement basis. It follows that consignments with a high M/W are likely to involve more cost per measurement ton and therefore the

---

1   Where both terms are measured in cubic feet per ton of 20 cwts.

M/W ratio is likely to be a factor which is explanatory of the structure of relative conference prices.

However, it does seem that conferences may not always act in accordance with this principle because there is evidence from the rating of particular commodities (see Table 7.4 below) that as M/W increases the rate of freight *per measurement ton* for the same commodity is reduced. Sometimes this follows bargaining between shippers and a conference.[1]

Table 7.4 *Rating according to volumetric measure*

Commodity	Volumetric measure	Rate of freight
	Cubic feet per weight ton of consignment, M/W	Shillings per measurement (M), or weight (W) ton at the ship-owner's option
1. Baths, not plastic	< 120	253/-
	> 120	174/6
2. Buoys, mooring	< 240	315/-
	> 240	258/6
3. Caravans, domestic, non-motorised	< 640	225/-
	> 640	194/-
4. Capsules for bottles	< 240	348/6
	> 240 < 480	258/6
	> 480	225/-

In the event these commodities would all be rated on a measurement basis, and therefore the rate of freight per measurement ton *declines* as M/W increases.

Bearing in mind that all measurement cargo involves some loss of stowage,[2] and inspection of Table 7.3 suggests that the more important and significant losses of stowage per measurement ton occur when $M/W \geqslant 100$. In the event the threshold in our model was set, rather arbitrarily, at $M/W \geqslant 80$, a $W{:}M$ ratio of $1{:}2$. It should be noticed at this point that ships' manifests and 'shipping notes' deal in M and in W, but not in S (stowage factor) which will tend to vary with type of ship.

To sum up, there appear to be two opposed influences at work here. The first is that indicated in Table 7.3 where it seems that loss stowage *per measurement ton* tends to rise with the M/W ratio. On the other hand, the evidence from Table 7.4, and that presented in case histories in Chapter 6, shows that in some instances conferences give away to shippers a part of the advantage they give themselves when they reserve to their members the option of charging on either a weight or a measurement basis whichever yields the highest revenue 'to the ship'. In our price model, which is applied later in this chapter, we have attempted to test the impact of the variable $M/W \geqslant 2$ [3] on relative prices (freight rates). This is done in order to try to discover the *net* influence on relative prices of the two influences described above.

1 See Chapter 6, where case histories describing the bargaining in such cases are given.

2 So also can weight cargo, when the quantity loaded reaches the level at which the vessel is 'down to marks' before it is full to space limits.

3 That is, where the measurement tonnage of any consignment is twice as great, or more than twice as great as its weight tonnage.

d. Hazardous cargo

Conferences take account of hazard when rates are made, but none could say what was the premium for hazard. A dummy variable was therefore included in our model for all items of hazardous cargo, as defined on shipping notes and manifests. The model then provided an estimate, given later, of the premium due to hazard.

e. Refrigerated and cool chamber stowage of cargo

The same process was adopted in these cases as for hazardous cargo.

f. Consignments priced by individual conference members

It has been noticed earlier in this chapter that 'open' rates are charged for some bulk cargoes. Such rates are set by the individual shipowner and conference member. Similarly, some very high unit value cargo is rated 'ad valorem', and the rate actually charged is determined by the shipowner (or his agent) on the basis of the best knowledge that can be obtained of the unit value of each such consignment. In these cases the price model has been applied to each of the items of cargo concerned.[1] By these means estimates are obtained of the negative or positive value to shipowners of these respective concessions and premia.

g. Residual and unknown influences

A constant term has been added to the price model and has been found in all cases, to be positive and significant. From this it may be concluded that other, unquantified factors are a net positive influence upon relative prices.

2. The results of applying the price model

The model in the form described earlier in this chapter was applied to data assembled from the cargoes of five conference liners. The vessels, the conferences in which they were sailing at the time of the cargo census and the dates of sailing are given below:

1. PRIAM,   sailed outward from Liverpool in the Far Eastern Freight Conference, 6 November, 1969.

2. ANCHISES,   sailed homeward from Singapore and Malaysian ports in the Far Eastern Freight Conference, March 1970.

3. PROTESILAUS,   sailed homeward from Japanese ports and HongKong in the Far Eastern Freight Conference, March 1970.

4. IBERIC,   sailed outward from Liverpool in the United Kingdom—Australia Conference, 11 June, 1970.

5. BOTANY BAY,   sailed outward from Antwerp (*quasi* Tilbury)[2] in the United
(a container ship)   Kingdom—Australia Conference, 14 April, 1970.

Within its limitations the model is both explanatory and predictive. It aims to explain the relative influence of the various factors, described earlier in this chapter,

---

1   See Section 2 below.

2   Due to a strike of stevedores at Tilbury, BOTANY BAY was loaded, with cargo ex-UK, at Antwerp. Freight rates and all other data related to this sailing have been adjusted to a 'Tilbury basis'.

upon the freight rates actually charged for the consignments which have moved in the vessels named above. Each component variable in the model is found to be of significant explanatory value in all but one term of one application of the model. Subject to its limitations, one of which is the 'goodness of fit', the model may be used as a predictor of freight rates, given the data on those characteristics of each item of cargo which comprise the terms of the model. These terms in the form in which they appear in the model are, for convenience, repeated at the foot of Table 7.5.

The model is in the form of a multi-variate regression equation, and the terms of it are additive. The results of applying the function to cross-sectional data of cargoes of five specified conference liner voyages are shown in Table 7.5.

At the upper and lower ends of the scale of unit values conferences generally allow members some, usually circumscribed, discretion in price-making. This is a practice which is normally more important in highly industrialised trades, and is particularly relevant in this survey in the case of the Far Eastern Freight Conference represented by the cargo of the PRIAM sailing. It may be argued that when, as in this case, individual conference members are given some latitude and discretion in making prices, then the resulting rates of freight are not conference prices. We have taken this view and have excluded 22 consignments from the cargo of PRIAM on these grounds. Of this number 12 items are in the class 'valuable, special stow', and six of them are rated at 3 per cent *ad valorem*. The remaining 10 consignments are of very low unit value, some of them are commodities shipped in bulk and are 'open' rated, meaning that members are free to make their own rates of freight. In these cases and in the case of other low-rated consignments, the rates charged are below the lowest class rate of the conference.

The model was then applied to these two groups of high — and low — rated consignments, in order to estimate the coefficients for these special groups and so their worth to the shipowners and shippers concerned.

In the case of the group of low-rated consignments the model yielded a co-efficient of -5.27, which may be taken to mean that on average the shipowner is giving way to the extent of £5.27 per B/L ton on the freight rate for such cargo. For the group of high rated, *ad valorem* consignments, the coefficient is $+16.08$, a measure of the premium on the rate of freight charged for this description of cargo.

As an alternative, and as a check, the model was re-constructed to include two additional variables, *VSS* and *LR*, to cover these two extremes. The original model (as set out in Table 7.5) and the extended model are given below.

Original model, as applied to the cargo of PRIAM

$$FR_1 = 2.81 + 2.80 \log_e V - 1.60T \geqslant 50 + 0.25\left(\frac{M}{W} \geqslant 2\right) + 7.11H$$

$$+ 20.03R + 8.87CC.$$

Extended model

$$FR_2 = 1.45 + 3.08 \log_e V - 1.16T \geqslant 50 + 0.16\left(\frac{M}{W} \geqslant 2\right) + 6.46H$$

$$+ 20.15R + 8.81CC - 4.91LR + 15.40VSS$$

Table 7.5 *Price Model in Practice*

1 Vessel	2 Conference	3 Industrialised (I) or non-industrialised (NI) trade	4 Rate of Freight FR =	5 The values of the coefficients for each term in the price model, with the standard error, SE(b) in brackets. Constant b_1	Unit Value $b_2(\log_e V)$	Tonnage $b_3(T>50)$	Bale $b_4(M/W>2)$	Hazard $b_5(H)$	Refrigeration $b_6(R)$	Cool Chamber Stowage $b_7(CC)$	6 Coefficients of Correlation $\bar{R}$	Determination $\bar{R}^2$	7 Number of Consignments n	8 Durbin–Watson Statistic DW
PRIAM	FEFC Outward	I	FR_a 1...n	+2.81 (0.84)	+2.80 (0.14)	−1.60 (1.06)	+0.25 (0.07)	+7.11 (0.90)	+20.03 (1.67)	+8.87 (1.86)	0.721	0.520	550	1.53
IBERIC	UK–Australia Outward	I	FR_b 1...n	+3.34 (1.09)	+3.04 (0.18)	−1.50 (1.23)	−0.11 (0.08)	+11.74 (3.37)	+15.20 (2.24)	+7.12 (5.84)	0.595	0.354	714	1.64
PROTESILAUS	FEFC Homeward	Mostly I	FR_c 1...n	+7.01 (0.61)	+1.84 (0.11)	−2.73 (0.55)	+0.12 (0.03)	+6.12 (1.00)	+7.63 (0.57)	–	0.602	0.363	1121	1.60
ANCHISES	FEFC Homeward	NI	FR_d 1...n	+10.76 (0.96)	+0.57 (0.24)	−2.78 (1.38)	+0.11 n.s. (0.21)	–	–	–	0.176	0.031	200	1.52
BOTANY BAY (a container ship)	UK–Australia Outward	I	FR_e 1...n	+7.29 (0.89)	+2.70 (0.14)	−3.10 (1.22)	+0.21 (0.06)	+3.63 (0.94)	+12.31 (1.15)	–	0.460	0.212	1774	1.90

Notes:

FR – the actual rate of freight charged for each consignment in the conference trade concerned.

b_1 – a constant

$b_2(\log_e V)$ – the natural logarithm of the unit value of each consignment.

$b_3(T>50)$ – the greater of consignment weight or measurement tonnage equal to or in excess of 50 tons.

$b_4(M/W>2)$ – the ratio of consignment weight to measurement tonnage wherever it is equal to or exceeds 2 measurement tons per weight ton.

$b_5(H)$, $b_6(R)$ and $b_7(CC)$ – separate estimators for hazardous, refrigerated and cool chamber consignments.

n.s. – non-significant.

Statistical Note to Table 7.5

The Durbin–Watson statistic (shown in col. 8 of Table 7.5) is a test for serial correlation of the residuals (the differences between the actual and predicted freight rates for each consignment). Having regard for the number of variables in the price function (k, in Durbin and Watson's notation) and the number of observations, n, the values for the DW statistic given here can be taken to show no evidence of serial correlation at the 5 per cent level of significance.

The coefficient of determination, $\bar{R}^2$, is 0.520 for the original, but only 0.406 for the extended model.

The coefficients for *LR* and *VSS* take on values which are close to those given when the original model is applied to the new data, but it is clear that the extended model does not fit the data so well. The extremes of high and low rates introduce distortions. The range of freight rates and of unit values is very wide when all observations are included. The highest rate of freight charged is £151.17 (an *ad valorem* rate), and the lowest £5.04. The highest unit value is £5,039 per B/L ton and the lowest £12. The two groups at the extremes of the unit value range account for only 0.38 per cent of the 'population' of consignments, yet their removal, for the reasons given earlier, effects a considerable improvement in the general explanatory value of the model.

An attempt is made next to show that when the basic model ($FR = b_1 + b_2 \log_e V$) is built up by the successive addition of the other variables, the addition of each has a certain measurable explanatory value. The explanatory effect is also measured in respect of each additional variable on its own with and, separately, without the unit value variable term ($b_2 \log_e V$). All this is set out in respect of each vessel in Table 7.6 and is followed by the conclusions which may be drawn from the application of this price model.

Table 7.6 *Table of Values of the Coefficient of Correlation ($\bar{R}^2$) between the Actual Rate of Freight Charged and One or More Variables Relating to the Cargo of Individual Conference Freight Liners*

			(Values of $\bar{R}^2$)
Constant and variables		PRIAM	
b_1 (a constant) +	Sequential build up of variables	Each variable on its own with b_1 and $b_2 \log_e V$	Each variable on its own excluding $b_2 \log_e V$
$b_2 \log_e V$, natural log of unit value	0.323	–	–
b_3, tonnage $\geqslant 50$	0.325	0.325	0.020
b_4, $\frac{m}{w} \geqslant 2$ ratio	0.327	0.325	0.003
b_5, Hazard (*H*)	0.365	0.357	0.020
b_6, Refrigeration (*R*)	0.506	0.459	0.112
b_7, Cool Chamber (*CC*)	0.525	0.339	0.013
$\bar{R}^2$ for the whole model	0.525	–	–
$\bar{R}^2$ for the model excluding $b_2 \log_e V$	–	–	0.176

Table 7.6 *Table of Values of the Coefficient of Correlation* ($\bar{R}^2$) *between the Actual Rate of Freight Charged and One or More Variables Relating to the Cargo of Individual Conference Freight Liners*

Constant and variables	ANCHISES		(Value of $\bar{R}^2$)
b_1 (a constant) +	Sequential build up of variables	Each variable on its own with b_1 and $b_2 \log_e V$	Each variable on its own, excluding $b_2 \log_e V$
$b_2 \log_e V$, natural log of unit value	0.019	–	–
b_3, tonnage $\geqslant 50$	0.035	0.035	0.009
$b_4, \frac{m}{w} \geqslant 2$ ratio	0.031	0.016	0.005
b_5, Hazard (H)	–	–	–
b_6, Refrigeration (R)	–	–	–
b_7, Cool Chamber (CC)	–	–	–
$\bar{R}^2$ for the whole model	0.031	–	–
$\bar{R}^2$ for the model excluding $b_2 \log_e V$	–	–	0.011

Table 7.6 *Table of Values of the Coefficient of Correlation* ($\bar{R}^2$) *between the Actual Rate of Freight Charged and One or More Variables Relating to the Cargo of Individual Conference Freight Liners*

Constant and variables	IBERIC		(Value of $\bar{R}^2$)
b_1 (a constant) +	Sequential build up of variables	Each variable on its own with b_1 and $b_2 \log_e V$	Each variable on its own, excluding $b_2 \log_e V$
$b_2 \log_e V$, natural log of unit value	0.300	–	–
b_3, tonnage $\geqslant 50$	0.299	0.299	0.004
$b_4, \frac{m}{w} \geqslant 2$ ratio	0.302	0.303	0.041
b_5, Hazard (H)	0.306	0.304	0.004
b_6, Refrigeration (R)	0.349	0.343	0.032
b_7, Cool Chamber (CC)	0.354	0.306	0.003
$\bar{R}^2$ for the whole model	0.354	–	–
$\bar{R}^2$ for the model, excluding $b_2 \log_e V$	–	–	0.089

Table 7.6 *Table of Values of the Coefficient of Correlation ($\bar{R}^2$) between the Actual Rate of Freight Charged and One or More Variables Relating to the Cargo of Individual Conference Freight Liners*

	PROTESILAUS		(Value of $\bar{R}^2$)
Constant and variables	Sequential build up of variables	Each variable on its own with b_1 and $b_2 \log_e V$	Each variable on its own, excluding $b_2 \log_e V$
b_1 (a constant) +			
$b_2 \log_e V$, natural log of unit value	0.224	–	–
b_3, tonnage $\geqslant 50$	0.243	0.243	0.036
$b_4, \frac{m}{w} \geqslant 2$ ratio	0.244	0.288	0.003
b_5, Hazard (H)	0.262	0.241	0.032
b_6, Refrigeration (R)	0.363	0.317	0.127
b_7, Cool Chamber (CC)	–	–	–
$\bar{R}^2$ for the whole model	0.363	–	–
$\bar{R}^2$ for the model excluding $b_2 \log_e V$	–	–	0.195

Table 7.6 *Table of Values of the Coefficient of Correlation ($\bar{R}^2$) between the Actual Rate of Freight Charged and One or More Variables Relating to the Cargo of Individual Conference Freight Liners*

Constant and variables	BOTANY BAY		(Value of $\bar{R}^2$)
b_1 (a constant) +	Sequential build up of variables	Each variable on its own with $b_2 \log_e V$	Each variable on its own, excluding $b_2 \log_e V$
b_1 (a constant) +			
$b_2 \log_e V$, natural log of unit value	0.153	–	–
b_3, tonnage $\geqslant 50$	0.157	0.157	0.016
$b_4, \frac{m}{w} \geqslant 2$ ratio	0.158	0.158	0.017
b_5, Hazard (H)	0.162	0.161	0.016
b_6, Refrigeration (R)	0.212	0.203	0.049
b_7, Cool Chamber (CC)	–	–	–
$\bar{R}^2$ for the whole model	0.212	–	–
$\bar{R}^2$ for the model excluding $b_2 \log_e V$	–	–	0.048

Conclusions

The following conclusions arise from the application of the price model which has been described in this chapter and applied to data drawn from the cargoes of five conference liners and comprising 4,359 individual consignments. The conclusions relate particularly to the results of analyses which are set out in Tables 7.5 and 7.6.

1. The explanatory value of the several variables of the model is greater for those cargoes which are largely composed of manufactured goods. Examples are PRIAM and IBERIC, where the constant has a relatively low value. This indicates that the variables of the model (which are significant in all cases) are of some explanatory value. An indication of the extent of explanation is given by the coefficient of determination (i.e. the coefficient of correlation squared). For PRIAM R bar is 0.721 and R bar squared is 0.520 and for IBERIC these coefficients are 0.595 and 0.354 respectively.

2. When the model is applied to a cargo of goods which are largely industrial raw materials and food, such a case is ANCHISES, then the variables of the model are either not significant, as is the case with $b_4(M/W) \geqslant 2$, or are of very little explanatory value. In this example the constant term b_1 is large in relation to the coefficients. This implies that the identified variable factors are either individually of minor importance or are of small net effect in total. An inspection of the results shown in Table 7.5 shows that both implications are supported. While b_3 and b_4 take values which are comparable with those of the other cargoes analysed, b_2 is much lower than any of the others. In the absence of the premia represented by b_5, b_6 and b_7, the low value for b_2 as well as for b_3 and b_4, shows that the relative freight rates charged for this cargo are poorly explained by this model. Although price differentiation, as measured by a ratio of commodities per separate price in the tariff, are high for the tariff of the Far East Freight Conference (in which ANCHISES is sailing on this voyage), this cargo will not bear high freight rates due to the relatively low unit value of the individual consignments which compose it. *Within such trades,* that is, those from developing countries, there is no source of surplus over average total unit cost from which the cross-subsidisation of even lower unit value cargo can be carried out. The average yield of gross revenue per B/L ton of cargo carried was only £11.98 for ANCHISES; and this may be compared with an average gross revenue yield of £17.22 per B/L ton for PRIAM, whose cargo was chiefly composed of manufactures ex-UK.

3. It may be noticed that $b_4(M/W \geqslant 2)$ is positive in all cases except IBERIC (see above), indicating that on balance the effect of a high M/W ratio is to increase the rate of freight. This bears out the indication seen earlier in Table 7.3, which suggested that the higher is M/W the greater is the loss of stowage *per measurement ton* of cargo; and that this factor is not outweighed by the tendency for unit value to be lower the higher is M/W, nor by the effect of the known practice of conferences[1]

1 Seen in Chapter 6.

159

of giving away to shippers a part of their advantageous option of charging for 'measurement cargo' on either a W or an M basis according to whichever yields the highest freight 'to the ship'. It is particularly interesting to note also that IBERIC is sailing in the Dolphin service. This service complements the container service to Australia[2] and for this reason the service carries a high proportion of cargo of awkward shape — such, in fact, as would not readily fit into a container. The shipper is denied the speed and other advantages of the container service, and there is some evidence that the conference is more ready to give way on individual freight rates for cargo with high M/W ratios in the case of this route.

4. The sign of $b_3(T \geqslant 50)$ is negative in all cases, as might be expected. Pricing does take some account of tonnage moving and some commodities, such as semi-manufactured chemicals (sodium carbonate, for example), usually, but not invariably, move in large consignments. It is the consignment sizes which are being recognised here.

5. For all the cargoes analysed, the coefficient of unit value carries a positive sign. For the cargo of ANCHISES the coefficient is, as noted at paragraph 2 above, much smaller than it is for the other cargoes examined here. As has been explained already, cargo from developing countries presents fewer opportunities for price differentiation. The conferences involved do try very hard to differentiate[3] their rates of freight with respect to the unit value, and other characteristics, of each commodity shipped, but there is far less scope for doing so than there is in the case of the industrial export cargoes of a developed country. The reason lies in the relatively low unit value of the goods shipped outwards by developing countries.

6. Of the hazardous, refrigerated and cool chamber cargoes, the highest coefficients (and here it should be recalled that we have used estimators for these variables in all cases) are to be found in the case of refrigerated cargo. This is deep frozen cargo, 'fish fingers' are an example, and the premium freight rate charged reflects, at any rate in part, the cost of providing this service for the three or four weeks taken by the voyages considered here. The temperature for cool chamber stowage is not nearly as low as that used for refrigerated cargo, and is used for the carriage of such commodities as chocolate and biscuits. Hazardous consignments vary in the degree of hazard. Dangerous acids, for example, are not charged as high a premium as explosives. Again the premium is cost-based, as it reflects the insurance and extra handling and stowage costs involved. In the United Kingdom—Australia service, it appears that consignments of the higher degree of hazard are sent by conventional freight liner, which is represented here by IBERIC; rather than by a container ship, represented by BOTANY BAY. The chief reasons for this are that the larger the vessel the greater is the hazard, and also the need to stow very dangerous cargo on deck. The deck space on container ships is taken up by containers. There is little or no 'free standing' space, as there is on conventional freight liners, which may be used for hazardous cargo and from which, if circumstances arise in which the cargo

2 The BOTANY BAY sailing is an example of this service.

3 See Chapter 4, Table 4.1.

becomes dangerous through fire or other cause, it may, in an emergency, most readily be dumped overboard with least damage to the ship or to other cargo.

7. From Table 7.6 it may be seen that the natural logarithm of the unit value term in the price model explains more of the structure of relative prices than any other identified term in the model. A summary of the results shown in Table 7.6 are set out below in percentage form.

Table 7.7 *Explanatory worth of unit value* (V), *and of all other identified factors* (*OIF*), *expressed as a percentage of* $\bar{R}^2$ *for each vessel*

(Percentages)			
1	2	3	4
Unit value (V) on its own	Other identified factors with V	Other identified factors without V	Value of the coefficient of determination, $\bar{R}^2$
PRIAM	62	38	34	0.520
[ANCHISES	61	39	36]	0.031
IBERIC	85	15	25	0.354
PROTESILAUS	62	38	54	0.363
BOTANY BAY	72	28	23	0.212

The special circumstances involved in the IBERIC sailing have already been noticed (at paragraph 3 above), and they have influence here. The ANCHISES results are shown in brackets because of the very poor total explanatory worth of the price model in the case of this vessel (Col. 4 of Table 7.7).

Subject to these qualifications, it is clear that the natural logarithm of unit value 'explains', in all the cases shown here, more than 60 per cent, and in some cases considerably more, of what can be explained by this model; and the proportion of the total that can be explained is measured by $\bar{R}^2$, the coefficient of determination.

From this it is reasonable to conclude that unit value, a demand-based factor in price making, is an important influence upon freight rates actually formed, but we cannot tell whether it is either a predominant influence accounting for more than half the explanatory value of all factors, or even the influence of greatest single importance. This cannot be determined because the price model contains undifferentiated and unknown residual factors which cannot at present be identified.

8. The influence of the identified factors in the model other than unit value may be traced through Table 7.6. These factors are all directly, or indirectly, cost-based. Collectively they are of less explanatory value than unit value alone, but with one exception in one vessel[1] they are of significant explanatory worth. If an average of the five cargoes is taken from Table 7.7, unit value explains 68 per cent of the total that can be explained by the model and all the other identified factors collectively explain the remaining 32 per cent. If unit value (V) is removed from the model, the remaining identified factors are able to explain, on average, 34 per cent of the total, or almost the same as they can when associated with unit value.

---

1   The 'bale' factor ($b_4(M/W) \geqslant 2$) for ANCHISES.

9. So it may be concluded that in so far as the price model can explain the relative prices made by conferences in the quite large samples involved here, demand-based factors (sometimes referred to as 'value of service' factors) account for approximately two-thirds of the explanation and a number of identified cost-based factors (also known as 'cost of service' factors) for the remaining one-third. The cost-based factors still account for approximately a third of the explanation when the demand-based factor is removed, and this tends to confirm the independence of the groups of explanatory variables (see also above the note on the Durbin—Watson statistic).

8 Some Economic and Financial Consequences of Conference Membership

This chapter is divided into three parts. The first is concerned with the extent to which the physical capital assets, i.e. the ships employed wholly in conference trades, are utilised. Utilisation is examined in terms of load factor and time utilisation. In the second part an examination is made of conference membership and of the membership links between adjacent conferences. The third part deals with the financial consequences of conference membership in aggregate for all members and, separately, for individual member lines. The averages of aggregate data are then compared with those for individual members over the period 1958–68.

1. The utilisation of physical capital

We are concerned primarily with the extent to which the capital in the form of ships is employed under the conference system. The ratio of capital to labour is relatively high in this industry and large quantities of capital are involved (see below). We do not attempt here a measure of capacity utilisation which would bring quantified labour into the calculation, but it is reasonable to assume in this industry that the labour/capital proportions are set by the currently employed techniques, and with given techniques this proportion is fixed within narrow limits. Where this is so, then a physical capital utilisation ratio will accurately reflect the wider *capacity* utilisation ratio. Over time as techniques change, as they have done in this sector in the years since 1968, principally by the introduction of containers, the level and movement in physical capital utilisation may no longer reflect accurately the concurrent movement in capacity utilisation in the fullest sense.

Rochdale[1] has calculated that United Kingdom cargo liners, nearly all of which operate within conferences, accounted for 6.8 million deadweight tons of shipping in 1968,[2] or about one-third of the total United Kingdom registered tonnage of 20.6 million[3] for that year. The depreciated current value of the whole fleet (ships only) was estimated at £1,500 million[4] in the same year. The unit value of cargo liners is higher than that of general purpose tramp shipping or of bulk dry cargo shipping or tankers and so, taking the lowest limit for this estimate, UK cargo liners

---

1   *The Report of the Rochdale Committee of Inquiry into Shipping.* H.M.S.O. Cmnd. 4337, London, 1970.

2   Rochdale op.cit. Table 8.1, p.140

3   Rochdale op.cit. Table 2.3, p.18

4   Rochdale op.cit., paragraph 135, p.39

may be valued at a minimum of £600 million (depreciated current value) in 1968. Rochdale, drawing on some data assembled by the Institute of Shipping Economics, Bergen, estimates[1] that UK registered liners 'would appear to provide almost one-quarter of the world liner services'. From these two very broad approximations we get an order of magnitude for the depreciated value in 1968 of the world total of all conference liners of between £2,000 and £3,000 million.

The degree of physical capital utilisation clearly affects unit cost very considerably in this industry where fixed costs, largely, but not wholly capital costs, are a very high proportion of total costs. Prices are therefore also influenced by capital utilisation, although imperfectly so in a conference system. But at least prices tend to move broadly with costs in those trades where bargaining between the conference and collective organisations representing shippers takes place on a basis of financial results, and evidence of this has been presented in Chapter 4. These aspects are examined in further detail later on in the third part of this chapter.

Physical capital utilisation is also a variable of more general economic importance in terms of the use of scarce resources, and particularly the degree of use which is made under the conditions of very imperfect competition which exist in this large section of the world shipping industry.

We have been able to make a detailed examination of two important and complementary 'deep sea' (i.e. long distance) conference routes in respect of physical capital utilisation and financial performance, in aggregate and in terms of the participation of each individual conference member. Three separate conferences are involved. They cover the maritime trade in general cargoes to and from the Continent of Europe and the United Kingdom at one end and Australia at the other.

The conferences are as follows:

1. United Kingdom–Australia Conference (Outward).
2. Outward Continent–Australia Conference.
3. Australia–Europe Conference (Homeward).

Details of the membership of these conferences, the areas they serve, and the tariff terms of these and of other main line conferences are given in Appendix A.

For an analysis of physical capital utilisation, conferences 1 and 2 above have been taken together, but in some parts of the analysis the results for the British member lines only have been aggregated to form a sub-group.

The conference group studied, comprising conferences 1, 2 and 3 above, covers routes on which there is some directional imbalance of trade in terms of physical volume. This is due partly to seasonal factors in the export trade of Australia in primary produce and partly to an excess in the freight tonnage of Australian conference-borne exports to Europe over imports from Europe over the period covered by this analysis, which is 1958–1968 inclusive.

The utilisation of physical capital is studied in sequential terms starting with the load factor for loaded vessels only and then going on to that for loaded vessels and for semi-ballast and ballast vessels taken together. Physical capital utilisation is then examined over time taking account of all vessels employed in the trade and of time spent in active employment and in unemployment. Beyond this it is shown what links conference members have with contiguous conferences. In the Australian trade

1 Rochdale op.cit. paragraph 326.

164

which, apart from the differences already referred to, is reasonably well-balanced in respect of 'round trade', the most important link for members to have is clearly the one which is within the conference group and which covers both directions. 'Cross trade' links to other trades are vital if membership of the main trade is one-way only, but clearly less so if it is two-way.

In Table 8.1 is shown the aggregate load factors (of loaded vessels only) of all members lines sailing outward and homeward in the UK/Continent–Australia trade. The membership of conferences 1 and 2 above are amalgamated for the purpose of this exercise.[1]

The degree of utilisation of loaded vessels is high by any standards and reflects considerable organisation and 'rationalisation' by the conferences concerned[2] and by individual member lines; and the time trend here, particularly in the outward direction, is to improve the level of utilisation still further. However these figures are only the aggregate load factor for a group of vessels, and they are incomplete as a measure of physical capital utilisation in these trades in a fuller sense. Next it is necessary to take account of the imbalance of the outward and homeward trades and the consequent need for vessels to sail 'in ballast' (ballasters). The picture in more detail and taking both separate and aggregated measures of loaded vessels and of ballasters and semi-ballasters together is given in Table 8.2, where it should be noticed that data in this amount of detail are available only for the British member lines of the UK/Continent–Australia conference group.

Table 8.1 *Load Factors of Loaded Vessels only* [a]

	Percentages of space (in cubic feet) utilised of total space offered, with an adjustment to deduct space 'vacant' but unavailable.[b]		
	Outward	Homeward	Total
1958	89.6	92.3	91.1
1959	82.7	96.1	90.3
1960	92.8	93.2	93.0
1961	85.1	94.1	89.5
1962	86.0	95.7	91.0
1963	92.0	94.9	93.5
1964	94.9	95.2	95.1
1965	94.5	94.2	94.3
1966	91.2	93.9	92.5
1967	94.8	96.0	95.4
1968	96.7	94.0	95.4

(a) Semi-ballast and ballast vessels are excluded from this table and included in Table 8.2.

(b) Due to 'loss of stowage', which in turn arises from awkward shape, from the fragility of some cargoes, and from the liability of some cargoes to taint other cargo. Such loss can also, though rarely, be due to vessels being loaded 'down to permitted marks' before being filled to maximum cubic capacity.

1 For the membership of these and of other conferences, see Appendix A.

2 See Chapter 3, Section 2(d), iii. for descriptions of the 'rationalisation' of these trades.

Table 8.2 Load Factors in the United Kingdom/Continent–Australia conference trades outward and homeward. Selected years. British member lines only

| | 1 Total cargo space. All vessels(a) sailing | | | 2 Space utilised by loaded vessels | | | 3 Space utilised by loaded vessels and semi-ballasters | | | 4 Space unutilised (Unadjusted) Column 1 – Column 3 | | | 5 Space unutilised (Adjusted)(b) | | | 6 Percentage utilised of total space of all vessels sailing (Unadjusted) (Col.3 ÷ Col.1) | 7 Percentage utilised of total space of all vessels sailing (adjusted)(b) (Col.3) ÷ (Col.1 – Col.4 + Col.5) | | |
	Outward Mn.cu.ft.	Homeward Mn.cu.ft.	Total Mn.cu.ft.	Outward Mn.cu.ft.	Homeward Mn.cu.ft.	Total Mn.cu.ft.	Outward Mn.cu.ft.	Homeward Mn.cu.ft.	Total Mn.cu.ft.	Outward Mn.cu.ft.	Homeward Mn.cu.ft.	Total Mn.cu.ft.	Outward Mn.cu.ft.	Homeward Mn.cu.ft.	Total Mn.cu.ft.	%	Total %	Outward %	Homeward %
1958	93.8	98.0	191.8	70.8	91.2	162.0	72.3	91.2	163.5	21.5	6.8	28.3	19.6	5.9	25.5	85.2	86.5	78.8	93.9
1961	84.7	87.0	171.7	62.4	80.2	142.6	63.3	80.2	143.5	21.4	6.8	28.2	16.8	6.0	22.8	83.6	86.3	79.0	93.0
1965	89.5	89.7	179.2	74.0	83.0	157.0	74.0	83.0	157.0	15.5	6.7	22.2	13.7	6.2	19.9	87.6	88.8	81.1	93.0
1968	79.6	64.3	143.9	69.7	59.3	129.0	70.7	59.3	130.0	8.9	5.0	13.9	7.3	3.3	10.6	90.3	92.5	90.6	94.7

(a) Comprises loaded, semi-ballast and ballast vessels
(b) For space vacant but unavailable, due to 'loss of stowage' (see Table 8.1. note (b)) in loaded and semi-ballast vessels.

The British member lines of this conference group accounted for 70.0 per cent of the total of 3.44 million bill of lading tons of cargo carried by the conference group in 1958, and for 55.6 per cent of the total of 3.62 million tons carried in 1968. The load factor (for loaded vessels) and the time utilisation of non-British members are slightly better than the corresponding ratios for British members, and this is shown in Table 8.3 (load factor) and 8.7 col 1. (time utilisation). The performance of the British lines as a whole may therefore be seen to be truly representative of that of the whole conference group.

The results up to this point of our analysis of physical capital utilisation may be summarised in Table 8.3 below.

Table 8.3 *Load factors*[a] *in the UK/Continent—Australia and the Australia—Europe conferences*

	1 All members	2 British members only			
		a	b		
	Percentage utilised of total space of *loaded vessels*	Percentage utilised of total space of *loaded vessels*	Percentage utilised of total space of *all British vessels sailing*:		
			(i) Both directions	(ii) Outward	(iii) Homeward
1958	91.1	92.6	86.5	78.8	93.9
1961	89.5	88.9	86.3	79.0	93.0
1965	94.3	92.6	88.8	81.1	93.0
1968	95.4	95.2	92.5	90.6	94.7

(a) In all cases these percentages are derived from data of cubic capacity adjusted to exclude capacity 'vacant but unavailable' (due either to 'loss of stowage' or, rarely, to vessels being loaded 'down to permitted marks' before being filled to maximum cubic capacity).

The difference in these percentages between col. 1. and col. 2a are not very great or very important; they show that in three of the four years included in the table the British lines were a little less successful than their fellow conference members in other countries (largely West European countries and Japan, but see Appendix A for a full list) in making use of the space of vessels they 'put on the berth'.[1]

The differences between col. 2a. and col. 2b(i) are larger and reflect some imbalance of trade outward and homeward; an imbalance which, it may be noted, has been declining over the period 1958 to 1968.[2]

The trade homeward is greater in physical volume terms than the trade outward at certain seasons of the year. Consequently, in order to meet the 'needs of the trade' the conferences concerned require their members to send vessels outward in ballast or semi-ballast. This occurs, for example, during the fruit harvesting season in Australia. The load factor of all vessels sailing in the outward direction is for this reason among others substantially lower than that for the homeward direction, and the extent of this difference in each of the four years specified is shown in col.2b(ii) and col.2b(iii) of Table 8.3.

1 Differences of this order of magnitude in the load factor of groups of member lines could be due to differences in the nature of the cargo loaded and they do not necessarily reflect different efficiencies in the use of resources.

2 See Figures 12 and 13 where time trends in these variables are illustrated.

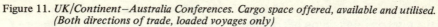

Figure 11. *UK/Continent–Australia Conferences. Cargo space offered, available and utilised. (Both directions of trade, loaded voyages only)*

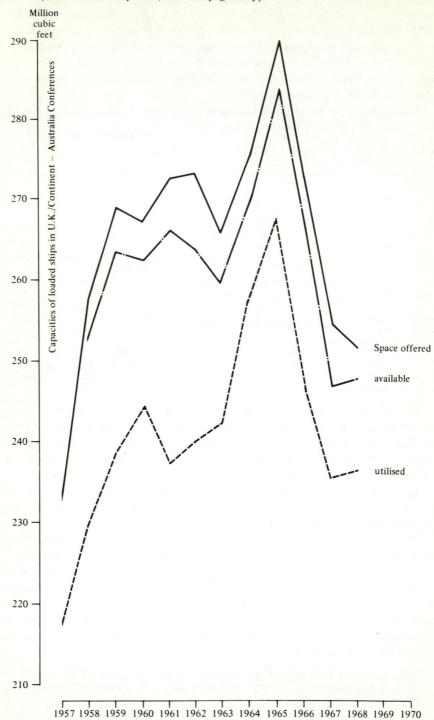

Figure 12. *UK/Continent–Australia Conferences. Cargo space utilised. (Both directions of trade, loaded voyages only)*

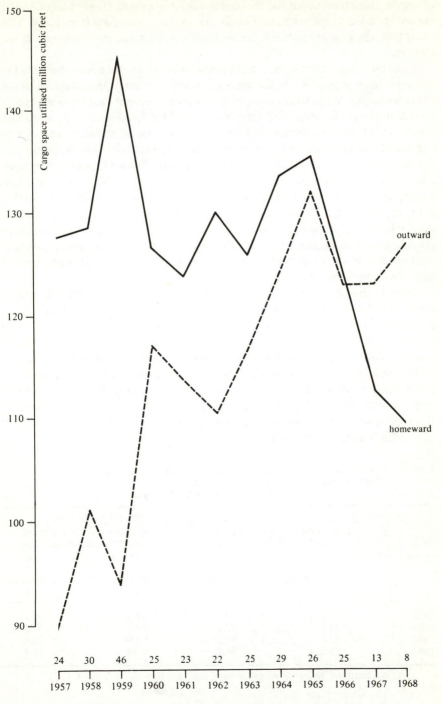

Note: Numbers of ballast and semi-ballast voyages shown above.

The higher total load factors in recent years are also partly due to a better balance between trade 'out' and 'home' (see Figure 13), and partly to the chartering of vessels, from sources outside the conferences concerned. These chartered vessels are not included in the conference, and data on their operations is excluded. Their use is typically to carry primary commodities, usually fruit, from Australia at peak seasons.

There are some material differences in the load factors between refrigerated and general cargo vessels when the former are employed to carry general goods, and this arises frequently in the trades to an from Australia. The outward trade is largely in manufactured goods of many different types, and the homeward trade is principally but, in recent years, far from completely in primary commodities. Of the primary commodities a substantial proportion require refrigerated stowage. So on the outward voyage vessels designed specifically for the carriage of frozen foods (chiefly meat and dairy products) have to be loaded with manufactured goods. There are sometimes loading and stowage problems in these circumstances and this can lead to a rather lower degree of utilisation of space than can be achieved when vessels designed to carry refrigerated commodities are loaded with this type of cargo. The load factors for refrigerated and general cargo vessels are shown in Table 8.4. Also shown is a time trend towards the better utilisation of refrigerated and general cargo space in both directions of trade.

Apart from a relatively poor level of utilisation in the outward trade in 1961, these load factors are high and improving. The trends in space offered, available and utilised over the period 1957–1968 may be seen in aggregate for these trades in Figure 11, and space utilised outward and homeward, on the same scale, with corresponding figures for the number of ballast and semi-ballast voyages in each year, 1957–1968, is shown in Figure 12. From this last-named graph the reduction of the imbalance in conference trade may be seen clearly. However this does not entirely dispense with the need for ballasters outwards because, in part, as already noticed, this need arises from the *seasonal peaks* in Australia's exports to the UK and Europe of perishable primary commodities.

Table 8.4 *Load factors*[a] *by type of vessel in Outward and Homeward directions of the UK/Continent–Australia Conference trades*:
Results for British member lines only

	OUTWARD % Utilised of total space of loaded vessels designed for:		HOMEWARD % Utilised of total space of loaded vessels designed for:	
	1 Refrigerated cargo	2 General cargo	1 Refrigerated cargo	2 General cargo
1958	91.8	89.7	97.4	90.1
1961	83.0	85.5	92.8	93.3
1965	92.8	91.1	93.0	93.0
1968	95.1	96.5	95.0	94.4

(a) Adjusted for 'space vacant but unavailable'. See note (b) to Table 8.1.

Some interest lies in the dispersion about the mean of the load factors of individual member lines. Even under conference conditions some non-price competition remains in terms of the speed and regularity of service offered to shippers. The pressures of this competition do at times conflict with the need, for financial reasons, for a high rate of physical capital utilisation. In Figure 13 are shown the weighted average load factors for the whole UK/Continent–Australia Conference group, for all the British member lines as a sub-group of the conference and the load factors for seven individual British members. Two other British lines with very small shares in this conference trade have been omitted in respect of their individual performance. The dispersion of the load factors of all the individual British member lines about the unweighted mean has been measured by both the standard deviation and by the coefficient of variation, which provides a *relative* measure of dispersion in addition to the *absolute* measure provided by the standard deviation. The results of this exercise are set out below in Table 8.5.

In general the load factors of individual member lines are not widely dispersed. With the exception of outward voyages in 1961, and homeward voyages in 1958, the dispersion about the unweighted mean, as measured by the coefficient of variation, is less than 5 per cent. Figure 13 depicts the dispersion of load factors about the weighted average load factor for British lines. This average was rather lower than the conference average for outward voyages, which is also shown, but in the homewards direction it was similar to that of the conference if the results for the four years are considered together.

Table 8.5 *Measures of the dispersion of the load factors of nine individual British member lines in the United Kingdom/Continent–Australia conference group*

	Standard deviation		Coefficient of variation. (%)	
	Outward	Homeward	Outward	Homeward
1958	3.50	4.86	3.85	5.14
1961	7.09	3.94	8.46	4.19
1965	2.66	4.50	2.88	4.81
1968	4.39	2.99	4.64	3.16

The load factor, that is, the proportional utilisation of ship space, with an allowance for space vacant but unusable for reasons of stowage or weight limitations, is only one dimension of capital utilisation. The second dimension is utilisation over time periods longer than a single voyage.

In Table 8.6 is set out an analysis of the operational and idle time of a group of conference liners. The data are for the United Kingdom/Continent–Australia conference trades, British lines only. Idle time includes ships' time allocated to this conference group on the basis of the proportion of each vessels's employment in the Australian trade. If, for example, a vessel is employed for two-thirds of the year in this trade and is idle for 30 days during that year, then 20 days of idle time is allocated to this trade.

It is reasonable to allow repairing and overhaul time to be counted as operational time. If this is done then we get the following time utilisation percentages which, when multiplied by the corresponding load factors, give a percentage for the utilisation of physical capital (Table 8.7).

Figure 13. *UK/Continent–Australia Conferences. Load factors of individual member lines in relation to weighted averages. (Loaded voyages only)*

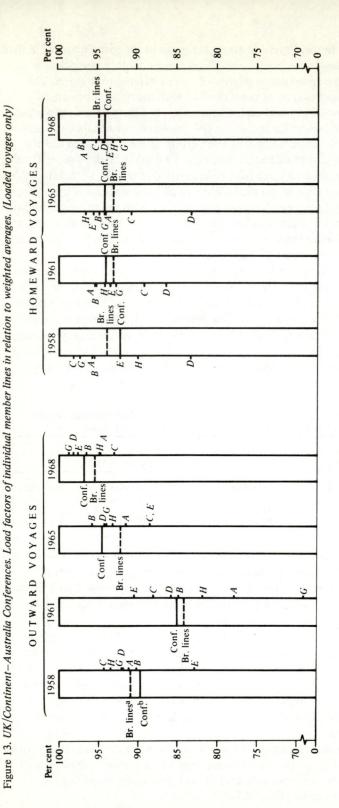

^a Weighted average load factor of all British member lines.

^b Weighted average load factor of all members of the UK/Continent–Australia Conferences.

Table 8.6 *An analysis of the employment of ships' time in United Kingdom/Continent–Australia conference trades. British lines only*

Percentages

	1	2	3	4 Idle time	
	Port loading and discharging time	Voyage time(a)	Repairing and overhaul time	a Occurring within these conference trades	b Occurring outside these trades but attributed proportionately to them
Outwards					
1958	41.4	47.8	6.4	2.4	2.0
1961	44.4	45.8	6.2	1.2	2.4
1965	49.4	43.5	4.6	1.1	1.4
1968	51.0	45.0	2.5	0.9	0.6
Homewards					
1958	46.0	44.9	5.4	1.8	1.9
1961	45.9	46.0	5.4	0.4	2.3
1965	53.0	42.0	3.7	0.3	1.0
1968	51.4	45.1	2.6	0.3	0.6

(a) Includes sea time during loading and discharging.

The physical capital utilisation percentages for both directions of the United Kingdom/Continent– Australia conference trade, which are given below, may be compared with some utilisation ratios for United Kingdom manufacturing industry as a whole.[1] The method, which is explained in the reference given, is basically that of selecting output levels at times when each industry is known to be operating at full capacity; joining these peaks by 'linear segments' and then extrapolating the segments at each end to cover the whole period. Estimates of potential output are then made for non-peak periods by reference to the straight line segments and their extrapolation. In conference shipping, full capacity operation is judged to be a 100 per cent effective[2] load factor associated with full time operation, including time spent on repairs and overhauls but with no allowance for idle time.

Table 8.7 *The utilisation of physical capital in the United Kingdom/Continent–Australia conference trades*

(Percentages)				
	1 Time Utilisation[a]		2 Load Factor of all vessels sailing[b]	3 Physical Capital Utilisation
	a Total Conference	b British Lines only	British Lines only	(Col. 1.b × Col. 2) British Lines only
Outward				
1958	97.0	95.6	78.8	75.3
1961	97.8	96.4	79.0	76.2
1965	98.5	97.5	81.1	79.1
1968	98.5	98.5	90.6	89.2
Homeward				
1958	97.0	96.4	93.9	90.5
1961	98.7	97.4	93.0	90.6
1965	98.8	98.7	93.0	91.8
1968	98.8	99.1	94.7	93.8
Both Directions				
1958	97.0	96.1	86.5	83.1
1961	98.3	96.9	86.3	83.6
1965	98.7	98.2	88.8	87.2
1968	98.6	98.8	92.5	91.4

(a) Specifically of loaded vessels. As used here, these figures carry the assumption that the idle time of ballast and semi-ballast vessels, of which there are relatively few on the outward leg and none on the homeward leg, is in approximately the same proportion to total time as is that of loaded vessels.

(b) Of all vessels sailing; includes loaded, ballast and semi-ballast vessels.

Within the nineteen industry groups there are some[3] which have utilisation percentage which in some of these years are lower than those for the example of conference shipping which is shown here, but conference shipping is undoubtedly a

1   Taylor, J., Winter, D., and Pearce, D. 'A 19 Industry Quarterly Series of Capacity Utilisation in the United Kingdom, 1948–1968'. *Bulletin of the Oxford University Institute of Economics and Statistics*, Vol. 32, No. 2, May, 1970.

2   That is, with an allowance for 'space vacant but unavailable'.

3   See Taylor J. et al. op.cit.

Table 8.8 *Comparative physical capital utilisation percentages for conference liner shipping in the UK/Continent—Australia trades and in nineteen UK industry groups*

	(Percentages) UK/Continent—Australia Conference Shipping (both directions of trade. British Lines only).	Nineteen UK industry Groups
1958	83.1	89.6
1961	83.6	94.3
1965	87.2	97.5
1968	91.4	94.8

'below average case' in respect of this measure. It is not, however, so far below the industry average as to indicate very serious under-utilisation of the capital factor of production employed in conference shipping as represented by this group of conference trades. It is, however, important to notice at this stage that a maintained high level of capital utilisation is a necessary but not a sufficient condition of the efficient operation of the factors of production engaged. Further aspects of efficiency as measured by relative net profitability and implied relative unit costs are examined in the third section of this chapter.

2. Inter-conference membership links and the continuity of employment of conference vessels

In the previous section of this chapter the degree of utilisation of the physical capital represented by the vessels in one conference group of substantial size and importance was studied in terms of load factors and time utilisation within a conference group. In that study an allowance was made for a *proportional* share, attributed to the conference group, of the idle time of conference vessels *throughout each year*. The relatively very small proportion of idle time spent outside the conference group (see Table 8.6) as a percentage of total conference time, plus this attributed external idle time, implies a high degree of continuity of employment of conference vessels. In this section the inter-conference links in terms of membership is explored in respect of the Europe[1]—Australia Conference group and also of the more complex Europe—Far Eastern areas group.

In Table 8.9 are shown the links of membership within the Europe—Australia Conference group. This group of three conferences is highly integrated. At the end of 1971 26 shipping lines were members of one or more of the three conferences in the group. Linkages within the group are virtually complete in directional terms; that is to say, nearly every member of one of the two, but not necessarily both, outward conferences is also a member of the single homeward conference. There are only two members who do not have these directional linkages. One, an old established British line, British India Steam Navigation Company, has 'rights' in the UK—Australia Conference outwards, but it cannot load in Continental ports and, what is more important, it has no rights in the Australia—Europe conference which governs the homeward trade. So, having sailed from the UK to Australia with cargo, this line appears to be faced with the prospect of returning in ballast or of using a

---

1 Includes the United Kingdom.

conference membership link which is external to the conference group being considered. In fact this line has provided itself with several conference membership links ex—Australian ports. These are as follows:

Australian—West Pakistan Outward Shipping Conference

Australia—East India Outward Shipping Conference

Australia—West India Outward Shipping Conference

Australia—Singapore and West Malaysia Outward Shipping Conference.

British India is chiefly concerned with the United Kingdom—India/Pakistan trade and the links defined above neatly join its operations in the UK—Australia outward trade with its two-way membership of a large group of area shipping conferences which cover trade in both directions between Europe, including the United Kingdom, and India and Pakistan.

The other line which has membership in only one direction, outwards from Australia, is the Australind Steam Shipping Company. This is a tiny British line operating only one or two ships and exercising its rights in the Australia—Europe Conference to the extent of only one voyage a year in some years, and in other years not at all. In earlier years, this line also had rights in one of the outward conferences. In more recent years it has arranged its outward voyages to Australia on routes which are outside the sphere of the Europe—Australia conference group.

Some other members of the Europe—Australia conference group have cross-trade links as well as membership of conferences which cover both directions of the Australian trade. For example, P. & O., who are members of all three conferences in the group, are also members of the cross-trade covered by the Australia—West India Outward Shipping Conference. Some other members do not have these outside links. For example, the Soviet Russian line, the Baltic Steamship Company, which joined conferences covering both directions of this trade in 1968, have no cross-trade links. Nor have the French line, Compagnie des Messageries Maritimes, nor the Dutch, Koninklijke Nedlloyd.

Australia is a relatively isolated continental block with a reasonably well-balanced conference trade with Europe. These factors make for a relatively simple group of conferences with largely over-lapping membership. A much more complex conference system covers the trade in both directions between Europe and the Far East, and this is now examined in terms of route coverage and the links which the shipping lines involved have between the eight 'main route' conferences principally concerned.

The Far East, as served by the 'main route' conference system, covers ports in Korea, Japan, Hong Kong, Taiwan, Malaysia, Singapore, the Philippines, Sabah, Brunei and Sarawak, and the inter-mediate area of the Gulf of Aden and Red Sea ports.[1] In Table 8.10 are set out the inter-conference membership links for four 'main route' uni-directional conferences and for two conferences, the Far Eastern Freight Conference and the Philippines—Europe Conference, which cover both directions of trade. The first-named of these two is the major conference in this trade and the principal shipping lines concerned are either full or associate members of it. Membership of a 'round trade' conference, such as this one is, clearly reduces

1 Further details of conference coverage including the coverage of European ports are given in Appendix A. Also shown there are data on membership and the terms on which various conferences quote rates and rebates.

Table 8.9 *Membership and inter-conference membership links within the Europe–Australia Conference Group. At December 1971*

Conference Members	Conference membership Outwards from Europe to Australia		Homewards to Europe from Australia
	1	2	3
	United Kingdom–Australia Conference	Outward Continent Australia Conference	Australia–Europe Conference
Actanz Line	√	√	√
Aktieselskabet Det Ostaslatiske Kompagni (The East Asiatic Co).		√	√
Associated Container Transportation (Australia)	√	√	√
The Australian National Line	√	√	√
Australia Europe Container Service (AECS)		√	√
The Australind Steam Shipping Co.			√
The Baltic Steamship Co.		√	√
Blue Star Line	√		√
British India Steam Navigation Co.	√		
The Clan Group	√	√	√
Compagnie des Messageries Maritimes		√	√
Dolphin Line	√	√	√
Ellerman and Bucknall Steamship Co.		√	√
Federal Steam Navigation Co.	√		√
Hapag–Lloyd Aktiengesellschaft		√	√
Jadranska Slobodna Plovidba		√	√
Koninklijke Nedlloyd		√	√
Lloyd Triestino		√	√
The Ocean Steam Ship Co.	√	√	√
Overseas Containers	√	√	√
Peninsular and Oriental Steam Navigation Co.	√	√	√
Port Line	√	√	√
Rederiaktiebologet Transatlantic		√	√
Scanaustral A.S.		√	√
Shaw, Savill and Albion Co.	√	√	√
Wilh. Wilhelmsen		√	√

Note:
The membership listed in this table include several container consortia which are composed of existing members who retain their membership in their own title or style as well as group membership under the title of the consortium. The following are consortia, with their membership.

continued

177

Note to Table 8.9 (continued)

Consortia	Membership of Consortia
Overseas Containers (OCL)	Federal Steam Navigation Co. The Ocean Steam Ship Company Peninsular and Orient Steam Navigation Co. Shaw, Savill and Albion Co. The Clan Group
Dolphin Line (This consortium carry cargo which cannot readily be loaded into containers. They run a 'conventional' service which is complementary to the container service run by OCL)	The same as given above for OCL.
Associated Container Transportation (Australia) (ACTA)	Blue Star Line Ellerman and Bucknall Steamship Co. Port Line
Actanz Line (This consortium has a function similar to that described above for Dolphin Line)	The same as given above for ACTA.

the need for lines to work for a system of inter-connected links into other conferences. Nevertheless most lines concerned with trading into the widespread Far Eastern area are members of all the main route conferences shown in Table 8.10, as well as of many smaller, cross-trade conferences which cover areas *within* the Far Eastern area, as defined above, and *between* parts of the Far East and other main areas such as Australia, and India and Pakistan. Some examples of members' cross-trade conference links are shown in Appendix A where 67 main route and cross-trade conferences[1] are identified in connection with the three trade routes: Europe—Australia; Europe—Far Eastern areas; and Europe—India and Pakistan.

It has been noted in general terms that the need for inter-conference membership links in order to ensure continuity of employment and a high level of capital utilisation is less in the Europe—Far Eastern trades because the Far Eastern Freight Conference (FEFC), one of the main ones involved, covers both directions of trade. Nevertheless the long-established lines have a wide membership of the main route conferences covering this trade, and also in most cases many membership links into cross-trade conferences. For example, P. & O. is a member of all of the eight main route conferences shown in Table 8.10. In addition (see Appendix A), it has membership of eight cross-trade conferences with ports or areas of origin within the Far East. These extend outside the area to India, Pakistan, the Persian Gulf, as well as providing several links within the area, such as from Hong Kong to the Philippines. Other old-established lines are similarly well connected. This is true of the Compagnie des Messageries Maritimes, the French line, and Mitsui OSK Lines, Japanese. But the newer lines established during the past few years by newly independent developing countries are less well connected. An example is Neptune Orient Lines, Singapore. This line began with membership of the important FEFC and UK—Far Eastern Freight Conference and later extended into membership of both

1 The list of 67 conferences is not exhaustive.

the Japan—Europe and Europe—Japan conferences. Its cross-trade conference
links were confined at the end of 1971 to the Singapore/West Malaysia—Australia
trade in both directions. Similar membership links may be seen in the cases of other
relatively new shipping lines, such as the Malaysian International Shipping Corporation, and the Orient Overseas Line.[1]

In Appendix A are set out further details of the membership, areas covered and
terms of rates and rebates of conferences covering the three trade routes from
Europe to Australia, to the Far East, and to India and Pakistan.

This analysis of conference membership and of the links which shipping lines
have built up for themselves in many conferences whose geographical spheres are
contiguous or over-lapping shows that the older shipping lines are very well connected
in this respect. If a main route conference does not cover trade in both directions
along the route, then lines are very commonly members of both of the uni-directional
conferences involved in the trade concerned. Where there are fairly rare exceptions
to this pattern, then the line which has membership in only one direction of trade
will be found to have membership of one or more cross-trade conferences which
link its operations at the end of an outward 'voyage leg' with the beginning of a
homeward leg in another trade, or possibly with a conference or conferences which
cover trades which lead the line's vessels to their home port by a trans-world route.
Newly formed shipping lines start in a small way in terms of conference membership,
but there is evidence that growth in establishing links and connections clearly takes
place. Continuity of employment of conference vessels is an obviously important
element, with load factors, in the degree of utilisation of the physical capital
employed in the world's conference shipping industry. We cannot conclude that
lack of conference membership never hampers the continuity of employment of
vessels, but it is clear that a high proportion of the shipping lines which *are already
conference members* are very widely connected in terms of conference membership,
and it is very doubtful, to say the least, that they are ever seriously constrained by
insufficient membership links into other conference trades.

3. Some financial consequences of conference membership
In this section tests are made of two hypotheses, as follows:
1. That the profitability of a large specified group of conference freight liner
   operations is low in relation to the profitability of other industries.
2. That freight shipping services organised by a specified conference group
   lead to widely dispersed results in terms of the net profitability of individual
   conference members.

The first of these tests is of a confirmatory nature. It is widely believed, particularly since the publication of the Rochdale report cited earlier, that the rate of return
on employed capital earned by 'liners basically cargo' is low relative to profitability,
similarly measured, in other industries. It is of some interest and importance to
check this point in relation to the conference group which is the subject of the
analysis made here.

---

1   See also Chapter 3, Section 2, (b) for a description of the criteria for entry to 'closed'
conferences.

Table 8.10 *Membership and inter-conference membership links within the United Kingdom/Europe–Far Eastern Conference Group. At December 1971*

Conference Members	Both Directions of Trade		Eastwards only		Westwards only			
	1 Far Eastern Freight Conference	2 Philippines/Europe Freight Conference	3 UK–Far Eastern Freight Conference	4 Europe/Japan Freight Conference	5 Japan/Europe Freight Conference	6 Sabah, Brunei and Sarawak Freight Conference	7 Japan-Gulf of Aden and Red Sea Ports Freight Conference	8 Far-Eastern Gulf of Aden and Red Sea Ports Freight Conference
A. Full Members								
Ben Line Steamers	✓	✓	✓	✓	✓	✓	✓	✓
Blue Funnel Line (The Ocean Steam Ship Co. The China Mutual Steam Navigation Co.)	✓	✓	✓	✓	✓	✓	✓	✓
Blue Star Line Ltd.	✓	✓		✓	✓	✓	✓	✓
Cie Maritime des Chargeurs Reunis	✓	✓		✓	✓	✓	✓	✓
Ellerman and Bucknall Steamship Co.	✓	✓		✓	✓	✓	✓	✓
Glen Line (Glen and Shire Joint Service)	✓	✓	✓	✓	✓	✓	✓	✓
Hapag-Lloyd Aktiengesellschaft[1]	✓	✓		✓	✓	✓	✓	✓
Lloyd Triestino S.p.A.N.	✓	✓		✓	✓	✓	✓	✓
Maersk-Kawasaki Line	✓	✓		✓	✓			
Malaysian International Shipping Corp. Berhad	✓	✓	✓	✓[4]	✓[4]	✓		
Maritime Company of the Philippines	✓	✓		✓	✓	✓		
Cie des Messageries Maritimes	✓	✓	✓	✓	✓	✓	✓	✓
Mitsui O.S.K. Lines	✓	✓		✓	✓[5]	✓	✓	✓
Koninklijke Nedlloyd N.V.[2]	✓	✓	✓	✓	✓[5]	✓	✓	✓
Neptune Orient Lines (Singapore)	✓	✓	✓	✓	✓	✓		
Nippon Yusen Kaisha	✓	✓		✓	✓	✓	✓	✓
Orient Overseas Line	✓	✓		✓	✓		✓	✓
A/S Det Østasiatiske Kompagni (The East Asiatic Co.)	✓	✓		✓	✓	✓	✓	✓
Peninsular and Oriental Steam Navigation Co.	✓	✓		✓	✓	✓	✓	✓
Polish Ocean Lines[3]	✓	✓		✓	✓	✓	✓	✓
A/B Svenska Ostasiatiska Kompaniet (The Swedish East Asia Co.)	✓	✓		✓	✓	✓	✓	✓
Wilh. Wilhelmsen	✓	✓		✓	✓	✓	✓	✓
B. Associate Members								
American President Lines	A	A			A			
Indonesian National Lines (P.N. Djakarta Lloyd	A	A						
P.T. Samudera Indonesia								
P.T. Trikora Lloyd								
P.T. Gesuri Lloyd)								
Jugoslavenska Linijska Plovidba	A	A						
Lauro Line	A							
Companhia Nacional de Navegaçao	A							
Rickmers-Linie	A	A		A	A		A	A

180

(1) 1970 merger between Hapag and Norddeutscher Lloyd
(2) 1970 merger between Hoal and Nedlloyd
(3) Became a full member in 1971, previously an associate member westbound
(4) Became a member 1.1.72
(5) Became a member 1.1.71

A. Associate member

Notes to Table 8.10

Conference coverage of areas and ports.

Conference reference number in Table 8.10	Eastbound	Westbound
1.	*From* Norway, Sweden, Finland, Poland, Denmark, Germany, Holland, Belgium and French ports from Dunkirk to St. Nazaire both inclusive, also Italian and Yugoslav ports. *To* States of Malaya, Singapore, Thailand, Hong Kong, Taiwan and Korea.	*From* **Korea, Hong Kong, Taiwan, States of Malaya and Singapore** *to* **Europe, Black Sea** ports (other than U.S.S.R. ports) and all non-European ports on the **Mediterranean Sea** and Moroccan ports on the **Atlantic Ocean.**
2.	*From* ports as in 1 above and U.K. and Eire *to* the Philippines.	*From* **Philippines** *to* ports as in 1 above.
3.	*From* U.K. and Eire *to* ports as in 1 above.	
4.	*From* ports as in 1 above and U.K. and Eire *to* Japan.	
5.		*From* Japan *to* ports as in 1 above
6.		*From* **Sabah, Brunei and Sarawak** *to* ports as in 1 above.
7.		*From* Japan *to* **Gulf of Aden and Red Sea** ports (excluding Israeli ports).
8.		*From* ports as in 1 above *to* ports as in 7 above.

The purpose of the second test is to investigate the range of financial consequences of conference membership across a number of individual conference
members, to consider individual members' experience in terms of the cargo they
lift, their relative performance and the implications of both of these aspects for conference operations and policies.

We have been permitted to study the financial results of the whole trade covered
by the Europe—Australia conference group, which comprises three separate conferences and a total of 26 member shipping lines of several nationalities, nearly all
European. These results have been made available to us in considerable detail, and
it has been possible to examine a sub-group of seven British member lines and to
use individual company data for some of our analyses.

The data examined arise from conference operations only. No other activities
or capital of the shipowning companies involved are included. A proportion of the
administrative costs incurred by each firm's membership of the conferences concerned are included, under the heading of disbursements, in the conference accounts;
and, in calculating replacement allowances and capital employed, so are payments
on account of new tonnage for future operation within these conferences.

a. Profitability of conference operations in aggregate

It is widely believed that the business of operating vessels under shipping conference
conditions yields a relatively low rate of profit. The Rochdale 'Committee of Inquiry
into Shipping' reported[1] average profitability of UK owned and registered 'liners
basically cargo' of 3.1 per cent per annum over the years 1959—69.[2] Profit, which
includes other income (net), is after depreciation but before tax, as a return on
capital employed. This was very slightly higher than the average percentage for all
British shipping, 3.0 per cent per annum over the same period, but very markedly
lower than the 'all British companies' average percentage[3] for the same period, of
13.4 per cent per annum.

In an appendix to the Rochdale report[4] some detailed data are given on the
financial results of operating United Kingdom owned and registered 'liners basically
cargo'. From this data have been compiled the figures shown in Table 8.11. Capital
employed is defined as 'ships at cost and valuation, less depreciation plus expenditure on new ship construction'. Profit is operating revenue after all disbursements,
depreciation and before other income (net), interest and tax. This definition is
labelled definition B. The percentage return upon actual capital employed in the
Europe—Australia conference group has been calculated on the same basis and the
two sets of results are shown together in Table 8.11, where a comparison is also
made with the Rochdale figures of return on capital employed by 'liners basically
cargo' on the definition, stated in the previous paragraph, which is the same as that
used in the calculation of the return on capital employed in British industry generally,
which is labelled definition A.

1   Rochdale op.cit. p.334—336.

2   Years to 31 March.

3   Quoted by Rochdale from *The Economist*

4   Appendix 13.

Table 8.11 *Percentage return on capital employed*

	1 In United Kingdom owned and registered 'liners basically cargo'.[a]		2 In liners of several different countries of registration, trading under the Europe–Australia conference group.
	Definition A	Definition B.	
1958	5.8	5.5	4.2
1959	2.9	2.3	3.8
1960	4.2	3.5	5.7
1961	1.4	0.7	5.5
1962	0.8	0.1	6.3
1963	2.3	1.7	6.6
1964	4.0	3.3	5.1
1965	3.3	2.5	3.0
1966	1.8	1.0	5.9
1967	1.9	1.4	8.9
1968	5.2	5.4	8.6
Annual average rates for the period 1958–68	3.1	2.5	5.8

(a) The figures given in this column are for the twelve months to 31 March in *the year following* the one shown. This is done to ensure a better comparison with the conference group figures which are for years to 31 December. The basic data are drawn from a sample which includes approximately 75 per cent of total UK owned and registered liner tonnage (see Rochdale op. cit. para. 1239).

The average annual return on capital employed over the eleven years shown in Table 8.11. is only 2.5 per cent for UK liners and 5.8 per cent for liners in the Europe–Australia conferences.

This is on the capital and profit definition labelled definition B, which applies both to UK owned and registered 'liners basically cargo' and to the liners in the Europe–Australia Conference group in this comparison.

The description 'liners basically cargo' implies that some passengers were involved and the very low return in the early 1960's is likely to be due in part to this component. Very few passengers were carried by vessels operated under the Europe–Australia conference group. 'Liners basically cargo' implies nothing about conference membership, although it is known that independent liners of UK registration are rare. The rate of return on capital employed in 'general purpose tramps' of UK ownership and registration was negative in the years, to March 31, 1960, 1962, 1963 and 1964 and was 0.1 per cent in 1961.[1] The return for passenger liners was also negative in the years, to March 31, 1962, 1963 and 1964.

The Europe–Australia conference group is highly organised, and in particular its financial machinery for monitoring the financial performance of the conference group as a whole and for employing those results in bargaining for 'across-the-board' freight rate increases is highly developed.[2] With the exceptions of 1959 and 1965, a fairly stable rate of return on actual capital employed was obtained.

1 Rochdale op.cit. p. 335, para 1261

2 Described in Chapter 4. Section 2 (e).

The rates of return on capital employed in the industry named UK owned and registered 'liners basically cargo' over the period 1958—68 are very similar which-ever of the two capital and profit definitions (described above) are adopted (see Table 8.11 Col.1). In comparison with the rate of return on all British industries, of 13.4 per cent on average over the years 1958 to 1968, the rate of return by UK owned and registered 'liners basically cargo' of 3.1 per cent per annum (definition A) and 2.5 per cent per annum (definition B) are both very low. The rate of return by the Europe—Australia conference group, which is calculated on definition B, is rather higher at 5.8 per cent per annum on average over the same period (1958—68), but the group remains a poor performer on the comparison with *The Economist's* figure for 'all British industries', of 13.4 per cent per annum. The average return for all UK owned and registered 'liners basically cargo' is so low that one wonders how the substantial amount of capital involved was retained in the industry over this period, as largely it was.[1]

It may be concluded from comparing the evidence presented in this study with that given in the Rochdale Inquiry that the conference group studied here is con-siderably above average in terms of rate of return on capital employed by UK 'liners basically cargo', but its rate is well below that for all UK companies.

The average rate of return on capital employed by the conference group has been shown to be 5.8 per cent per annum over the period 1958—1968. This is a highly capital intensive industry; it employs physical capital of considerable longevity, the average life of vessels is 25 years which is at least twice as long as that normally assumed for plant, machinery and land vehicles. In these circumstances the decision to invest is particularly influenced by the rate of return on capital valued at current replacement values. This is shown in Table 8.12 in comparison with the return on the historical cost of ships employed *less* depreciation *plus* expenditure on new ship construction. Percentages are given separately for each direction of trade.

The return on capital, in terms of ships only, valued at current replacement prices is indeed low, at an *average* figure over the period 1958—68 of 3.2 per cent. Of course at any time the fleet employed is composed of vessels of various ages, and the year by year replacement allowances, estimated at current replacement values, will be insufficient in total under inflationary conditions to meet the cost of new vessels. There are complications both of extra financing for future technical progress as well as for past and likely future increases in shipbuilding costs. The only comfort for shipowners in this and other conference trades would appear to be the even lower returns yielded by other types of ship operation, except ore carriers and, in recent years, other types of bulk carrier except oil.[2]

The results set out in Table 8.12. also show the consistently higher profitability of the outward trade compared to the homeward. The greater fragmentation of the European market for conference shipping services and the greater collective bargain-ing power of Australian shippers are factors which go some way towards explaining these differences. Further studies of differences between the outward and homeward trades are described in Chapter 5, particularly Tables 5.1 and 5.2., where it is shown

1 See Rochdale, op. cit. Table 8.1 p. 140, for data of the tonnage of this type of shipping owned and registered in the United Kingdom over this period.

2 See Rochdale op.cit. Table 18.4, p. 335.

Table 8.12 *Europe–Australia conference group. Return on capital employed valued at historical and at replacement cost*

	Percentages					
	1 Return upon capital employed valued at historical cost of ships *less* depreciation *plus* expenditure on new ship construction.			2 Return upon capital employed valued at replacement cost of ships at prices current in each year.		
	Outwards	Homewards	Total	Outwards	Homewards	Total
1958	8.1	1.4	4.2	3.9	0.7	2.1
1959	3.8	3.8	3.8	2.0	1.9	2.0
1960	8.0	3.7	5.7	4.2	2.0	3.0
1961	7.0	4.2	5.5	3.9	2.5	3.2
1962	8.3	4.7	6.3	4.8	2.8	3.7
1963	7.7	5.7	6.6	4.2	3.4	3.8
1964	7.5	3.1	5.1	4.0	1.7	2.7
1965	6.4	0.1	3.0	3.3	0.1	1.6
1966	8.1	4.0	5.9	3.9	2.2	3.0
1967	11.3	6.6	8.9	6.2	3.9	5.1
1968	12.0	5.3	8.6	7.4	3.4	5.4
Average annual rates for the period 1958–68	8.0	3.9	5.8	4.3	2.2	3.2

that the freight rates in the outward direction rise faster than those in the homeward direction. Most, but not all costs are common to both directions of trade, so this differential price trend is one factor which is explanatory of the differential profitability which appears above in Table 8.12.

The financial consequences, in aggregate conference terms, of membership of the Europe–Australia conference group are presented in further detail in Table 8.13. The methods used by this conference group to bargain with organised Australian shippers for 'across-the-board' freight rate increases has been described in Chapter 4.[1] One aspect of the bargaining mechanism is the 'profit allowance' (defined in the notes to Table 8.13). In the years 1964–68 inclusive this allowance was agreed at 8 per cent of actual capital employed. In earlier years different rates of profit allowance were agreed between the conferences and shippers.[2] An important result here is that although these various rates of profit were agreed, they were never earned in the homeward trade and were earned in the outward trade only in 1962, 1966, 1967 and 1968. It was only in 1967 and 1968 that this agreed rate of profit was earned in total trade.

The relatively low rate of return upon capital employed, valued at historical cost written down, has already been noticed, as has the rate of return on capital at replacement cost in each direction of trade. Profitability is also shown here (Table 8.13.) in terms of gross and net margins (definitions are given in the notes to this table). The gross margin reflects the high capital intensity of this industry and the net margin, after replacement allowance confirms the low profitability which is shown by the return on employed capital. Also confirmed by the net margin

1 Section 2.e.

2 Shown in the notes to Table 8.13.

Table 8.13 *Europe–Australia Conference Group financial results of voyages 1957–68*

		1957 Outward	Homew'd	Total	1958 Outward	Homew'd	Total	1959 Outward	Homew'd	Total	1960 Outward	Homew'd	Total	1961 Outward	Homew'd	Total	1962 Outward	Homew'd	Total
A.	**Employed capital and the return upon it**																		
1. Actual capital employed, ships only.[a]	£'s m.	28.41	44.25	72.66	34.64	48.45	83.09	35.00	50.95	85.95	38.31	43.98	82.29	42.80	48.12	90.92	39.34	48.80	88.14
2. Replacement value of capital employed.	£'s m.	61.33	96.47	157.80	71.08	98.26	169.34	65.74	99.93	165.67	72.51	82.95	155.46	75.05	80.45	155.50	68.44	83.02	151.46
3. Agreed profit allowance.[b]	£'s m.	3.41	5.31	8.72	4.16	5.81	9.97	3.04	4.45	7.49	3.37	3.86	7.23	3.32	3.72	7.04	3.09	3.83	6.92
4. Surplus or (deficiency)[c]	£'s m.	(1.17)	(3.53)	(4.70)	(1.36)	(5.12)	(6.4)	(1.73)	(2.52)	(4.25)	(0.29)	(2.24)	(2.53)	(0.38)	(1.68)	(2.06)	0.17	(1.52)	(1.35)
5. Net Profit, before interest and tax.[d] (Row 3 + row 4)	£'s m.	2.24	1.78	4.01	2.80	0.69	3.49	1.31	1.92	3.23	3.07	1.63	4.70	2.94	2.04	4.98	3.26	2.31	5.57
6. Net Profit as % of actual capital employed (Row 5 ÷ Row 1)	%	7.88	4.02	5.52	8.08	1.42	4.20	3.74	3.77	3.76	8.01	3.71	5.71	6.87	4.24	5.48	8.29	4.73	6.32
7. Net Profit as % of replacement value of fleets. (Row 5 ÷ Row 2)	%	3.65	1.85	2.54	3.94	0.70	2.06	1.99	1.92	1.95	4.23	1.97	3.02	3.92	2.54	3.20	4.76	2.78	3.68
B.	**Gross and net profitability**																		
1. Bill of Lading tons carried	m. tons	1.60	1.67	3.27	1.70	1.74	3.44	1.47	1.94	3.41	1.97	1.72	3.69	1.87	1.74	3.61	1.80	1.84	3.64
2. Gross freight revenue.[e]	£'s m.	18.34	28.59	46.93	20.47	27.92	48.39	17.90	29.82	47.72	23.12	26.44	49.56	23.90	26.99	50.89	23.26	29.82	53.08
3. Gross trading profit before deducting expenditure on improvements and modifications.	£'s m.	4.37	5.07	9.44	5.32	4.28	9.60	3.62	5.54	9.16	5.66	4.63	10.29	5.40	4.72	10.12	5.55	5.11	10.66
4. Net profit before interest, tax and expenditure on improvements and modifications.[d]	£'s m.	2.29	1.87	4.16	2.86	0.80	3.66	1.37	2.01	3.38	3.14	1.70	4.84	2.99	2.12	5.11	3.33	2.41	5.74
5. Gross margin (Row 3 ÷ row 2)	%	23.83	17.73	20.12	25.99	15.33	19.84	20.22	18.58	19.20	24.48	17.51	20.76	22.59	17.49	19.89	23.86	17.14	20.08
6. Net margin (Row 4 ÷ row 2)	%	12.49	6.54	8.86	13.97	2.87	7.56	7.65	6.74	7.08	13.58	6.43	9.77	12.51	7.85	10.04	14.32	8.08	10.81

TABLE G13 (continued)

		1963 Outward Homew'd	1963 Total	1964 Outward Homew'd	1964 Total	1965 Outward Homew'd	1965 Total	1966 Outward Homew'd	1966 Total	1967 Outward Homew'd	1967 Total	1968 Outward Homew'd	1968 Total
A. Employed capital and the return upon it													
1. Actual capital employed, ships only.[a]	£'s m.	39.35 / 48.60	87.95	40.78 / 50.00	90.78	43.69 / 51.63	95.32	37.27 / 46.21	83.48	41.46 / 44.60	86.06	52.77 / 53.71	106.48
2. Replacement value of capital employed.	£'s m.	71.66 / 81.03	152.69	77.19 / 93.29	170.48	85.48 / 97.88	183.36	77.78 / 86.84	164.62	75.24 / 75.42	150.66	85.21 / 83.73	168.94
3. Agreed profit allowance.[b]	£'s m.	3.14 / 3.86	7.00	3.26 / 4.00	7.26	3.50 / 4.13	7.63	2.98 / 3.70	6.68	3.32 / 3.57	6.89	4.22 / 4.30	8.52
4. Surplus or (deficiency)[c]	£'s m.	(0.13) / (1.09)	(1.22)	(0.22) / (2.44)	(2.66)	(0.69) / (4.08)	(4.77)	0.03 / (1.83)	(1.80)	1.36 / (0.61)	0.75	2.10 / (1.44)	0.66
5. Net Profit, before interest and tax.[d] (Row 3 + row 4)	£'s m.	3.02 / 2.76	5.78	3.05 / 1.55	4.60	2.81 / 0.05	2.86	3.01 / 1.87	4.88	4.67 / 2.96	7.63	6.32 / 2.86	9.18
6. Net Profit as % of actual capital employed (Row 5 ÷ Row 1)	%	7.67 / 5.68	6.57	7.48 / 3.10	5.07	6.43 / 0.10	3.00	8.08 / 4.05	5.85	11.26 / 6.64	8.87	11.98 / 5.32	8.62
7. Net Profit as % of replacement value of fleets. (Row 5 ÷ Row 2)	%	4.21 / 3.41	3.79	3.95 / 1.66	2.70	3.29 / 0.05	1.56	3.87 / 2.15	2.96	6.21 / 3.92	5.06	7.42 / 3.42	5.43
B. Gross and net profitability													
1. Bill of Lading tons carried	m. tons	1.87 / 1.79	3.66	2.10 / 1.88	3.98	2.22 / 1.92	4.14	2.03 / 1.74	3.77	2.08 / 1.49	3.57	2.19 / 1.43	3.62
2. Gross freight revenue.[e]	£'s m.	24.21 / 30.14	54.35	27.13 / 33.23	60.36	30.19 / 33.57	63.76	28.46 / 29.75	58.21	30.37 / 30.49	60.86	36.57 / 34.44	71.01
3. Gross trading profit before deducting expenditure on improvements and modifications.	£'s m.	5.39 / 5.53	10.92	5.87 / 4.97	10.84	5.96 / 3.71	9.67	5.90 / 5.16	11.06	7.55 / 5.78	13.33	9.59 / 6.03	15.62
4. Net profit before interest, tax and expenditure on improvements and modifications.[d]	£'s m.	3.12 / 2.88	6.01	3.16 / 1.73	4.89	3.03 / 0.30	3.33	3.22 / 2.11	5.33	4.87 / 3.11	7.98	6.57 / 3.06	9.63
5. Gross margin (Row 3 ÷ row 2)	%	22.26 / 18.35	20.09	21.64 / 14.96	17.96	19.74 / 11.05	15.17	20.73 / 17.34	19.00	24.86 / 18.96	21.90	26.22 / 17.51	22.00
6. Net margin (Row 4 ÷ row 2)	%	12.89 / 9.56	11.06	11.65 / 5.21	8.10	10.04 / 8.94	5.22	11.31 / 7.09	9.16	16.04 / 10.20	13.11	17.97 / 8.89	13.56

Notes a. Historical cost of fleets *less* depreciation of 90 per cent over twenty-five years (leaving 10 per cent over twenty-five years residual value undepreciated), *plus* payments on account of new tonnage, *plus* improvements and modifications written down.

b. This is named the 'capital allowance' in the conference 'formula' accounts. It is the allowance agreed between the conference and Australian shippers' organisations for the remuneration of the capital employed in the trade. The allowance was agreed at 12 per cent in 1958; at various percentages between 7.74 and 8.79 over the period 1959–63 inclusive (when a basic rate and a half-life rate were combined), and at 8 per cent each year from 1964 to 1968.

c. This is net profit, as defined at row 5, subtracted from the 'profit allowance' (row 3). It shows that the profit allowance was, in the event, hardly ever earned.

d. This is net profit after all disbursements. Included with disbursements in this definition (which is the one adopted by the conference in its 'formula' accounts) is expenditure on 'improvements and modifications'. It should be noticed that this last-named item is excluded from disbursements, and therefore included with net profit, in section B of this Table. This is done because section B is the basis upon which the results of conference operations as a whole are compared with the results of operations by individual British member lines. In the accounts for individual lines, expenditure on 'improvements and modifications' is, with some basis in logic, not deducted from net profit.

e. Includes a tiny amount of passage money which is inseparable.

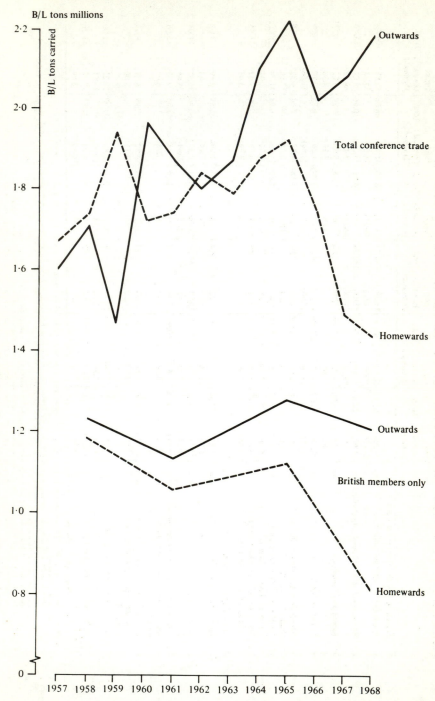

calculations is the considerably poorer profitability performance of the voyages homewards.

This part of our analysis validates the first hypothesis we set out to test.

'That the profitability of a large specified group of conference freight liner operations is low in relation to the profitability of other industries'.

Several measures of profitability have been employed in this test and the results are in accord with each other.

b. Relative profitability of individual conference members

We now turn to examine the second hypothesis:

'That freight conference shipping services organised by a specified group lead to widely dispersed results in terms of the net profitability of individual conference members'.

First, the total trade flows and a sample of individual members' trade in relation to total conference trade is examined. In Figure 14 are shown the trends in the trade carried by the vessels of the Europe—Australia conference group in the period 1957—68 and an indication of the trend of the trade carried by the British members of this group. In total the trade is in substantial volume averaging 3.7 million bill of lading tons per annum over this period of twelve years.[1] In the four years for which individual data are available the British share of total trade, from which the individual data are taken, ranges from 70.0 per cent, or 2.41 million bill of lading tons, in 1958 to 55.6 per cent, or 2.01 million bill of lading tons, in 1968. So our sample, in all the years examined, exceeds 55 per cent of total conference trade and in no year is the total absolute size of the sample less than 2 million bill of lading tons of trade.

In composition this sample is wide-ranging. It includes an exceptionally extensive range of British and European industrial finished and semi-finished goods. The United Kingdom—Australia freight tariff contains over 7,000 entries and is the largest of the several tariffs examined in the course of this research. In the homeward direction a very considerable range of relatively high unit value primary commodities of both agricultural and mineral origin are included.

In directional terms the sample, comprising the British share of total conference trade, is also substantial. It is in both cases a declining share, but it does not fall below 55 per cent in any of the years in which operations are examined here. This is shown in Table 8.14. Furthermore, the British members do constitute a complete conference in themselves. This is the UK—Australia conference; and its membership is given in Appendix A. The data on British members' operations which is subject to analysis in this chapter relate to 'conventional' conference operations before the container consortia were formed by some members in 1968 and 1969. These consortia also appear in Appendix A.

There are nine British member lines which took part in the operations of this conference over the period 1957 to 1968 inclusive. Two members operated on a very small scale and in some years did no operations at all or operated only in one direction. These members' operations have been included in the aggregate results for British, and all conference members, but they have been omitted from the individual results which are now considered.

1 See also Figure 11 where cargo space utilised by this conference is illustrated in total.

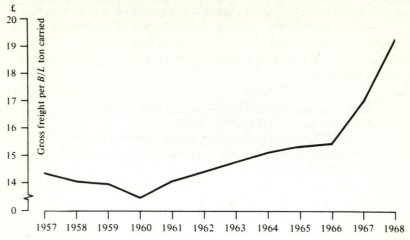

Figure 16. *Gross freight per B/L ton carried. Total conference trade outward and homeward*

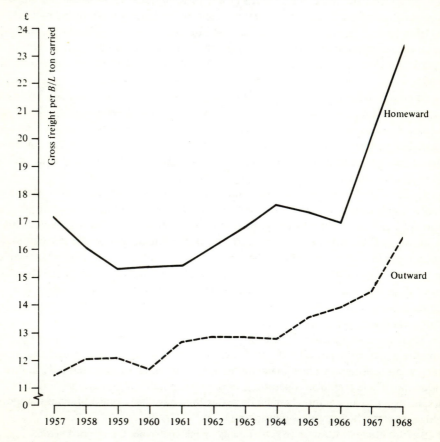

Table 8.14 *Europe–Australia Conference Group. British shares in total conference trade measured in bill of lading tons*

	Percentages Outwards	Homewards	Total Trade
1958	71.5	68.5	70.0
1961	60.7	60.8	60.7
1965	57.8	58.5	58.1
1968	55.1	56.3	55.6

In a typical market situation for conference shipping services market fragmentation and consequent price differentiation are found to a greater or lesser extent according to type of export trade, degree of industrialisation of the exporting country, and other factors. The Europe–Australia conference trade takes place between highly industrialised, and therefore typically fragmented markets, at the European end and less industrialised, less fragmented and more shipper-organised markets at the Australian end. There are therefore considerable differences and contrasts between the trades in each direction covered by this conference group. The trend, shown in Figure 15, of average gross freight revenue per B/L tons of cargo carried reflects changes in freight rates 'across the board' and individually, and changes in the volume and composition of the trade. This trend moves sharply upwards in 1967 and 1968 when the greatest influence was freight rate increases and surcharges (see Table. B.1. Appendix B) made at the time or shortly after the Arab–Israeli war of June 1967, and the devaluation of sterling later in the same year. In itself this trend explains little, but if it is split into directional trades, as it is in Figure 16, it can be seen that the average freight revenue per B/L ton carried in the homeward direction is substantially greater than that obtained outward. The main influences governing these differences in the average *level* of freight revenue are price and cost; the homeward trade is quite largely in commodities such as meat and dairy products, which require refrigerated stowage. This involves higher capital and operating costs to conference members. Of course these aspects alone tell us nothing about the profitability of outward and homeward trade, but when consideration is given to the financial consequences of conference membership to individual member lines, these circumstantial trading aspects need to be borne in mind.

Of great importance when individual members' results are compared, are the differences between them in their average gross freight per B/L ton carried. In order to be able to test the second hypothesis, stated above, we need to examine the range of profitability of member lines. This may be done in terms of net profit per unit of physical output or per unit of sales in money terms (the net margin), but in each case care must be taken to exclude differences in net profit per unit of output which are due not to any inter-member differences in the efficiency with which members conduct their operations, but to differences which exist between members in the average unit value per B/L ton of cargo which they load. The loading experiences in this respect for the principal seven British members of the Europe–Australia conference group is shown in Figure 19, which illustrates the outward and homeward experiences separately, and in both cases comparisons are also made with the average experience of the whole conference.

Figure 17. *Europe–Australia Conference Group. Gross freight per B/L ton carried*

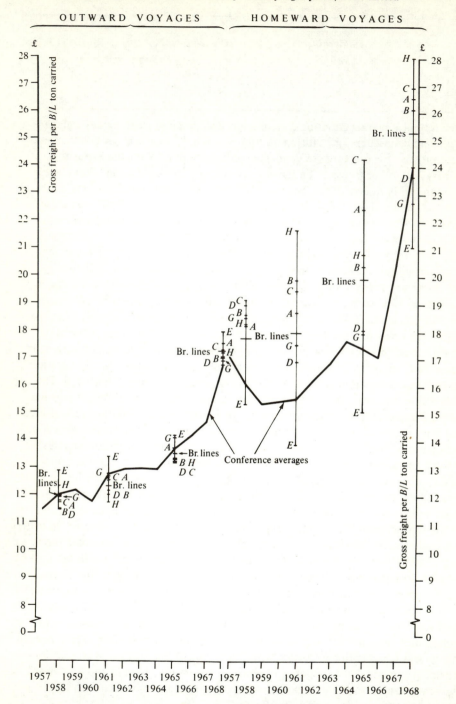

In the outward trade the British lines load chiefly in the United Kingdom, although some also have 'rights' to load in Continental ports, and these rights are exercised.[1] The cargoes loaded are almost entirely composed of industrial goods — finished manufactures, semi-finished goods and processed industrial intermediate goods. The data displayed in Figure 17 indicate that the average gross freight per B/L ton of cargo carried outwards from Europe by British member lines does not differ greatly between members. In the homeward trade, however, these differences appear to be greater, as judged by eye from Figure 17. As calculated by finding the coefficient of variation, V (the standard deviation divided by the mean), the outward and homeward trades compare as follows.

Table 8.15 *Individual British members of the Europe—Australia Conference Group. Coefficients of variation, V, in average gross freight per B/L ton carried*

	Percentages Outward	Homeward
1958	4.0	6.5
1961	4.1	12.7
1965	2.8	14.5
1968	2.0	9.5

In each of these four years the coefficient of variation is greater in the homeward than it is in the outward trade; it ranges from one and a half to more than five times greater on a comparison of each year's figures.

The variation is small in the outward trade and this indicates that members' loading 'rights',[2] which are chiefly on a geographical basis, result in a cargo mix which yields nearly the same average gross freight per B/L ton carried by each member. This calculation leaves us in a good *prima facie* position to study the differences which exist between members in the profitability of their outward trade. This is so because differences between members in average gross freight per B/L ton carried are relatively small, as measured by the coefficient of variation, and are unlikely to have very much influence upon the differences which exist between members in various comparisons of profitability. However, this tentative conclusion needs a further statistical test in the form of a regression analysis. This is set out in Table 8.16.

The values for R^2 are found to be lower for the outward direction of trade than for the homeward. This is so in respect of each of the four years shown in Table 8.16 and in repsect of both measures of profitability, i.e. gross margin of profit and net profit per B/L ton carried. Furthermore, the values of T relating to the term bx in the regression equations (see above the Statistical Note to Table 8.16), is below unity in five out of the total of eight examples of this calculation in the outward direction. This means that in the five cases where $T < 1$ the influence of the term bx, representing gross freight per B/L ton carried, upon the term y, representing one of the two measures of profitability, is without 'significance' in the statistical sense. In the homeward direction, however, not only is it true, as has been noted already,

1   See Table 8.9 in section 2 of this chapter for membership details.

2   See Chapter 3. Section 2 (d).

Table 8.16 *Europe–Australia Conference Group. Coefficients of determination, R^2, from the regression of: (a) Gross margin and (b) Net profit per B/L ton carried on gross freight per B/L ton carried.*

British member lines only. (In brackets, the value of T, see Statistical Note below)

| | Outwards | | Homewards | |
	(a)	(b)	(a)	(b)
1958	.064	.038	.099	.238
	(0.59)	(0.44)	(0.74)	(1.25)
1961	.144	.206	.457	.568
	(0.92)	(1.14)	(2.05)	(2.56)
1965	.179	.283	.459	.362
	(1.04)	(1.41)	(2.06)	(1.68)
1968	.040	.094	.480	.404
	(0.46)	(0.72)	(2.15)	(1.84)

Statistical Note to Table 8.16
The regression equations are in the form $Y = a + bx$. Y, the dependent variable, is in this case successively the measure of profit designated (a) and (b) in this table. x is the independent variable, in this case gross freight per bill of lading ton carried. In brackets under each value of R^2, (the coefficient of determination), is given the value for T. T is found by dividing the constant term b by the standard error of the b term, SE(b). Where T is less than one, bx is not 'significant', in the statistical sense. For the implications of this see the text.

that the values for R^2 are substantially higher than in the corresponding calculations outwards, but the values of T are in all cases except one greater than unity. This indicates that the influence of the term bx upon y is 'significant' in the seven instances where $T \geqslant 1$.

From this statistical exercise it may be concluded that the differences between member lines in the average gross revenue per B/L ton which they receive for cargo they lift from the European end of this conference trade has practically no influence upon the differences which exist between them in respect of two separate measures of profitability. This conclusion was likely to be found as soon as we knew from the results of calculations shown in Table 8.15. that there was very little variation between members in their average gross receipts per B/L ton carried.[1] So the conclusions now drawn from Table 8.16. are confirmatory.

The results of the regression analysis on the data relating to the homeward trade are quite different from those for the outward trade. The values for R^2, the coefficient of determination, are considerably higher in every year than they are in the outward trade; furthermore they are of greater statistical significance, as measured by the values for T (given in brackets in Table 8.16). It may therefore be concluded that in this direction of this conference trade the differences which exist between member lines in respect of their average gross revenues per B/L ton of cargo lifted from Australian ports does influence their absolute level of profitability, and also their profitability relative to each other. The coefficients of variation shown in Table 8.15. foreshadow this conclusion, for they range in value from 6.5 to 14.5 per cent and are, on average, 3.4 times greater than those found in the outward

1 V, the coefficient of variation, ranged from 2.0 to 4.1 per cent over the four selected years, 1958, 1961, 1965 and 1968.

194

trade in respect of differences between member lines in their average gross freight per B/L ton of cargo carried.

These intermediate conclusions must be borne in mind as we come next to consider the range and dispersion of differences in the profitability of individual member lines operating under conference conditions of common pricing, combined arrangements for rebates and a substantial extent of output sharing among existing members.

What follows is a range and dispersion analysis of the consequences of conference membership for the profitability of individual members of the conference and, following from that, the consequences of differential individual profitability performance for conference bargaining and the pricing of its services.[1]

The trends in the profitability of outward, homeward and total conference trade is shown in fully comparable terms in respect of the gross margin in Figures 18 and 19. On average over the twelve years 1957–1968, the gross margin for the whole conference trade has been 19.7 per cent with swings downwards in 1965 to a low point of 15.2 per cent, and up to a high point of 22.0 per cent in 1968 (Figure 18). Gross margins in the outward trade are invariably above the average for the total trade and reach as high as 26.2 in 1968. In the homeward trade gross margins are on average invariably lower than in total trade; the smallest gross margin, 11.0 per cent was reached in the homeward trade in 1965 (Figure 19).

The performance of the British lines in relation to the whole conference is shown in Figure 20 for trade outward and homeward. The British average gross margin is below that of the conference in all the years shown, except for 1968 in the homeward direction. This finding is in line with that shown later on net profit per B/L ton of cargo carried, but it runs contrary to the data (shown on Figures 17) of the British lines' average gross freight revenue per B/L ton carried. This suggests that as a group British lines are less successful in financial terms than the conference group as a whole. This point is further substantiated in Table 8.17.

Table 8.17 *Europe–Australia Conference Group. Shares of all British member lines in total group operations outward and homeward*

| | Percentages | | |
	Total B/L tonnage carried	Gross freight Revenue	Net profit before interest, tax and expenditure on 'improvements and modifications'
1958	70.0	73.9	69.2
1961	60.7	64.8	41.3
1965	58.1	62.3	18.9
1968	55.6	57.9	50.1

The performance of the British lines in aggregate for both directions of trade taken together, as measured by net profit per B/L ton carried, is below the average

1 It should be noticed here that when the profitability performances of British member lines on average and individually are compared with those of the Europe–Australia Conference Group as a whole, a particular measure of gross and net profit is employed for reasons of comparability. The differences between this measure of profit and that used in the aggregate conference analysis made in Section 3 (a) is explained in the notes to Table 8.13.

for the whole conference group (Figure 21). This is so also in respect of gross profit margins (see Figure 20). This relatively poor performance by the British group, which are subject to the more detailed analysis by individual line which follows, needs to be borne mind.

The performance of individual British member lines is illustrated by three measures of profitability; these are, gross margin, net profit per B/L ton carried and net margin.[1] The range of the performance of individual lines is illustrated in respect of outward and homeward trade separately in Figures 20 (gross margin); 21 and 23 (net profit per B/L ton carried) and 24 (net margin).

The 'scores' of individual member lines in terms of above or below average performance in respect of each of these measures is shown in Table 8.18. From section 1 of this table, which shows the position for voyages outward from Europe, lines B, D and G emerge as relatively strong performers. Lines A, C and H are relatively weak, and E shows mixed but fairly evenly balanced scores.

It has been shown a little earlier in this chapter that in the homeward trade the average gross freight per B/L ton varies considerably between members. So in section 2, Homeward, of Table 8.18. scores for the average yield of homeward cargo, as measured by average gross freight per B/L ton carried, are shown alongside members' scores in the measures of profitability. Of the relatively high scorers outward, line B, with an above average yield of cargo homeward, scores above average in all four years. Line G gets a below average yield from its cargo but, remarkably, manages to score above average profitability. Line D gets a below average yield and scores below average profitability. Of the two relatively weak performers outward, line A gets an above average yield homewards and scores above average profitability, and the experience and performance of line C is similar. Line E picks up low-rated cargo on average and performs badly in the profitability scores. Line H loads above average rated cargo and performs below the average in profitability.

Section 2 of the analysis in Table 8.18, which is concerned with homeward trade, confirms the results of earlier analyses in showing that the gross revenue per B/L ton of cargo loaded by individual lines does have *some* influence on their profitability, although there is one case here of a line which achieved above average profitability in the face of below average revenue per ton of cargo lifted, and one which manages the reverse of this. This suggests the presence of other factors which have influence upon relative net profitability and these are now examined.

Average profitability in this conference group has been shown earlier in this section to be relatively low. The question now posed is whether and, if so, to what extent does the average rate of profitability (given by various different measures) conceal widely different rates of profit earned by individual member lines. First the 'means' (arithmetic averages) are compared with the 'ranges' (the two extreme values of each series and the difference between them) in Table 8.19.

---

1 Gross margin is gross profit before depreciation, expenditure on 'improvements and modifications', interest and tax divided by gross freight revenue: Net profit is profit before expenditure on 'improvements and modifications', interest and tax; and net margin is net profit divided by gross freight revenue.

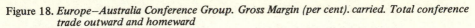

Figure 18. *Europe–Australia Conference Group. Gross Margin (per cent). carried. Total conference trade outward and homeward*

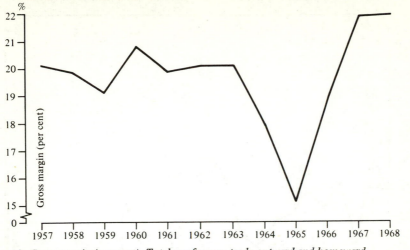

Figure 19. *Gross margin (per cent). Total conference trade outward and homeward*

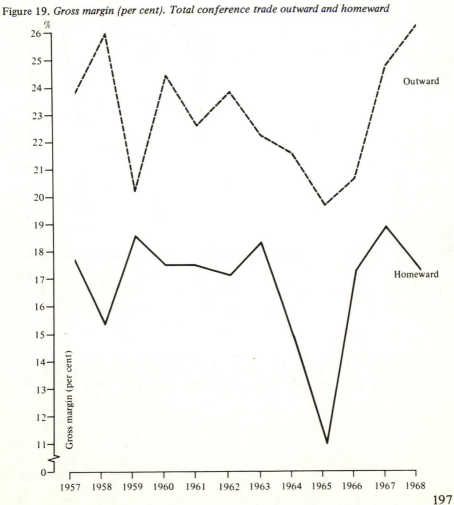

Figure 20. *Europe–Australia Conference Group. Gross margin (per cent)*

OUTWARD VOYAGES   HOMEWARD VOYAGES

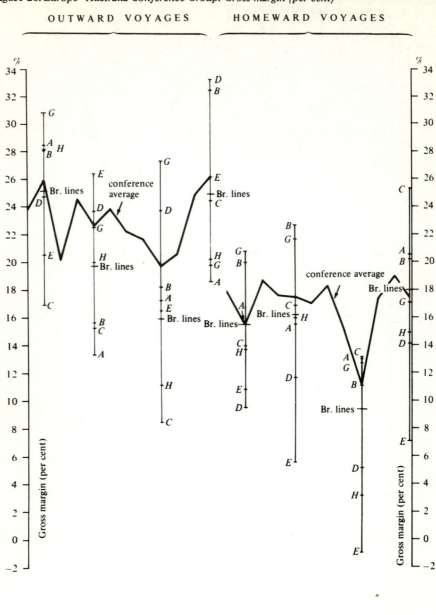

Figure 21. *Europe–Australia Conference Group. Net profit per B/L ton carried. Total conference trade outward and homeward*

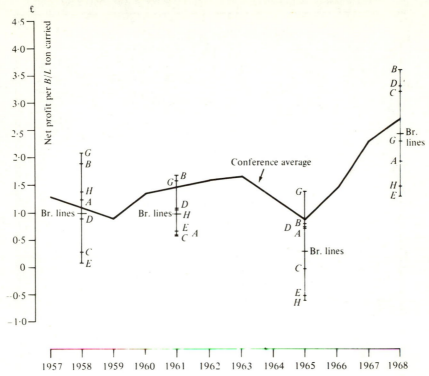

Figure 22. *Net profit per B/L ton carried. Total conference trade outward and homeward*

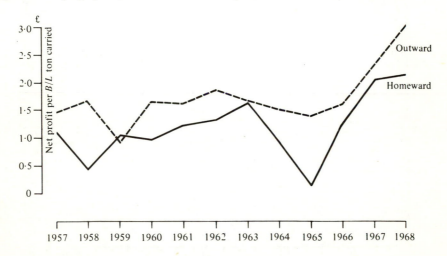

Figure 23. *Europe–Australia Conference Group. Net profit per B/L ton carried*

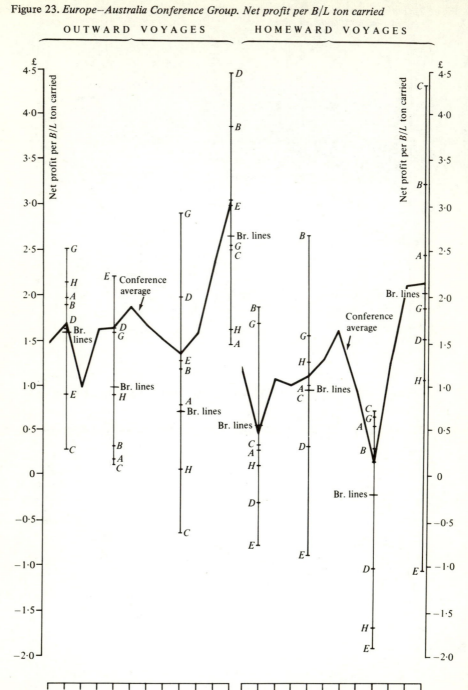

Figure 24. *Europe–Australia Conference Group. Net margin (per cent)*

OUTWARD VOYAGES   HOMEWARD VOYAGES

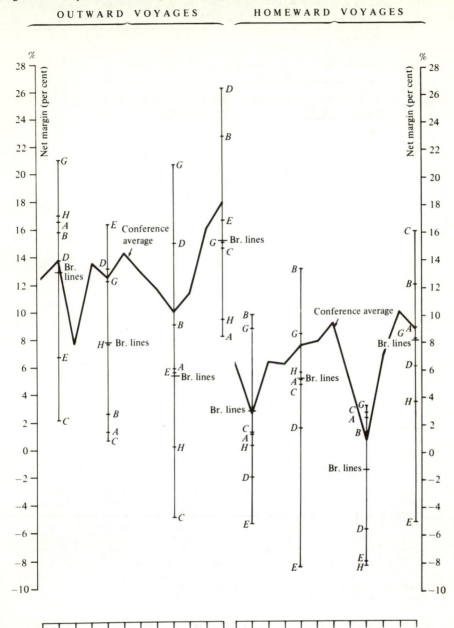

Table 8.18 *Europe–Australia Conference Group. Above and below average 'scores' in profit-ability in four selected years 1958, 1961, 1965 and 1968. British members only. Unweighted average measures of profitability*

1.OUTWARD

Individual Member Lines	Gross margin a. Above average	Gross margin b. Below average	Net profit per B/L ton a. Above average	Net profit per B/L ton b. Below average	Net margin a. Above average	Net margin b. Below average
A	1	3	1	3	1	3
B	3	1	3	1	3	1
C	0	4	0	4	0	4
D	3	1	3	1	4	0
E	2	2	3	1	2	2
G	3	1	3	1	3	1
H	2	2	1	3	1	3

2.HOMEWARD

	Gross margin a	Gross margin b	Net profit per B/L ton a	Net profit per B/L ton b	Net margin a	Net margin b	Average revenue yield per unit of cargo carried — Gross Freight per B/L ton a	Gross Freight per B/L ton b
A	3	1	3	1	3	1	4	0
B	4	0	4	0	4	0	4	0
C	3	1	2	2	3	1	4	0
D	0	4	0	4	0	4	1	3
E	0	4	0	4	0	4	0	4
G	4	0	3	1	4	0	1	3
H	1	3	1	3	1	3	4	0

Note on choice of years

The years selected for detailed financial analysis in this section of Chapter 8 were chosen for the following reasons.

The years of highest and lowest profitability for the whole Europe–Australia Conference Group. From Table 8.13. it may be seen that for total trade profitability, as measured by net profit as a percentage of the replacement value of fleets, gross profit per £ of gross revenue and net profit per £ of gross revenue, was highest in 1968 and lowest in 1965. The year 1958 was chosen because it is the first year of the period studied and 1961 was chosen as a year of average, or typical profitability; net profit as a percentage of actual capital employed in total conference trade was 5.5 per cent in 1961 and 5.8 per cent per annum on average over the period 1958–68, and net profit as a percentage of the replacement value of fleets was 3.2 per cent in 1961 and the same on average over this period (see Table 8.12).

In a highly capital intensive industry, such as this is, the gross margin is not a good measure of realised profitability. However this analysis of gross margin is use-ful in that it does show, at the extremes, e.g. at the low point of the range in the homeward trade in 1965, that one member, and there was only one, was incapable of replacing any capital consumption out of current gross profit in that year. In

Table 8.19 *Europe–Australia Conference Group. 'Mean' and 'range' of profitability of individual British member lines*

Outward Voyages   **Homeward Voyages**

A Gross Margin. (Gross profit per £ of gross Revenue. New pence)

	Mean	Range			Mean	Range		
		High	Low	H–L		High	Low	H–L
1958	25.4	30.9	17.0	13.9	14.8	20.7	9.4	11.3
1961	19.6	26.5	13.4	13.1	15.7	22.6	5.5	17.1
1965	17.6	27.4	8.5	18.9	8.2	13.1	−1.0	14.1
1968	25.1	33.4	18.7	14.7	17.0	25.3	7.1	18.2

B Net Profit per B/L ton carried (£s)

	Mean	Range			Mean	Range		
		High	Low	H–L		High	Low	H–L
1958	1.58	2.50	0.25	2.25	0.44	1.86	−0.79	2.65
1961	0.97	1.60	0.09	1.51	0.99	2.69	−0.88	3.57
1965	1.07	2.90	−0.64	3.54	−0.34	0.70	−1.91	2.61
1968	2.75	4.46	1.41	3.05	1.91	4.35	−1.07	5.42

C Net Margin (Net profit per £ of gross revenue. New pence)

	Mean	Range			Mean	Range		
		High	Low	H–L		High	Low	H–L
1958	13.3	21.1	2.1	19.0	2.3	10.0	−5.1	15.1
1961	7.7	16.4	0.7	15.7	4.6	13.6	−8.3	21.9
1965	7.3	20.6	−4.9	25.5	−1.6	3.6	−8.1	11.7
1968	16.0	26.3	8.1	18.2	7.3	12.3	−5.1	17.4

more general terms, the relatively large allocations required for depreciation, on the replacement basis employed in this conference, tend to obscure the profitability differences between members when the gross margin is used as a measure (see Table 8.20, where measures of dispersion are applied to the three measures of profitability shown in Table 8.19.).

In terms of net profit per unit of physical output, or per unit of gross revenue, we get a more accurate view of the relative profitability of member lines at the extremes of the range in each of the four years examined. On this measure the year 1968 was the best for profitability. In the outward trade the most profitable member was 1.62 times, or 62 per cent more profitable than the average member in terms of net profit per B/L ton carried, and the least profitable member was about half as profitable as the average. In terms of net profit per £ of gross revenue the results for 1968 were very nearly the same as this.

Profitability difference between members at the extremes of the range widen considerably in a poor year. In 1965 unit costs rose much faster than freight charges and profitability was generally much lower than in 1968, and it was particularly low in the homeward trade. But taking first the outward trade, we find that the leading member's profitability (in terms of net profit per B/L ton carried) was 171 per cent greater than the average, while the trailing member was making a loss on every ton he carried and this rate of loss was more than half as much as the average rate of profit. In the homeward trade there was in this year a loss on average for the British lines as a group. The leading member achieved a low rate of profit, but the trailing member's loss was 5.6 times as great as the average.

Shipping conferences are cartel-type organisations which set common prices and share out the available business between members. The profitability of the weakest member must be of considerable importance in conference price making processes, whether these are based on the 'formula' method (discussed in Chapters 3 and 4) used in the Europe—Australia trades, or on the less formalised methods used in other conferences, for example, the rough estimates of cost changes gathered and analysed by the Far Eastern Freight Conference as described in Chapter 4, Section 2(e).

It has been shown earlier in this section that the outward trade is practically free of influences upon profitability which stem from differences in the revenue yield per unit of cargo loaded by individual member lines. In this direction of trade in the years 1958, 1961, 1965 and 1968, the strongest member's rate of profit, as measured by net profit per £ of gross revenue, was respectively 1.6, 2.1, 2.8 and 1.6 times the average rate of profit, and in the same terms the weakest member's rate of profit or loss was 0.16, 0.09, a rate of loss more than half as great as the average rate of profit, and 0.51 respectively.

So profitability *differentials* within this membership are wide and of course the *average* rate of profit conceals them. These differences are even wider in the home-ward trade, partly because the average gross yield of cargo lifted by individual members varies more widely than it does in the outward trade.

Although it is the strongest and weakest member's rate of profit which is of particular interest and importance in price making, it is also necessary to calculate the extent of dispersion of the rates of profit of all members about their mean. This calculation is needed because the extremes might be very extreme and all the other members' rates of profit might be closely bunched around the mean. So in Table 8.20 is shown the *standard deviation*[1] from the mean net profit rate for the British member lines trading regularly in the Europe—Australia Conference Group in the period 1958—68.

Also shown in this table are the related *coefficients of variation*. This coefficient is the *standard deviation* for each series divided by the *mean* for that series. Its use is to enable comparisons to be made between series which have means which are widely different from one another in different years, as is the case here.

It will be remembered that it is in the outward trade that relative profitability is uninfluenced by differences between members in the average gross freight revenue they receive per B/L ton of cargo they carry because these differences are very small.[2] The outward trade is examined first.

1   The standard deviation is the square root of the sum of the squares of the differences of each rate of profit from the mean, or arithmetic average, rate.

2   In Table 8.15. it is shown that the coefficient of variation in respect of this series is very low. At its highest, in 1961, it is 4.1 per cent, and is only 2.0 per cent in 1968.

Table 8.20 *Europe–Australia Conference Group. Standard deviation and coefficient of variation for two measures of net profitability. British member lines*

	Net profit per B/L ton carried			Net margin (Net profit in new pence per £ of gross revenue)		
	1	2	3	4	5	6
	Mean	Standard Deviation	Coefficient of variation (%)	Mean	Standard Deviation	Coefficient of variation (%)
	(£'s)	(£'s)	Col 2 ÷ Col 1	(new pence)	(new pence)	Col 5 ÷ Col 4
A. Outward Voyages						
1958	1.58	0.71	44.9	13.28	6.08	45.8
1961	0.97	0.77	79.4	7.69	5.91	76.9
1965	1.07	1.09	101.9	7.29	7.96	109.2
1968	2.75	1.03	37.3	16.01	6.11	38.2
B. Homeward Voyages						
1958	0.44	0.91	206.8	2.26	5.09	225.2
1961	0.99	1.02	103.0	4.59	6.24	134.9
1965	−0.34	1.07	314.7	−1.59	4.95	311.3
1968	1.91	1.59	83.2	7.28	6.25	85.9

In good years for profitability[1] in the outward trade, such as 1968 and, to a lesser extent 1958, the coefficient of variation, V, is just under 40 per cent. In 1961, the year selected as typical in terms of net profitability of the whole period 1958–68, this coefficient rises to nearly 80 per cent; and in a bad year, such as 1965, the pressure of rapidly rising costs spreads out the performance of individual members into an extensive array of profitability ratios which are dispersed to the extent of over 100 per cent in relation to their mean.

In the homeward trade, where net profitability is influenced by the differences between members in the average gross freight revenue which each receives per B/L ton of cargo carried (see Tables 8.15 and 8.16), the coefficients of variation of net profit are between 2 and 3 times greater than they are in the corresponding years in the outward trade, and the coefficient of variation rises to over 300 per cent in the poor year, 1965.

Even if we discount the fact, which has been shown earlier, that the highest and lowest net profitability performances within this group of British members are even more dispersed about the mean than are the members as a whole (as measured by V), a dispersion of 80 per cent in an average year, rising to 100 per cent in a poor year, is a substantial degree of variation of net profitability of members.

If we now take the average variation (from Table 8.20) of the representative good and poor years for net profitability it may be noticed that in outward trade net profits are dispersed to the extent of about 70 per cent, and homewards by about 199 per cent around the mean. This is a substantial degree of general dispersion of profitability among British member lines.

We must now recall that the differences between the mean rate of profit and the extreme high and low profit earners in the British group is even greater. In section C of Table 8.19. are shown the highest and lowest net margins of profit of British

---

1 As best measured comparatively between years by the net margin (shown in the right hand section of Table 8.20).

members. In operations in the year 1961, which represents average performance over the period 1958—68, the highest ratio in outward trade was 2.1 times the mean ratio, and the lowest ratio was only 9 per cent of the mean, so the leading member's rate of net profit per £ of gross revenue was 23 times that of the least profitable member. In a poor year, such as 1965, the leading member's rate of *net profit* was 2.8 times the mean, and at 20.6 new pence per £ of gross revenue was greater than the average *gross margin* for all British members (which was 17.6 new pence of gross profit per £ of gross revenue). In 1965 the least profitable member made a loss of 4.9 new pence on each £ of gross revenue.

It may be concluded that the second hypothesis we set out to test in this section of the chapter is validated, that is:

'That freight shipping services organised by a specified conference group lead to widely dispersed results in terms of the net profitability of individual conference members.'

This conclusion requires further specification as follows:

(i) The general degree of dispersion of the rate of net profitability among individual conference members is wide in the terms measured by the coefficient of variation (the standard deviation divided by the mean or arithmetic average rate of profitability). It is even wider when the extremes of high and low profitability are considered in relation to the mean profitability of the group, and it is this latter conclusion which is particularly relevant to conference price formation.

(ii) The dispersion about the mean of the net profit rates of individual conference members is greater in years of lower average profitability than it is in years of higher average profitability among members.

(iii) The dispersion about the mean of the net profit rates of individual conference members is greater in homeward trade than it is in outward trade. This is due in part to the much greater variation between members in the average gross freight revenue they receive per B/L ton of cargo they carry in the homeward trade. In the outward trade the variation in this factor is uninfluential upon the variations between members in their net profitability.

4. Implications of the dispersion of individual members' net profit rates for conference price making.

The shipping conference type of industrial combination, as represented by this example, embraces members which differ widely from one another in their net profitability. These profitability differences do not necessarily reflect a similar range of differences in the efficiency with which each line is managed. In attempting to trace the causes of the differences in relative net profitability we examined the following possibly causative factors.

　　a. Scale of operations in the trade.
　　b. Time spent in port.
　　c. Port charges.
　　d. Replacement allowances per £ of gross freight revenue.
　　e. Capital utilisation.
　　f. Gross freight revenue per B/L ton of cargo loaded.

In outward trade the only one found to be explanatory of net profitability was d. In homeward trade d. and f. were found to be of explanatory value. Factor f. has already been discussed and its influence is obvious and direct. Factor d., relative replacement allowances per unit of gross revenue, reflects the relative age structure of the fleets employed in the trade by each member and, following from that, differences in the average speed of vessels. We have not attempted to trace the wide differences in net profitability in outward trade any further back than this.

The implications for conference price making of the wide range of differences in net profitability among member lines must be that some pressures for higher freight rates do arise from members with relatively low rates of net profit (or even losses in some cases) at times when other members are making profits which are two or three times the mean rate of profit, and it is the conference organisation which enables this to occur.

A further important point, in the nature of a qualification to this conclusion, arises in the homeward trade where, for the reasons already explained, variations between the profitability of individual member lines is particularly great. If revenue pooling is applied to gross earnings in such situations, as it has been in these conferences in the homeward direction in the years 1966, 1967 and 1968,[1] then the variations between members in their profitability is reduced, and so is the pressure for higher freight rates from members with low rates of profit. On the other hand, as has been shown in Chapter 3, revenue pooling is accompanied by 'rationalisation', that is, the trade from certain smaller ports is handled by one or perhaps two members only and differentials in their gross revenue due to this allocative process is subject to balancing out by the pooling arrangements. Such rationalisation results in less choice by shippers than would otherwise be the case, and so in less non-price competition generally within the conference. When pooling is applied, variations in net profitability within the conference are reduced and along with this result goes a reduction in pressure for price (freight rate) increases from members with lower than average profitability. Against this general economic gain, for such it must be counted, should be set the rather intangible economic losses which come from the accompanying reduction in inter-conference non-price competition and reduction in consumer choice.

In sum, the conference system embraces an extensive range of net profitability among its members. Since, in this period of ten years in which conference operations are studied, none of the weaker conference members dropped out, and generally conference members continue in business over very long periods, it may be concluded that one effect of conference operations is to protect the weaker members and in so doing the average profitability is pulled down; but, as has been shown, this average conceals rates of profit which are much higher. Since prices are common and the average gross revenue of members per B/L ton is approximately the same in outward trade; the higher net profitability of some members in that trade reflects lower unit costs. These, in turn, may be due to many different reasons which have already been discussed.

---

1 The financial effects of pooling are not included in the analyses made in this chapter.

Summary

1. Physical capital resource utilisation is measured in terms of both load factor and ship's time utilisation in the UK/Continent—Australia Conference trade. On average for both directions of this trade utilisation ratios for British member lines for the representative years 1958, 1961, 1965 and 1968 range from 83.1 per cent to 91.4 per cent. These percentages may be compared with capital utilisation ratios for nineteen British industries in the same years, where the range is from 89.6 per cent to 97.5 per cent.

2. The share of British member lines in the total trade of this conference group ranges from 70.0 per cent of the total cargo of 3.44 million bill of lading tons carried in 1958 to 55.6 per cent of the total of 3.62 million B/L tons in 1968. The load factor and time utilisation ratios of non-British member lines are slightly better than the corresponding British ratios, so it may be concluded that on the basis of this substantial sample of conference trade the capital resources employed — £84 million at replacement prices in 1968 — are utilised at a level which is below, but not greatly below the average ratio of capital utilisation in British industry in the same years.

3. The high degree of continuity of conference shipping operations, which is entailed by the utilisation ratios given above implies a well-organised system of of linking the end of one voyage with the start of the next. Our investigation into inter-conference membership links confirms the existence of a closely integrated web of membership links into conferences covering contiguous areas.

4. Members of 'main route' outward conferences will nearly always also be members of the corresponding homeward conference which covers the route in the reverse direction. Shipowners who are members in one direction only get home by their membership of cross-trade conferences which link them into other main route conferences which enables them to complete their circuits. Cross-trade conferences are also joined by shipowners who are members of main route conferences covering both directions of trade; this is done particularly in cases where the main route trades are unbalanced for seasonal or other reasons.

5. The long-established shipping lines from developed, industrialised countries are usually very widely connected in terms of conference membership. The more recently formed shipping lines from developing countries and other countries began with less extensive but viable membership links, and there is evidence that such members do grow by establishing further links into more conferences.

6. The profitability of the UK/Continent—Australia conference group, as measured by the rate of return on actual physical capital employed (in the form of existing ships and new ships on order and under construction, all at cost less depreciation) was 5.8 per cent annum on average over the period 1958—68. The Rochdale average figure for UK owned and registered 'liners basically cargo' on the same definition over the same period was only 2.5 per cent per annum. On an alternative capital and profit definition 'UK liners basically cargo' had a rate of return of 3.1 per cent and 'all British industries' a rate of 13.4 per cent over this period. This conference

group is therefore considerably more profitable on average than all UK cargo liners, but for both groups the rate of return is very far below that of 'all British industries' as defined.

7. In terms of physical capital utilisation the conference group which has been studied uses the large amount of physical capital it employs to a reasonably full degree in comparison with other British industries and there is not very much variation between members in this respect.

8. A maintained high level of capital utilisation is a necessary but not a sufficient condition of efficient operation, and when various financial measures of efficiency are applied to the same conference group it is found that not only is profitability very low, in comparison with other British industries, but it also varies widely between members. If capital utilisation by members had been at a lower level, profitability would inevitably have been even worse than it was. It has been shown that relative profitability is very low indeed for the weaker members.

9. The general dispersion of the rates of net profitability among individual conference members is wide, as measured by the coefficient of variation. It is also wide when the extremes of the profitability range are considered in relation to the mean profitability of the group.

10. The dispersion of the net profitability rates of individual members is greater in years of lower average profitability than it is in years of higher average profitability, and it is greater in the homeward trade than it is in the outward trade. This latter finding is due in part to the wide differences between members in the average gross freight revenue they receive per bill of lading ton of cargo they carry in the homeward direction. In the outward trade the differences between members in respect of this factor is very small and is found to be uninfluential upon the relative net profitability of individual members.

11. Since members make prices in common, and the average unit revenue of each member is approximately the same in the outward trade as is also capital utilisation, the wide range of high and low net profitability of individual members in this trade reflect wide variations in unit costs.

12. In the ten year period studied, 1958–1968, none of the weaker members has dropped out of the conference group studied in this chapter, and generally conference members continue in business over long periods of time . When this finding is coupled with that given under paragraph 11, it may be concluded that the conference operates, as do similar combinations in other industries, to ensure the financial viability of all members. In doing so the average profitability of the group is pulled down, but it has been shown that this average conceals some rates of profit which are far above it.

13. On the other hand the conference works to ensure that members with less fortunate experiences in terms of the average unit revenue per B/L ton of cargo loaded are compensated by more fortunate members. This is done by a system of 'rationalisation' and 'pooling'. This works to reduce the differences between members in their net profitability when these differences are due to this cause, and thereby the pressure by low profitability members for freight rate increases is reduced.

9   Conclusion

Introduction

1. A summary or note of conclusion has been written at the end of each chapter of this book. In this final chapter the main conclusions are drawn together and the principal arguments are presented. Wherever it seems appropriate reference is made to substantiating or otherwise relevant evidence which is set out in the main body of the text. For convenience some supporting material is included in square brackets in this conclusion.

2. This is a study of 'deep sea' (long distance) freight shipping conferences in respect of their origins in the last century, their development, recent and present organisation and economic practices. The work is both descriptive and analytical and is founded upon more information about conferences than it has been possible to assemble before.

3. It has not been our aim to reach prescriptive solutions to problems in the general field of maritime economics, but rather to attempt to add to the previously somewhat slender body of knowledge and analysis of this large and very complex sector of the world shipping industry.

4. In geographical terms the conferences studied here are those which cover the 'general cargo'[1] trade in both directions between Europe and Australia, Europe and the Far East, and Europe and India/Pakistan. Main route conferences in these trades number 35, and a further 32 cross-trade conferences covering trade connected in some way with the main routes are also included. These are 'closed'[2] conferences. The estimated world total of shipping conferences is 360, inclusive of 'open'[2] conferences.

5. In terms of tonnage of cargo carried the main route conferences, in the three trades which have been named, carried approximately 14.7 million Bill of Lading tons in 1965.

A. Formation, Development and Organisation of Shipping Conferences

6. On the basis of the investigations we have carried out in the course of this study, it seems to us that one of the most significant factors which led to the formation of shipping conferences was the very rapid increase in the supply of shipping space relative to the demand for that space. This increase in supply was due to a number of factors, but the most important was the technical development in ships; not only

---

1   That is, all cargo which does not normally travel in bulk in complete shiploads.

2   Defined in Chapter 1 p.1 and footnote.

were larger ships being built but more cubic capacity became available through improvement to engine design (Chapter 2. Section 1.b.), the improved engines enabled ships to reduce the time taken for their journeys and the opening of the Suez Canal was a further factor which enabled journeys to and from the East to be completed in a much shorter time. Increases in trade were of course also taking place, but on the estimates we have made the increase in effective shipping capacity far outstripped the increase in demand (Figure 1, Chapter 2).

7. The excess supply of shipping space relative to the demand was reflected in the late 19th century in falling freight rates and profits as well as in the fierce competition for cargo which took place. The shipping industry was not the only industry which was to experience competitive pressures due to the technical changes which were taking place at the end of the 19th and early 20th centuries, and the response of the shipping industry in forming a combination of owners to regulate both prices and 'output' was not unique. But whereas in some other industries more complete monopolistic organisation was possible through forward and backward integration, this was not a feature of the shipping industry and conferences of shipowners have never enjoyed complete monopoly of their markets. What is remarkable about the system of shipping conferences is that the organisation has remained intact and almost unchanged for nearly 100 years.

8. In their early organisation the conferences in the Eastern trades differed in the degree to which they exercised control over their members in the extent of their ties with shippers. They did for the most part, however, follow the practices of combinations in other industries; that is, they fixed the price of their output (service), they attempted to regulate the total output and the output of each individual member, and they gave incentives in the form of rebates to their customers (the shippers) to use their service exclusively. Forms of output sharing varied from control over the number of sailings and ports of call to the sharing of revenue obtained for a large part of the cargo carried. The shipping conferences did not, and still do not, have a complete monopoly of shipping services; some alternative means of shipment were and are available, chiefly from aspiring conference members. Nor have conference members always been convinced of the advantages (for them) of a common tariff and limited sailings. Throughout their existence conferences have had to cope with recalcitrant members and with shippers who were dissatisfied – in one way or another – with the service offered.

9. There has been no radical change in the conference organisation, however, since its inception, but pressures have been exerted in one form or another so that gradual changes have taken place both in the internal organisation of conferences and in their relations with shippers.

10. Detailed information on conference organisation and practice has not previously been available. We have seen (Chapter 3, Section 2.a.) how the development of the areas and ports which conferences serve has been partly historical and partly economic. The organisation of conference services into different types of ports is a post-war development and the rationalisation of services, although an aim since the early days of conferences, has been more successfully achieved in the last 15 years.

11. Up to the 1950's, the importance of British shipowners in the conference system was still evident, but since that time the increase in membership of national flag lines (state-owned or state-subsidised lines) has meant that British shipowners

have become relatively less important and their influence on the conference system has somewhat diminished. Physically most conference organisations remain in the UK.

12. Competition from 'outsider' shipping lines have provided shippers with alternative means of shipment, although on a much less regular basis, but the ways in which conferences have dealt with such competition have undergone some change. Such practices as selective rate cutting, 'port blanketing' and other devices (Chapter 3. Section 2.c.) have been used in the postwar period but conferences have been reluctant to take action against individual shippers. A notable feature of the 1960's was the establishment of conciliation machinery to settle disputes not only between shippers and the conference but between the conference and aspiring members. This conciliation machinery has been assisted by the formation of shippers' councils in the UK and some European countries, but although this form of shippers' organisation has developed it is not yet very widespread except in Australia (where it is very comprehensive) and in some parts of the Far East.

13. The system of output sharing and revenue pooling has reached a high level of sophistication and is now more comprehensive than at any time in the history of conferences. Although conferences were started by British shipowners, they are now international organisations and are a good example of agreements across national boundaries that have operated, for the most part successfully, for a long period of time. What we do not yet know, however, is how far the conference system will have to undergo radical change as a result of the introduction of container ships. It may be that this development will provide another watershed in the organisation of deep sea transport.

B. Price Formation

General price changes

14. Conferences change prices chiefly in two ways. First, they make general, across-the-board changes by a stated, single percentage which applies to all, or nearly all, freight rates listed in the tariff. Second, they change individual prices in negotiation with individual shippers, or associations of shippers. Sometimes these individual rate changes take place at the time of a general rate change but also at other times. They also make freight rates for new products, and products not previously shipped, as they come forward for shipment.

15. A considerable volume of evidence has been assembled, and reported in Chapter 4, to show that general rate changes are substantially cost-based, rather than demand-based. The processes by which conferences collect, collate, and analyse cost data from individual member lines is fully described.

16. Individual exemptions from a general rate increase are fairly common. Individual exceptions which involve raising some rates by more than the percentage of a general rate increase are rare.[1] In both cases such prices are demand-based. That is to say, the pricing process respects the elasticity of demand, and other demand conditions, for the transport service in the individual case, whether that is reflective of the elasticity of demand for the product shipped in the market area of destination,

---

1 An example is given in Chapter 6. Case history 3.

or of the proportion which the freight charge bears to the unit c.i.f. value of the commodity, or whether it reflects the elasticity of supply of the product shipped.

17. There are also some higher rates of freight charged for cargo of particular types. Examples are hazardous cargo and cargo which requires refrigeration. There are also extra charges, known as 'additionals', for cargo requiring the use of heavy lifting gear, transhipment or direct delivery to 'outports' (ports not on the schedule of regular calls.) All these particular, extra components of final freight rate are cost-based.

18. So, general, across-the-board freight rate changes by conferences are essentially cost-based (sometimes called the 'cost of service' pricing principle), with some modifications which are demand-based (also known as the 'value of service' pricing principle), and a few which are in the nature of cost-based extras. Relative conference prices are a separate matter. Our conclusions on them are given under paragraphs 32—43.

Price bargaining in individual cases

19. Freight rate bargaining takes place between conferences and shippers acting individually or, in some instances, collectively. This process occurs at any time, usually on the initiative of the shipper. A number of case histories of rate bargaining are studied in some depth in Chapter 6. The factors which appear from our studies of cases to be important influences upon the formation of freight rates in bargaining of this type have been related to theoretical considerations which are explained below.

a. The higher is the cost of transport measured as a proportion of the total landed c.i.f. price of the commodity shipped the higher is the elasticity of demand for the transport service concerned, and *vice versa.*

b. The price elasticity of demand for the service of transport varies directly, but not proportionately, with the price elasticity of demand for the goods shipped by such services into markets in the area of destination.

c. The greater the competition in the product market the higher is the price elasticity of demand in that market and, following from b. above, the higher is the price elasticity of demand in the related transport service market and *vice versa.*

d. The elasticity of demand for the service of transport varies directly, but not proportionately, with the elasticity of supply of the product shipped.

The evidence from the case histories of individual freight bargaining shows that attention is paid to relationships a., b. and c. above. The evidence about relationship d. is inconclusive.

Price movements

20. The three conference groups which have been studied raised their basic rates of freight (excluding surcharges) on average for *both* directions of trade (outward and homeward) by 6.8 per cent per annum over the period 1948—1970 (Chapter 5, Table 5.4).

21. Because of exemptions from general rate increases, and individual rate bargaining (see above paragraphs 16 and 19) which occurs at other times and which hardly ever lead to a rate increase and frequently result in rate reductions, the above

213

unweighted trend in conference freight rates is overstated. A test of this has been made by taking account of all freight rate changes in one conference. Weights were then allocated according to the freight revenue yield of each commodity (Chapter 5. Section 2). The result is an average weighted rate of change of 6.5 per cent per annum compared with an unweighted movement of 6.9 per cent over the period 1948–1970. So, on this evidence, freight rate changes which are unweighted in this sense overstate the true movement in conference freight rates, but not by very much.

22. From 1948 to 1970 basic, unweighted conference freight rates rose by 169 per cent, and rates including a surcharge (due to Suez Canal closure) by 187 per cent. Over the same period U.K. retail prices rose by 137 per cent and wholesale prices of all manufactured goods by 103 per cent. World commodity prices barely changed at all between the beginning and the end of this period and time-chartered tramp shipping rates rose by 34 per cent. The weighting of conference rate increases, in the way referred to above, would, if generally applied, reduce the combined conference basic rate increase from 169 to about 159 per cent over the period 1948 to 1970.

23. Conference freight rates have risen faster in the outward direction of trade than they have in the homeward direction.[1] Over the period 1948–60 outward, basic, unweighted freight rates for the three conference groups rose by 6.78, and homeward rates by 6.21, per cent per annum. For the next period, 1960–1970, the difference between the movements of the two sets of freight rates was less: 5.27 per cent per annum outwards and 5.08 homewards. The price movement homewards as a proportion of outwards was 91.6 per cent in the first period and 96.3 in the second period.

24. Trade in the homeward direction from the Far East is very largely in industrial goods. If we omit both directions of the Europe–Far East conference group from our calculation, we get a price movement homewards as a proportion of outwards of 81.8 per cent in the first period and 94.4 per cent in the second. So, the general cargo trade outwards from developed, industrialised countries has faced a faster rise in conference freight rates than the general cargo trade outwards from less developed economies. This finding is linked (at paragraph 66) with others given later in this summary.

25. Time-chartered tramp vessels fully compete with conference liners only over the relatively narrow section of the market for conference shipping services which comprises some 'parcels' of bulk commodities in the form of raw or semi-manufactured materials, and manufactured goods which normally travel in amounts sufficient to fill a whole ship. Time-chartered hiring rates fluctuated very widely over the period 1948–70, particularly so in the first half of this period, due in large part to the Korean war and the first Suez crisis. On a comparison of time-chartered tramp and conference line rates, the liner rates have risen much faster than time-charter tramp rates over the whole period.[2] In the more recent period, 1960–70, both sets of prices moved up at about the same rate, with some evidence pointing in the same

1 See Figure 6 in Chapter 5.

2 On a comparison of the gradients of the fitted least squares regression line.
See Chapter 5, Table 5.4.

214

direction as the results of earlier research[1] which found that conference liner rate movements lag movements in tramp rates. (See Chapter 5, Table 5.5.)

26. A comparison, in terms of absolute cost levels, of operating a conference freight liner and a time-chartered liner (not a bulk cargo carrier) of similar type, size and performance and carrying a similar amount of cargo over the Europe—Far East trade route in both directions, revealed that, subject to the narrowness of the data base, the cost of the conference liner, £9.92 per bale ton of space available, was closely similar to the average total cost of hiring and operating, including all 'on-costs', a time-chartered vessel under conference conditions, which was £9.67. The hiring rate included in this calculation is the average of the highest and lowest rates over the year to July 1971. Assuming other involved costs unchanged, the highest and lowest hiring rates imply a highest total unit cost of £11.29 per bale ton and a lowest cost of £8.05 for the chartered vessel.

27. Conference freight rates are very much more stable than time-chartered shipping rates. On a precise calculation of the relative degrees of variation from average it is shown (Chapter 5, Table 5.11) that the time-chartered rates varied from their average by about twice as great a percentage as conference liner freight rates did from their average.

Nature of demand for conference shipping services

28. Market demand for conference shipping services may be divided in three sectors. At the top end of the range of prices (freight rates) competition from air freight transport services introduces greater price elasticity into the demand for conference services to commodities which are chiefly of very high unit value. At the lower end of the scale of price, competition, and therefore greater price elasticity, is again met by conferences, this time in the form of the services offered by specialised bulk carriers and time-chartered tramp vessels. In between these upper and lower market sectors lies an extensive middle ground. Here the conference reigns very largely supreme and unchallenged. Air transport and independent tramp vessels compete with conferences only over the narrow extreme fringes of the whole market, and thus may be seen as largely 'non-competing groups'.

29. In this middle ground the market is very fragmented, due to lack of buyers' knowledge, and demand is relatively inelastic. In the higher-middle ranges, below the sector where air freight transport competition enters, demand is particularly inelastic because the rate of freight is a relatively small proportion of the c.i.f. landed unit value of the commodities shipped. On the same principle, in the lower-middle range, above the sector where competition from bulk carriers enters, demand is more elastic. [These propositions are founded upon Marshall's law of derived demand[2] and are supported by evidence assembled in the course of this research[3]].

Price differentiation

30. Shipping conferences differentiate between their customers in the prices they

---

1 D.L. McLachlan op.cit., at Chapter 5, p. 111.

2 Developed and applied to transport problems by A.A. Walters, op.cit. at Chapter 6, p. 140.

3 Presented in Chapter 6, and briefly summarised above at paragraph 19.

charge. This practice is possible because, first, the service of shipping is not re-sale-able; second, entry to 'closed' shipping conferences is restricted; and, third, because buyers' knowledge of the market is generally limited to that section of it which is concerned with the shipment of their own and their competitors' products.

31. On a measure of price differentiation which is in terms of the number of listed commodities per separate price quoted in the freight tariff, it is found that conferences carrying cargo outwards from developed, industrialised countries are on average less differentiated with respect to price (39 commodities and commodity groups per separate price) than are the corresponding conferences homewards on the same trade routes (5 commodities per separate price).[1] These latter trades are largely, but not wholly, from less economically developed areas of the world. Partly this difference is due to the administrative difficulties and cost involved in making separate prices for several thousand separate commodities included in the tariffs covering trade outwards from highly industrialised countries,[2] where a very wide variety of goods is involved; in the trade from developing countries a much smaller number of specific commodities and shippers are involved.

The structure of relative prices

32. The practice of price differentiation by shipping conferences produces a wide band of relative prices. The motives and criteria which guide the price makers are of great interest, and those who have previously studied the economics of shipping conferences have almost invariably been particularly drawn to this aspect. In this respect we are no exception.

33. The conceptual and practical basis for our computable model of the structure of relative prices is fully described in Chapter 7, where the reader will also find a summary of the conclusions reached from its applications. A brief note of the main features of the model and a highly condensed summary of the main results of applying it to conference data are given below.

34. The price model finally employed was developed from a series of experimental and iterative processes. The relative rate of freight charged per B/L ton for any consignment carried by a conference was found to be a function of the following variables, among others

    a. The unit value of the consignment, per bill of lading ton.

    b. The weight or measurement tonnage (according to whichever is used as a basis for rate setting) of the consignment, where this exceeds 50 W or M tons (as the case may be).

    c. The ratio of measurement to weight tons of the consignment, wherever this exceeds 2.

    d. Certain special characteristics of consignments wherever these are relevant to price setting, including hazardous nature, and requirements for refrigeration, cool chamber stowage, and safe stowage for consignments of very high unit value.

A constant term was added to these variable terms of the model.

---

1 See Table 4.1 in Chapter 4.

2 The greater use of 'block pricing' in these conferences reflects this problem.

35. This model was applied separately to the cargoes of five conference vessels sailing in various conferences on routes covered by this study. A total of 4,359 consignments were included, and a total of approximately 15,000 observations were computed.

36. It was found that the model had much greater explanatory value when it was applied to cargoes which were very largely composed of manufactured goods, than it had when it was applied to cargoes composed chiefly of industrial materials and food products. (see Table 7.5 in Chapter 7). [The value of $\overline{R}^2$, the coefficient of determination, for the application of the model to the cargo of PRIAM (sailed ex-Liverpool outwards in the Far Eastern Freight Conference) was 0.520 with a constant term of $+2.81$. While in the opposite direction of trade on the same route the application of the model to the cargo of ANCHISES (sailed ex-Singapore and Malaysian ports homewards to Europe) produced a value of $\overline{R}^2$ of only 0.031, and a constant term of $+10.76$. The PRIAM's cargo, yielding an average of £17.22 of gross freight revenue per B/L ton was composed very largely of manufactured goods. The cargo of ANCHISES, on the other hand, yielded an average of £11.98 of gross freight revenue per B/L ton and was chiefly composed of primary commodities — industrial raw materials largely, and some food products. For ANCHISES the variable terms of the model were of small explanatory value, both individually and collectively.]

37. Although, as has been shown (paragraph 31), price differentiation is practised to a higher degree in homeward conference trades from developing countries, and this one is no exception, the commodities travelling cannot bear high freight rates due, among other factors, to their relatively low unit value. In such trades as these the scope for the cross-subsidisation of even lower unit value commodities is not great.

38. In its application to the cargoes of five conference liners, the price model indicated that the unit value of individual consignments was in all cases statistically significant and explanatory, in some degree, of the relative rates of freight in a positive sense — the higher the unit value the higher the rate of freight. In the case of ANCHISES, see example at paragraph 36, the degree of explanatory value, although significant, was very low.

39. The variable of consignment size was in all cases significant and of negative sign. The price makers do take some account of the amount of tonnage moving and some, but not all, commodities which move in large quantities also move in large consignments. It is consignment size which is recognised by the model.

40. The measurement/weight ratio, the M/W term in the model, was statistically significant in all cases except one and was of positive sign. Analyses of other evidence (given in Chapter 7) confirm that the higher is M/W the greater is the loss of stowage *per measurement ton,* and that this effect is reflected in higher relative rates of freight. This effect is not outweighed by the tendency for unit values to be lower the higher is M/W.

41. The variables which represent other particular physical characteristics of commodities are all significant and of positive influence upon the rate of freight.

42. In sum, unit value explains more of the structure of relative conference prices than any other variable in the model, and more than all the other variables together. Unit value accounts for about two-thirds of the total explained by the model and

the other identified factors together for the remaining third. This remains broadly true whether the other factors are associated in the model with unit value or whether their explanatory worth is separately assessed without the unit value term being associated with them in the model (Table 7.6 in Chapter 7).

43. The unit value variable is a demand-based factor, and all the other variables which have been identified are cost-based. So it is concluded that, subject to the limitation imposed by the degree of explanatory worth of the model, the structure of relative conference prices owes more to demand-based than it does to cost-based factors. General movements of conference prices, on the other hand, are predominantly cost-based (see paragraph 15). It must, however, be recognised that the price model offers only a part of an explanation of the structure of relative conference prices. There are most probably other, so far unidentified factors which may have influence upon this structure. Where, as in the case of ANCHISES, the model explains little, then the large value of the constant term in the model suggests that basic unit cost, which is not greatly differentiated by the other terms in this model, is the chief determinant of price; but it must be noticed that this is not to offer any explanation of the structure of *relative* prices.

Conference prices related to costs

44. The short run cost structure of conference liner operation, and indeed of all ship operation, is distinguished for its very high proportion of fixed, inescapable costs. This entails steeply falling (and rising) average and marginal cost curves. In these circumstances great importance attaches to optimum capacity utilisation; a level which is just below the maximum possible utilisation of physical space because of the high unit loading and unloading costs of getting the last five per cent or so of cargo into and out of the vessel.

45. Even more important is the long run cost structure of a freight conference liner shipping industry serving a particular 'deep sea' trade. Under these conditions average and marginal costs are constant as a succession of liners are carefully organised onto 'the berth' by the conference, loaded (usually at or near to their optimum utilisation ratio),[1] and despatched on regular services into a network of conference trades in which the vessel's owner has previously arranged inter-connecting membership links which ensure the continuity of the vessel's employment over time.[2]

46. Unit cost and prices have been related in this study and it is shown (Chapter 4, Figure 5) that price differentiation leads to cross-subsidisation between shippers (and possibly also between their customers). Welfare gains and losses follow from this pricing practice, and this involves a re-distribution of welfare – a statement which is subject to the usual qualifications with which welfare concepts are hedged about – such qualifications do not negate the reality which is that commodities rated above average long run unit cost make possible the transport of other commodities at rates below average long run unit cost which would not otherwise travel by regular conference liner services.

47. It is shown[3] that the net profitability of outward voyages from highly

1 Load factors are given in Chapter 8, Section 1.

2 Chapter 8, Section 2.

3 In respect of one conference group. See Chapter 8, Table 8.13.

industrialised countries is *consistently* better than that of homeward voyages from much less developed economies. This is no more than suggestive that cross-subsidisation takes place from developed, industrialised economies — where high unit value manufactured goods pay relatively high freight rates — to developing economies which are linked to them by conference shipping services and where generally lower unit value commodities are shipped in the homeward direction. Although, as has been shown, price differentiation is greater in degree in the trade from developing countries, the nature of that market in terms of the preponderance of relatively low unit value commodities is such that it is not capable of bearing such high rates of freight as the trade in manufactures (see paragraph 36).

C. Some Economic Effects of Conferences

Resource use

48. Physical capital resource utilisation is assessed from a combined measure of load factor and ship's time utilisation. In the UK/Continent—Australia conference group the average of this combined measure for both directions of trade for all British members in the years 1958, 1961, and 1968 ranged from 83.1 per cent to 91.4 per cent. This performance may be compared with that of nineteen British industries in the same years, where the range was from 89.6 per cent to 97.5 per cent.

49. The share of British member lines in the total trade of this conference group ranges from a high point of 70.0 per cent of the total cargo of 3.44 million bill of lading tons carried in 1958 to a low of 55.6 per cent of the total of 3.62 million B/L tons in 1968. The load factor and time utilisation ratios of non-British member lines are slightly better than the corresponding British ratios, so it may be concluded that on the basis of this substantial sample of conference trade the considerable volume of capital resources employed — £84 million at replacement prices in 1968 — are utilised at a level which is below, but not greatly below the average ratio of capital utilisation in British industry in the same years.

50. The high degree of continuity of conference shipping operations, which is suggested by the utilisation ratios shown in paragraph 48, implies a well-organised system of linking the end of one voyage with the start of the next. Our investigation into inter-conference membership links confirms the existence of a closely integrated web of membership links into conferences covering contiguous areas.

51. Members of 'main route' outward conferences were found to be nearly always also members of the corresponding homeward conference which covers the route in the reverse direction. Shipowners who are members in one direction only get home by their membership of cross-trade conferences which link them into other main route conferences which enable them to complete their circuits. Cross-trade conferences are also joined by shipowners who are members of main route conferences covering both directions of trade; this is done particularly in cases where the main route trades are unbalanced for seasonal or other reasons.

52. The long-established shipping lines from developed, industrialised countries are usually very widely connected in terms of conference membership. The more recently formed lines from developing countries and other countries began with less extensive but viable membership links, in terms of circuit completion, and there is

evidence that such members do grow by establishing further links into more conferences.

Return upon capital employed

53. The profitability of the UK/Continent—Australia conference group, as measured by the rate of return on actual physical capital employed (in the form of ships in use and new ships on order and under construction, all at cost less depreciation) was 5.8 per cent per annum on average over the period 1958—68. The Rochdale average figure for UK owned and registered 'liners basically cargo' on the same definition over the same period was only 2.5 per cent per annum. On an alternative capital and profit definition 'UK liners basically cargo' had a rate of return of 3.1 per cent and 'all British industries' a rate of 13.4 per cent over this period. This conference is therefore considerably more profitable on average than all UK cargo liners, but for both groups the rate of return is very far below that of 'all British industries' as defined.

54. In terms of physical capital utilisation the conference group which has been studied uses the large amount of physical capital it employs to a reasonably full degree in comparison with other British industries, and there is not very much variation between members in this respect.

55. A maintained high level of capital utilisation is a necessary but not a sufficient condition of efficient operation, and when various financial measures of profitability are applied to the same conference group it is found that not only is profitability very low, in comparison with other British industries, but is also varies widely between members. If capital utilisation by members had been at a lower level, profitability would inevitably have been even worse than it was; and profitability was very low indeed for the weaker members (see Chapter 8, Table 8.19).

Range of relative net profitability of conference members

56. The general dispersion of the rates of net profitability (net profit per B/L ton carried) among individual conference members was wide. In the years 1958, 1961, 1965 and 1968 the lowest coefficient of variation among seven British members of the UK/Continent—Australia Conference Outwards was 37 per cent, and the highest 102 per cent. In the lowest case, which occurred in the year 1968 the average rate of return upon capital employed (by the whole conference) was relatively high at 12.0 per cent, while in 1965, the year of greatest dispersion of those examined, the rate of return upon conference capital in this direction of trade was relatively low at 6.4 per cent. [A regression of each member's revenue yield per bill of lading ton on net profit per B/L ton is non-significant in outward trade, and so this variation in net profitability remains to be explained by other relative factors. Those others examined include scale of operations in the trade, time spent in port, port charges, replacement allowances per £ of gross freight revenue, and capital utilisation. None is of substantial influence upon relative net profitability, except replacement allowances per £ of gross freight revenue. This factor, in turn, reflects relative age structure of fleet employed and, following from that, the average speed of ships. We have not attempted to trace the causes of the wide differences in net profitability in outward trade any further back than this.]

57. The dispersion of the net profitability rates of individual members, as measured by the coefficient of variation, is greater in years of lower average profitability than it is in years of higher average profitability, and it is greater in the homeward than it is in the outward trade. This latter finding is due in part to the wide differences between members in the average gross freight revenue they receive per bill of lading ton of cargo they carry in the homeward direction. In the outward trade the differences between members in respect of this factor is very small and is found to be uninfluential upon the relative net profitability of individual members (paragraph 56 and, for full details, Chapter 8, Section 3.b.).

58. The extremes of the range of net profit per B/L ton carried are widely separated, and this range is examined as well as the average dispersion about the mean rate of net profitability (as measured by the coefficients of variation given at paragraph 56). In a relatively good year, 1968, the highest rate of net profit per B/L ton carried outwards was £4.46, the lowest £1.41 and the mean £2.75. In a relatively poor year, 1961, the corresponding figures were £1.60, £0.09 and £0.97. In homeward trade the range is wider; for 1968 the figures were £4.35, *minus* £1.07, and £1.91; and for 1961 £0.70, *minus* £1.91 and *minus* £0.34.

59. Since members make prices in common, and the average unit revenue of each member is approximately the same in outward trade, as is also capital utilisation, the wide range of high and low net profitability of individual members in this trade reflect wide variations in unit costs. This implies pressures from weaker members in the price making process.

60. In the ten year period studied, 1958—1968, none of the weaker members has dropped out of the conference group studied in this chapter, and generally conference members continue in business over long periods of time. When this finding is coupled with that given under paragraphs 58 and 59, it may be concluded that the conference operates, as do similar combinations in other industries, to ensure the financial viability of all members. In doing so the average profitability of the group is pulled down, but it has been shown that this average conceals some rates of profit which are far above it.

61. On the other hand the conference works to ensure that members with less fortunate experiences in terms of the average unit revenue per B/L ton of cargo loaded are compensated by more fortunate members. This is done by a system of 'rationalisation' and 'pooling'. (See paragraph 13 and also Chapter 3, Section 2.d and 2.e). This works to reduce the differences between members in their net profitability when these differences are due to this cause, and thereby the pressure by low profitability members for freight rate increases is reduced.

D. Some Problems of Redistribution

62. We have no means of measuring the gains or losses due to the cross-subsidisation which arise from the differential pricing processes of shipping conferences, but it is clear that the re-distribution is arbitrary and is to be deplored on those grounds alone. Conferences are in effect taxing some of their customers and giving subsidies to others.

63. These welfare losses *tend* to be offset by welfare gains, and this type of re-distribution between customers is preferable to the re-distribution carried out by other types of monopolist which involves re-distribution from customers to monopoly

profit. It has been made clear (paragraph 53) that conferences considered as a whole do not make profits of monopoly dimensions, but it is necessary to be careful here not to beg any questions about the efficiency of conference operations from this statement.

64. In the upper middle range of conference prices in outward conferences it has been suggested (paragraph 29) that price elasticity is likely to be very low. This makes it likely, but not certain, that the differential pricing process *in this sector of the price range* ensures the 'satisfaction of marginal conditions', that is to say, no more or very few more of the goods rated in this range would travel if freight rates were lower. The same is unlikely to be true of the lower middle range of conference prices, where elasticity is greater because the freight cost forms a greater proportion of the total c.i.f. price.

65. In sum, the welfare losses due to pricing above, in some cases far above, long run marginal cost (equal to long run average cost) are partly offset by the welfare gains of cross-subsidisation Moreover, the likely satisfaction of marginal conditions in the area of welfare losses is some mitigation of those losses in respect of their indirect, loss of trade effects. On the other hand, the arbitrary re-distribution of welfare remains, and the taxing role which conferences assume is the way in which this re-distribution is carried out.

66. There is some evidence in the results of this study to support the view that not only is there cross-subsidisation between shippers within the developed, industrialised countries, but that such transfers also take place from some shippers (those who pay freight rates above the long run average cost of carriage) in developed countries to those in developing countries, linked to them by conference services, who pay rates of freight which are below the long run average cost of shipment. The evidence for this proposition may be summarised as follows:

    a. Rates of freight have moved up faster in the outward than they have in the homeward direction of trade in the post-war period. This suggests that manufactures can better bear price increases than primary products (paragraph 23).

    b. Average gross revenue per bill of lading ton is markedly higher for outward cargoes composed chiefly of manufactures than it is for homeward cargoes composed chiefly of primary commodities (other than those requiring special treatment, such as refrigeration),(paragraph 36).

    c. Application of our price model to cargoes of manufacturers shows that the unit value of goods shipped is the chief explanatory factor, accounting for about two-thirds of the total explanation offered by the model. When the same model is applied to a cargo composed largely of primary commodities being shipped to Europe from a developing country, its explanatory value is very poor, indicating that unit value (along with the other terms in the model) is of very little explanatory worth.

    d. The net profitability of a homeward conference, carrying primary commodities chiefly, was *in every year* of the period 1958–1968 lower than the net profitability of the corresponding conference outward from developed countries, which carried manufactures over the same period.

67. Primary commodities, being of relatively low unit value, cannot bear the higher freight rates charged upon high unit value manufactures. Since, for reasons given at

paragraph 29, there is a high price elasticity in the demand for the transport of goods of relatively low unit value, then the demand for the transport of primary commodities is relatively more price elastic. Furthermore, it will remain so whether or not their rates of freight are cross-subsidised, and marginal conditions cannot be satisfied in the case of this class of goods at any rate of freight in excess of zero. More of these goods will travel the lower is the rate of freight.

68. The evidence presented does suggest that much cargo under the general description of low unit value manufactures and primary commodities is carried by conferences at rates of freight which are below long run average and marginal cost. Some other evidence (presented in Chapter 4, Section 4.) supports the conclusion that occasionally 'open rated' and other very low rated cargo is carried at rates which are even lower than short run marginal cost (which includes only the cost of stevedoring, selling and marginal ship's time cost).

69. The supply of goods or services at prices *below* marginal cost can be justified on economic grounds only when such action causes substantial external benefits to arise. These externalities might either take effect as a reduction of diseconomies which are being produced by a substitute for the service concerned (see Chapter 1, p. 7 footnote (1)), or they might be in the form of benefits arising from stimulation to other economic activity leading to benefits which are greater than the loss incurred by production below cost. When shipping conferences price some of their services below the cost of carriage they are causing the second type of external effect to arise in the shape of international trade promotion. In so far as marginal conditions are satisfied on shipping services priced above the cost of carriage, and they are likely to be satisfied in many cases, then these external benefits will not then be offset by any corresponding dis-benefits. There are however some offsetting effects which arise when conferences charge, as they sometimes do, rates of freight which are very far below cost in order either to defeat actual competitors or to discourage potential competitors. Furthermore, the conference practice of pricing in common causes some mal-distribution of income and some support for conference members of relatively low economic performance.

70. Redistribution and the problems associated with it do not end with the application of a particular pattern of differentiated freight rates. The market conditions governing the transport and sale of each commodity will be influential in determining the proportions in which the total transport charge is borne by buyer and seller. This proportion will vary between each commodity and each market. All that can be stated in general terms is that the greater is the elasticity of demand in the *market for commodities* the greater will be the proportion of the freight charge that will be borne by the seller. The competitiveness of markets for the goods shipped is one of the chief determinants of price elasticity of demand. Both manufactures and primary commodities enter some markets which are highly competitive. Evidence has been presented (in Chapter 6) which shows that this occurs and that conferences do tend to give way to shippers, in both developed and developing countries, in respect of freight rates on commodities which enter markets where competition is especially great. There is also evidence of conferences giving preferential promotional freight rates to new commodities and to commodities not previously shipped into overseas markets where competition is expected to be particularly keen.

71. The provision of scheduled shipping services linking many countries necessarily

involves some multi-national organisation which can link together in a harmonious pattern the operations of many private and nationalised shipowning companies. Shipping conferences have filled this role continuously for a hundred years. Their origins were strongly influenced by the impact of technical change and their current evolution is also under influence from the same general source. It is too early yet to predict the effects of recent and current technical change in the shape of container-isation, except to point out that as the loosely-organised collective monopoly of, typically, 20 members gives place to a conference made up of fewer but much larger units, the barriers to entry rise, the ties with shippers become stronger, the extent of external competition and of internal, non-price competition both decline and there is a strong probability of larger economies of scale. Our conclusion on some redistributional effects of shipping conference operations points to some public benefits and losses without attempting a judgement as to which group outweighs the other. Recent structural changes in the shipowning industry and in shipping con-ferences seem likely to increase the potential for both gains and losses of the types we have identified.

Appendix A
Conference Membership and
Route Coverage

The purpose of this appendix is threefold. First, to name and to group together the conferences which operate in the trades which form the basis of this study; second, to provide information of the areas covered by the conferences named in the first section and to add details of their membership and the terms on which they are prepared to do business; third and last, to provide the names and areas only of 'cross trade' conferences which connect the three conference groups described earlier, and to show in respect of some representative conference members the extent of their membership of main and 'cross trade' conferences.

A. Main route conferences in the Australian and Eastern trades

I. Europe–Australia trade
    1. United Kingdom–Australia conference
    2. Outward Continent–Australia conference
    3. Australia–Europe conference

II. Europe–Far East trade
    4. The Far Eastern Freight Conference.[1]
    5. Philippines–Europe Freight Conference.[1]
    6. United Kingdom–Far Eastern Freight Conference.
    7. Italy–Far East Conference.
    8. Entente de fret en sortie de Marseille et ports annexes sur la Malaisie, la Thailand, les Philippines, Hong Kong, la Chine et Taiwan, la Coree et le Japon.
    9. Conference des Charentes.
    10. Europe–Japan Freight Conference.
    11. Spain–Far East Freight Conference.
    12. Japan–Europe Freight Conference.
    13. Sabah, Brunei and Sarawak Freight Conference.
    14. Japan–Gulf of Aden and Red Sea Ports Conference.
    15. Far East–Gulf of Aden and Red Sea Ports Conference.

III. India and Pakistan trade
    16. United Kingdom–India/Pakistan Eastbound Conference.

---

1 Covers both directions of trade, outward and homeward.

17. Continent—India/Pakistan Eastbound Conference.
18. Western Italy—India and Pakistan Conference.
19. Entente de fret en sortie des Ports du Sud de la France sur Ceylon, L'Inde et le Pakistan.
20. Chittagong and Pussur River—United Kingdom and Eire Conference .
21. Chittagong and Pussur River—Continental Conference.
22. Calcutta—United Kingdom and Eire Conference.
23. Calcutta—Continental Conference.
24. Karmahom—United Kingdom and Eire Conference.
25. Karmahom—Continental Conference.
26. Madras—Homeward Freight Conference.
27. Madras and Pondicherry—Continental Conference.
28. Madras Coast—United Kingdom and Eire Conference.
29. Madras Coast—Continental Conference.
30. Malabar Coast—United Kingdom and Eire Conference.
31. Malabar Coast—Continental Conference.
32. Tuticorin—United Kingdom and Eire Conference.
33. Tuticorin—Continental Conference.
34. Visakhapatnam—United Kingdom and Eire Conference.
35. Visakhapatnam—Continental Conference.

B. Conference route coverage, terms of business and membership
Information on these matters is given below for all the main route shipping conferences which operate in the trades to and from Europe, Australia the Far East and India and Pakistan. 'Cross trade' conferences operating on routes between Australia, the Far Eastern areas and India and Pakistan are included in the next section.

The data are as at the date shown in each case.

(A) signifies associate conference member.

1. United Kingdom—Australia Conference
Area: From United Kingdom ports to Australia and Tasmania
Terms: Contract: Tariff rate net
Non—Contract: Tariff rate plus 10%, less 10% 6 months deferred
(Rebate periods: 1 Jan—30 June and 1 July—31 Dec.)
Members (July 1971)
Actanz Line
*Associated Container Transportation (Australia)
The Australian National Line
Blue Star Line
British India Steam Navigation Co.
The Clan Group
Dolphin Line
Federal Steam Navigation Co.
The Ocean Steam Ship Co.
*Overseas Containers
Peninsular and Oriental Steam Navigation Co.

Port Line
Shaw, Savill and Albion Co.

*These are container consortia. Their membership is as follows:

ACTA   Blue Star Line
Ellerman and Bucknall
Port Line

OCL   Federal Steam Navigation Co.
The Ocean Steam Ship Co.
Peninsular and Oriental Steam Navigation Co.
Shaw, Savill and Albion Co.
The Clan Group
In addition it should be noticed that the Actanz Line is a consortium of 'conventional carriers' with the same membership as ACT. The Dolphin Line is similar and has the same membership as OCL.

2. Outward Continent–Australia Conference

Area: From Norway, Sweden, Denmark, Finland, Poland, Germany, Holland, Belgium, France, Italy and Portugal to ports in Australia.

Terms: Contract: Net Rates
Non–Contract: Rates plus 10%, less 10% 6 months deferred.
(Rebate periods: 1 Jan–30 June and 1 July–31 Dec)

Members (December 1971):

Actanz Line
A/S Det Ostasiatiske Kompagni (The East Asiatic Co.)
Associated Container Transportation (Australia)
The Australian National Line
Australia Europe Container Service (AECS)
The Baltic Steamship Co.
Compagnie des Messageries Maritimes
Dolphin Line
Ellerman and Bucknall Steamship Co.
Hapag–Lloyd Aktiengesellschaft
Jadranska Slobodna Plovidba
Koninklijke Nedlloyd
Lloyd Triestino
The Ocean Steam Ship Co.
Overseas Containers
Peninsular and Oriental Steam Navigation Co.
Port Line
Rederiaktiebologet Trans-atlantic
Scanaustral A.S.
The Scottish Shire Line
Shaw, Savill and Albion Co.
Wilh. Wilhelmsen.

3. Australia–Europe Shipping Conference

Area: From ports in Australia to ports in the Mediterranean Adriatic Sea, Aegean Sea, Turkey, Black Sea, United Kingdom and Eire, Continent (France to Germany range), Portugal and Spanish Atlantic Coast, Scandinavia and Baltic Sea.

Terms: Net Rates (no rebates).

Members (October 1971):

Actanz Line
A/S Akotieselskabet Det Ostasiatiske Kompagni (The East Asiatic Co).
Associated Container Transportation (Australia)
The Australian National Line
Australia Europe Container Service (AECS)
The Australind Steam Shipping Co.
The Baltic Steamship Co.
Blue Star Line
The Clan Group
Compagnie des Messageries Maritimes
Dolphin Line
Ellerman and Bucknall Steamship Co.
Federal Steam Navigation Co.
Hapag–Lloyd Aktiengesellschaft
Jadranska Slobodna Plovidba
Koninklijke Nedlloyd
Lloyd Triestino
The Ocean Steam Ship Co.
Overseas Containers
Peninsular and Oriental Steam Navigation Co.
Port Line
Rederiaktiebolaget Transatlantic
Scanaustral A.S.
Shaw, Savill and Albion Co.
Wilh. Wilhelmsen

4. The Far Eastern Freight Conference

Area: *Westbound.* From Korea, Hong Kong, Taiwan, the States of Singapore and Malaysia to Europe, Black Sea ports (other than U.S.S.R. ports) and all non–European ports on the Mediterranean sea and Moroccan ports on the Atlantic Ocean.

Eastbound. From Norway, Sweden, Finland, Poland, Denmark, Germany, Holland, Belgium and French ports from Dunkirk to St. Nazaire (both inclusive). Also Italian and Yugoslav ports to States of Malaya, Singapore, Thailand, Hong Kong, Taiwan and Korea.

Terms: Contract: Tariff less 9½% immediate
Non–Contract: Tariff less 10% 6 months deferred
(Rebate periods 1 Jan.–30 June and 1 July–31 Dec).

Members (September 1971):

  Ben Line Steamers
  Blue Funnel Line
   (The Ocean Steam Ship Co.
   The China Mutual Steam Navigation Co).
  Blue Star Line (Loads only at Singapore)
  Cie. Maritime des Chargeurs Reunis
  Ellerman & Bucknall Steamship Co.
  Glen Line (Glen and Shire Joint Service)
  Hapag—Lloyd Aktiengesellschaft
  Koninklijke Nedlloyd N.V.
  Lloyd Triestino S.P.A.N.
  Maersk—Kawasaki Line
  Malaysian International Shipping Corp. Berhad.
  Cie. Des Messageries Maritimes
  Mitsui OSK Lines
  Neptune Orient Lines (Singapore)
  Nippon Yusen Kaisha
  Orient Overseas Line
  A/S Det Ostasiatiske Kompagni (The East Asiatic Co).
  Peninsular & Oriental Steam Navigation Co.
  Polskie Linie Oceaniczne (Polish Ocean Lines)
  A/B Svenska Ostasiatiska Kompaniet (The Swedish East Asia Co).
  Wilh. Wilhelmsen
  Also
(A) American President Lines
(A) Companhia Nacional de Navegacao (to Portuguese Ports only)
(A) Indonesian National Lines (Loading at Singapore only)
(A) Jugoslavenska Linijska Plovidba — to Yugoslavia, Albanian, Rumanian ports, Trieste, Egypt, Syria, Lebanon, Israel, Cyprus.
(A) Lauro Line
(A) Rickmers—Linie

5. Philippines—Europe Conference

Area: *Westbound* from the Philippines to Europe, Black Sea ports (other than USSR ports) and all non-European ports on the Mediterranean Sea and Moroccan ports on the Atlantic).

  Eastbound from United Kingdom and Eire, Norway, Sweden, Finland, Poland, Denmark, Germany, Holland, Belgium and French ports from Dunkirk to St. Nazaire both inclusive, also Italian and Yugoslav ports to the Philippines.

Terms: Contract and Non—Contract rates net. (No rebates).

Members (September 1971):

  Ben Line Steamers
  Blue Funnel Line

(The Ocean Steam Ship Co.
The China Mutual Steam Navigation Co).
Cie. Maritime des Chargeurs Réunis
Ellerman & Bucknall Steamship Co.
Glen Line (Glen and Shire Joint Service)
Hapag—Lloyd Aktiengesellschaft
Koninklijke Nedlloyd N.V.
Lloyd Triestino S.p.A.N.
Maersk—Kawasaki Line
Maritime Company of the Philippines
Cie. des Messageries Maritimes
Mitsui OSK Lines
Nippon Yusen Kaisha
A/S Det Ostasiatiske Kompagni (The East Asiatic Co).
Peninsular & Oriental Steam Navigation Co.
A/B Svenska Ostasiatiska Kompaniet (The Swedish East Asia Co).
Wilh. Wilhelmsen
Also

(A) American President Lines

(A) Jugoslavenska Linijska Plovidba to Yugoslav and Albanian ports, Trieste, Port Sudan, Egypt, Syria, Lebanon, Israel and Cyprus.
Also timber to Venice.

(A) Rickmers—Linie

6. United Kingdom—Far East Freight Conference

Area: From United Kingdom and Eire ports to ports in States of Malaya and Singapore, Thailand, Hong Kong, Taiwan and Korea.

Terms: Contract: Tariff less 9½% immediate
Non—Contract: Tariff less 10% 6 months deferred
(Rebate periods: 1 Jan.—30 June and 1 July—31 Dec).
Also ex-gratia special rebate (varies with commodity and destination).

Members (September 1971):
Ben Line Steamers
Blue Funnel Line
(The Ocean Steam Ship Co.
The China Mutual Steam Navigation Co).
Ellerman & Bucknall Steamship Co.
Glen Line (Glen and Shire Joint Service)
Malaysian International Shipping Corp. Berhad.
Cie. des Messageries Maritimes
Neptune Orient Lines (Singapore)
Nippon Yusen Kaisha
A/S Det Ostasiatiske Kompagni (The East Asiatic Co).
Peninsular & Oriental Steam Navigation Co.
Also
(A) Orient Overseas Line

7. Italy—Far East Conference

Area: From Italian and Yugoslav ports to ports in Hong Kong, Japan, Korea, States of Malaya, Singapore, Philippines, Taiwan and Thailand.

Terms: Contract: Tariff rates, less 9½% immediate
Non—Contract: Tariff rates, less 10% 6 months deferred
(Rebate periods: 1 Jan.—30 June and 1 July—31 Dec).

Members (June 1971):

A/S Det Ostasiatiske Kompagni (East Asiatic Co).
Lauro Line
Hapag—Lloyd AG
Jugoslavenska Linijska Plovidba (Jugolinija)
Koninklijke Nedlloyd nv
Lloyd Triestino S.p.A.N.
Mitsui—O.S.K. Lines
Nippon Yusen Kaisha
Peninsular & Oriental Steam Navigation Co.
Rickmers—Linie
A/B Svenska Ostasiatiska Kompaniet (Swedish East Asia Co).
Wilh. Wilhelmsen

8. Entente de Fret en Sortie de Marseille et ports annexes sur la Malaisie la Thailand, les Philippines, Hong Kong, La Chine et Taiwan, la Coree et le Japon

Area: From Marseilles etc., to Malaysia, Thailand, the Philippines, Hong Kong, China, Taiwan, Korea and Japan.

Terms: Contract: Tariff rates less 9½% immediate
Non—Contract: Tariff rates less 10% 6 months deferred except for the Philippines.
(Rebate periods: 1 Jan.—30 June and 1 July—31 Dec).

Members (July 1971):

The East Asiatic Co.
Ellerman Bucknal Steamship Co.
Koninklijke Nedlloyd n.v.
Compagnie Maritime Des Chargeurs Reunis
Cie des Messageries Maritimes
Mitsui O.S.K. Lines
Nippon Yusen Kaisha
Peninsula & Oriental Steam Navigation Co.
The Swedish East Asia Co.
Wilh. Wilhelmsen

9. Conference Des Charentes

Area: From on board vessel La Rochelle Pallice, Tonnay-Charente or Bordeaux to India, Pakistan, Ceylon, Burma, Singapore and Malaya, Indonesia, Taiwan, Thailand, China, Philippines and Japan.

Terms: Net Rates
(Rebate periods: No rebates)

Members (October 1970):

The Ben Line Steamers
Bibby Bros. & Co.
Blue Funnel Line
   (Ocean Steamship Co.
   China Mutual Steam Navigation Co.
   Nederlandsche Stoomvaart Maatschappij 'Ocean')
The British India Steam Navigation Co.
Thos. & Jno. Brocklebank
Compagnie Maritime des Chargeurs Reunis
Compagnie des Messageries Maritimes
Deutsche Dampfschiffahrts—Gesellschaft 'Hansa'
The East Asiatic Company
Ellerman & Bucknall Steamship Co.
The General Steam Navigation Co.
Glen Line
Hamburg Amerika Linie
Henderson Line
India Steamship Co.
Indonesian National Lines
   P.N. Djakarta Lloyd
   P.T. Gesuri Lloyd
   P.T. Samudera Indonesia
   P.T. Trikora Lloyd
Mitsui O.S.K. Lines
Moss Hutchinson Line
Nippon Yusen Kaisha
Peninsular and Oriental Steam Navigation Co.
The Scindia Steam Navigation Co.
The Shipping Corporation of India
The Swedish East Asia Co.
Wilh. Wilhelmsen

10. Europe–Japan Freight Conference

Area: From ports in the UK, Eire and ports in Norway, Sweden, Finland, Poland
Denmark, Germany, Holland, Belgium, and France (from Dunkirk to
St. Nazaire, both inclusive), also Italy and Yugoslavia, to ports in Japan.

Terms: Contract: Tariff less 9½% immediate
Non—Contract: Tariff less 10% six months deferred
(Rebate periods 1 Jan.–30 June and 1 July–31 Dec).

Members (December 1971):

Ben Line Steamers
Blue Funnel Line
   (The Ocean Steam Ship Co.
   The China Mutual Steam Navigation Co).
Cie. Maritime des Chargeurs Reunis
Ellerman & Bucknall Steamship Co.

Glen Line (Glen and Shire Joint Service)
Hapag—Lloyd Aktiengesellschaft
Koninklijke Nedlloyd N.V.
Lloyd Triestino S.p.A.N.
Maersk—Kawasaki Line
Malaysian International Shipping Corp. Berhad
Cie. des Messageries Maritimes
Mitsui OSK Lines
Neptune Orient Lines (Singapore)
Nippon Yusen Kaisha
A/S Det Ostasiatiske Kompagni (The East Asiatic Co).
Peninsular & Oriental Steam Navigation Co.
Polish Ocean Lines
A/B Svenska Ostasiatiska Kompaniet (The Swedish East Asia Co).
Wilh. Wilhelmsen
Also
   (A) Rickmers—Line

11. Spain—Far East Freight Conference

Area: From Spanish ports to ports in the State of Malaysia, Singapore, Thailand, Hong Kong, Taiwan, Philippines, Korea and Japan.

Terms: Contract: Tariff rates less 9½% immediate
Non—Contract: Tariff rates net
(Rebate periods: No rebates)

Members (February 1972):
Cie. Maritime des Chargeurs Reunis
Cie. des Messageries Maritimes
The East Asiatic Co.
Mitsui O.S.K. Lines
Nippon Yusen Kaisha
The Swedish East Asia Co.
Wilh. Wilhelmsen.

12. Japan—Europe Freight Conference

Area: From ports in Japan to Europe, the Black Sea Ports (excl. USSR), all non-European ports on the Mediterranean Sea and Moroccan ports on the Atlantic Ocean.

Terms: Contract and Non—Contract rates: Former 9½% below latter. 2½% Fidelity Rebate (4 months deferred) for shippers who confine f.o.b. shipments to conference vessels. (Payable to Contract Shippers Only).

Members (September 1971):
Ben Line Steamers
Blue Funnel Line
   (The Ocean Steam Ship Co.
   The China Mutual Steam Navigation Co).
Ellerman & Bucknall Steamship Co.
Glen Line (Glen and Shire Joint Service)

Hapag—Lloyd Aktiengesellschaft
Koninklijke Nedlloyd N.V.
Lloyd Triestino S.p.A.N.
Maersk—Kawasaki Line
Malaysian International Shipping Corp. Berhad.
Cie. des Messageries Maritimes
Mitsui OSK Lines
Neptune Orient Lines (Singapore)
Nippon Yusen Kaisha
Orient Overseas Line
A/S Det Ostasiatiske Kompagni (The East Asiatic Co).
Peninsular & Oriental Steam Navigation Co.
Polskie Linie Oceanicszne (Polish Ocean Lines)
A/B Svenska Ostasiatiska Kompaniet (The Swedish East Asia Co).
Wilh. Wilhelmsen
Also
(A) American President Lines
(A) Lauro Line

13 Sabah, Brunei and Sarawak Freight Conference

Area: From Sabah, Brunei and Sarawak to Europe, Black Sea Ports (other than USSR Ports) and all non-European ports on the Mediterranean Sea and Moroccan ports on the Atlantic Ocean.

Terms: Contract: Tariff rates less 9½% immediate.
Non—Contract: Tariff rates less 10% 6 months deferred
(Rebate periods: 1 Jan.—30 June; 1 July—31 Dec).

Members (January 1972):
Ben Line Steamers
Blue Funnel Line
(The Ocean Steam Ship Co.
The China Mutual Steam Navigation Co).
Ellerman & Bucknall Steamship Co.
Glen Line (Glen & Shire Joint Service)
Hapag—Lloyd Aktiengesellschaft
Koninklijke Nedlloyd N.V.
Lloyd Triestino S.p.A.N.
Malaysian International Shipping Corp. Berhad.
Cie des Messageries Maritimes
Mitsui O.S.K. Lines
Nippon Yusen Kaisha
A/S Det Ostasiatiske Kompagni (The East Asiatic Co).
Peninsular and Oriental Steam Navigation Co.
A/B Svenska Ostasiatiska Kompaniet (The Swedish East Asia Co).
Wilh. Wilhelmsen.
Also
(A) Jugoslavenska Linijska Plovidba

14. Japan–Gulf of Aden and Red Sea Ports Conference

Area: From ports in Japan to Gulf of Aden and Red Sea ports (including Suez but excluding Israeli ports).

Terms: Contract and Non–Contract rates, the former being 9½% below the latter. (Rebate periods: No rebates)

Members (June 1971):

Ben Line Steamers
Blue Funnel Line
   (The Ocean Steam Ship Co.
   The China Mutual Steam Navigation Co).
Ellerman and Bucknall Steamship Co.
Glen Line (Glen and Shire Joint Service)
Hapag–Lloyd Aktiengesellschaft
Koninklijke Nedlloyd N.V.
Lloyd Triestino S.p.A.N.
Cie Maritime des Chargeurs Reunis
Cie des Messageries Maritimes
Mitsui O.S.K. Lines
Nippon Yusen Kaisha
Orient Overseas Line
A/S Det Ostasiatiske Kompagni (The East Asiatic Co).
Peninsular and Oriental Steam Navigation Co.
A/B Svenska Ostasiatiska Kompaniet (The Swedish East Asia Co).
Wilh. Wilhelmsen
Also

(A) American President Lines
(A) Jugoslavenska Linijska Plovidba for shipments to Aden
   Djibouti, Assab, Port Sudan and Suez
(A) Polskie Linie Oceaniczne

15. Far East–Gulf of Aden and Red Sea Ports Conference

Area: From Hong Kong, Taiwan, the States of Singapore and Malaya to ports in the Gulf of Aden and Red Sea (including Suez)

Terms: Tariff rates: less 10% 6 months deferred. (Rebate periods: 1 Jan.–30 June; 1 July–31 Dec).

Members (May 1971):

Ben Line Steamers
Blue Funnel Line
   (The Ocean Steam Ship Co.
   The China Mutual Steam Navigation Co).
Ellerman and Bucknall Steamship Co.
Glen Line (Glen and Shire Joint Service)
Hapag–Lloyd Aktiengesellschaft
Koninklijke Nedlloyd N.V.
Lloyd Triestino S.p.A.N.
Cie des Messageries Maritimes
Mitsui O.S.K. lines

Nippon Yusen Kaisha
Orient Overseas Line
A/S Det Ostasiatiske Kompagni (The East Asiatic Co).
Peninsular and Oriental Steam Navigation Co.
A/B Svenska Ostasiatiske Kompaniet (The Swedish East Asia Co).
Wilh. Wilhelmsen
Also
(A) American President Lines
(A) Jugoslavenska Linijska Plovidba for shipments to Aden
    Djibouti, Assab, Port Sudan and Suez
(A) Polskie Linie Oceaniczne

16. United Kingdom–India/Pakistan Eastbound Conference
Area: From United Kingdom ports and Eire to all ports in India and Pakistan.
Terms: Contract: Tariff less 9½% immediate
         Non–Contract: Tariff less 10% 4 months deferred
         (Rebate periods: 1 Jan.–30 Apr., 1 May–31 Aug. and 1 Sept.–31 Dec.).
Members (October 1971):
        Anchor Line
        Bibby Line
        British India Steam Navigation Co.
        Thos. & Jno. Brocklebank (Owners of the Anchor (Calcutta service)
           Brocklebank and Brocklebanks' Well Lines)
        The City Line
        The Clan Line Steamers
        Ellerman's Wilson Line
        Hall Line
        India Steamship Co.
        National Shipping Corporation
        Pakistan Shipping Line
        Peninsular and Oriental Steam Navigation Co.
        Scindia Steam Navigation Co.
        The Shipping Corporation of India

17. Continent–India/Pakistan Eastbound Conferences
Area: From Norway, Sweden, Finland, Denmark, Germany, Holland, Belgium
        and all ports on the Channel and Atlantic Coasts of France, north of and
        including Nantes, to ports in India and Pakistan
Terms: Contract: Tariff rates, less 9½% immediate
         Non–Contract: Tariff rates, less 10% 4 months deferred
         (Rebate periods: 1 Jan.–30 Apl., 1 May–31 Aug., 1 Sept.–31 Dec.).
Members (October 1971):
        British India Steam Navigation Company
        Brocklebanks' Well Line
        The Clan Line Steamers
        Compagnie Maritime Belge (Lloyd Royal) S.A.
        A/S Det Ostasiatiske Kompagni (East Asiatic Co.)

Deutsche Dampfshiffahrts-Gesellschaft 'HANSA'
Hall Line
India Steamship Company
Koninklijke Nedlloyd N.V.
Cie des Messageries Maritimes
National Shipping Corporation of Karachi
Pakistan Shipping Line
Peninsular & Oriental Steam Navigation Co.
Scindia Steam Navigation Co.
The Shipping Corporation of India
A/B Svenska Ostasiatiska Kompaniet (Swedish East Asia Co).
Wilh. Wilhelmsen
VEB Deutsche Seereederei

18. Western Italy–India and Pakistan Conference

Area: From Western Italy to ports in India and Pakistan
Terms: Contract: Tariff rates, less 9½% immediate
Non–Contract: Tariff rates, less 10% 6 months deferred
(Rebate periods: 1 Jan.–30 June and 1 July–31 Dec).
Members (June 1971):
British India Steam Navigation Co.
A/S Det Ostasiatiske Kompagni (E.A. Co).
Deutsche Dampfshiffahrts-Gesellschaft 'HANSA'
Holland-Bombay-Karachi Lijn
Holland-Bengalen-Burma Lijn
India Steamship Co.
Lloyd Triestino S.p.A.N.
Pakistan Shipping Line
Peninsular & Oriental Steam Navigation Co.
Shipping Corporation of India
The Scindia Steam Navigation Co.
The Clan Line Steamers
A/B Svenska Ostasiatiska Kompaniet (S.E.A. Co).
Wilh Wilhelmsen

19. Entente de Fret en Sortie des Ports du Sud de la France sur Ceylan, l'Inde et le Pakistan

Area: From ports in the south of France to ports in Ceylon, India and Pakistan
Terms: Contract: Tariff rates less 9½% immediate
Non–Contract: Tariff rates less 10% 4 months deferred
(Rebate periods: 1 Jan.–30 Apl., 1 May–31 Aug., 1 Sep.–31 Dec).
Members (August 1971):
Anchor Line
British India Steam Navigation Co.
Deutshe Dampfschiffahrts Gesellschaft 'HANSA'
The East Asiatic Co.
India Steamship Co.

Koninklijke Nedlloyd N.V.
Compagnie Maritime des Chargeurs Reunis
Cie des Messageries Maritimes
National Shipping Corporation, Karachi
Peninsular & Oriental Steam Navigation Co.
Scindia Steamship Co.
Shipping Corporation of India
Swedish East Asia Co.
Wilh. Wilhelmsen

20. Chittagong and Pussur River—United Kingdom & Eire Conference

Area: From all ports in East Pakistan to the United Kingdom of Great Britain and Northern Ireland, and Eire.

Terms: Contract: Tariff rates less 9½% immediate
Non—Contract: Tariff rates less 10% 3 months deferred
(Rebate periods: 1 Jan.—31 Mar., 1 Apl.—30 June, 1 July—30 Sept., 1 Oct—31 Dec).

Members (October 1971):
British India Steam Navigation Company
Thos. & Jno. Brocklebank
The City Line
The Clan Line Steamers
India Steamship Company
National Shipping Corporation
Pakistan Shipping Line
Peninsular & Oriental Steam Navigation Company
Scindia Steam Navigation Company
The Shipping Corporation of India

21. Chittagong and Pussur River—Continental Conference

Area: From all ports in East Pakistan to all ports in Greece (west of longitude 22°E), Albania, Yugoslavia, Italy, France, Spain, Portugal Belgium, Holland, Germany, Denmark, Norway, Sweden and Finland

Terms: Contract: Tariff rates less 9½% immediate
Non—Contract: Tariff rates less 10% 3 months deferred
(Rebate periods: 1 Jan.—31 Mar., 1 Apl.,—30 June, 1 July—30 Sept., 1 Oct.—31 Dec).

Members (October 1971):
British India Steam Navigation Company
Thos. & Jno. Brocklebank
The City Line
The Clan Line Steamers
The East Asiatic Company
Deutsche Dampfshiffahrts-Gesellschaft 'HANSA'
India Steamship Company
Koninklijke Nedlloyd N.V.
Lloyd Triestino S.p.A.N.

Marasia S.A.
Compagnie des Messageries Maritimes
National Shipping Corporation
Pakistan Shipping Line
Peninsular & Oriental Steam Navigation Company
Scindia Steam Navigation Company
The Shipping Corporation of India
Swedish East Asia Company
VEB Deutsche Seereederei
Wilh Wilhelmsen

22. Calcutta–U.K. & Eire Conference

Area: From Calcutta to ports in the U.K. & Eire
Terms: Contract: Tariff rates less 9½% immediate
Non–Contract: Tariff rates less 10% 3 months deferred
(Rebate period: 1 Jan.–31 Mar., 1 Apl.–30 June, 1 July–30 Sept.,
1 Oct.–31 Dec).

Members (January 1972):
British India Steam Navigation Co.
Thos. & Jno. Brocklebank
The City Line
The Clan Line Steamers
India Steamship Co.
National Shipping Corporation
Pakistan Shipping Line
Peninsular & Oriental Steam Navigation Co.
Scindia Steam Navigation Co.
The Shipping Corporation of India

23. Calcutta–Continental Conference

Area: From Calcutta to all ports in Belgium, Denmark, Finland, Germany,
Holland, Norway and Sweden.
Terms: Contract: Tariff rates less 9½% immediate
Non–Contract: Tariff rates less 10% 3 months deferred
(Rebate periods: 1 Jan.–31 Mar., 1 Apl.–30 June, 1 July–30 Sept.,
1 Oct.–31 Dec).

Members (February 1972):
British India Steam Navigation Co.
Thos. & Jno. Brocklebank
The Clan Line Steamers
The East Asiatic Co.
Deutsche Dampfschiffahrts-Gesellschaft 'HANSA'
India Steamship Co.
Koninklijke Nedlloyd N.V.
National Shipping Corporation
Pakistan Shipping Line
Peninsular & Oriental Steam Navigation Co.,

Scindia Steam Navigation Co.
The Shipping Corporation of India
Swedish East Asia Co.,
VEB Deutsche Seereederei
Wilh. Wilhelmsen

24. Karmaham—U.K. & Eire Conference

Area: From all ports on the coasts of West Pakistan and India between Karachi
in the north and Karwar in the south, both ports inclusive, to the
United Kingdom and Eire.

Terms: Contract: Tariff rates less 9½% immediate
Non—Contract: Tariff rates less 10% 3 months deferred
(Rebate periods: 1 Jan.–31 Mar., 1 Apl.–30 June, 1 July–30 Sept.,
1 Oct.–31 Dec).

Members (January 1972):

Anchor Line
British India Steam Navigation Co.
The City Line
The Clan Line Steamers
Ellerman's Wilson Line
Hall Line
India Steamship Company
National Shipping Corporation
Pakistan Shipping Line
Peninsular & Oriental Steam Navigation Company
Scindia Steam Navigation Company
The Shipping Corporation of India

25. Karmahom—Continental Conference

Area: From all ports on the coasts of West Pakistan and India, between Karachi
in the north and Karwar in the south, both ports inclusive, to Gibraltar,
all ports in Greece (west of longitude 22°E), Yugoslavia, Italy, France,
Spain, Portugal, Belgium, Holland, Germany, Denmark, Norway, Sweden
and Finland.

Terms: Contract: Tariff rates less 9½% immediate
Non—Contract: Tariff rates less 10% 3 months deferred
(Rebate periods: 1 Jan.–31 Mar., 1 Apl.–30 June, 1 July–30 Sept.,
1 Oct.–31 Dec).

Members (February 1972):

American Export Lines
American President Lines
Anchor Line
British India Steam Navigation Company
The City Line
The Clan Line Steamers
Compagnie Maritime Belge (Lloyd Royal) S.A.
Deutsche Dampfschiffahrts-Gesellschaft 'HANSA'

The East Asiatic Company
Ellerman's Wilson Line
Hall Line
India Steamship Company
Jugoslavenska Linijska Plovidba
Koninklijke Nedlloyd N.V.
Lloyd Triestino S.p.A.N.
Compagnie des Messageries Maritimes
National Shipping Corporation
Pakistan Line
Peninsular & Oriental Steam Navigation Company
Scindia Steam Navigation Company
The Shipping Corporation of India
The Swedish East Asia Co.
VEB Deutsche Seereederei
Wilh. Wilhelmsen

26. Madras Homeward Freight Conference

Area: From Madras and Pondicherry to ports in the United Kingdom and U.K. Transhipment.

Terms: Contract: Tariff rates less 9½% immediate
Non—Contract: Tariff rates less 10% 3 months deferred
(Rebate periods: 1 Jan.—31 Mar., 1 Apl.—30 June, 1 July—30 Sept., 1 Oct.—31 Dec.).

Members (January 1972):
British India Steam Navigation Co.
The Clan Line Steamers
Hall Line
India Steamship Co.
National Shipping Line
Pakistan Shipping Line
Peninsular & Oriental Steam Navigation Co.
The Scindia Steam Navigation Co.
The Shipping Corporation of India

27. Madras and Pondicherry—Continental Conference

Area: From Madras and Pondicherry to Genoa and all ports in France, Belgium, Holland, Germany, Denmark, Norway, Sweden and Finland.

Terms: Contract: Tariff rates less 9½% immediate
Non—Contract: Tariff rates less 10% 3 months deferred
(Rebate periods: 1 Jan.—31 Mar., 1 Apl.—30 June, 1 July—30 Sept., 1 Oct.—31 Dec.).

Members (February 1972):
British India Steam Navigation Company
The Clan Line Steamers
The East Asiatic Co.
Hall Line

Deutsche Dampfschiffahrts-Gesellschaft 'HANSA'
India Steamship Co.
Koninklijke Nedlloyd N.V.
Cie des Messageries Maritimes
National Shipping Corporation
Pakistan Shipping Line
Peninsular & Oriental Steam Navigation Co.
Scindia Steam Navigation Co.
The Shipping Corporation of India
The Swedish East Asia Co.
V.E.B. Deutsche Seereederei
Wilh. Wilhelmsen

28. Madras Coast–U.K. & Eire Conference

Area:　From Madras Coast ports to ports in the United Kingdom and U.K.
　　　　transhipment.

Terms:　Contract: Tariff rates less 9½% immediate
　　　　Non–Contract: Tariff rates less 10% 3 months deferred
　　　　(Rebate periods: 1 Jan.–31 Mar., 1 Apl.–30 June. 1 July–30 Sept.,
　　　　1 Oct.–31 Dec).

Members (January 1972):

The Clan Line Steamers
India Steamship Co.
National Shipping Corporation
Pakistan Shipping Line
Scindia Steam Navigation Co.
The Shipping Corporation of India

29. Madras Coast–Continental Conference

Area:　From Madras Coast ports to Le Havre, Dunkirk, Antwerp, Rotterdam,
　　　　Amsterdam, Hamburg and Bremen

Terms:　Contract: Tariff rates less 9½% immediate
　　　　Non–Contract: Tariff rates less 10% 3 months deferred
　　　　(Rebate periods: 1 Jan.–31 Mar., 1 Apl.–30 June, 1 July–30 Sept.,
　　　　1 Oct.–31 Dec).

Members (February 1972):

The Clan Line Steamers
Deutsche Dampfshiffahrts-Gesellschaft 'HANSA'
India Steamship Co.
Koninklijke Nedlloyd N.V.
National Shipping Line
Pakistan Shipping Line
Scindia Steam Navigation Co.
The Shipping Corporation of India
VEB Deutsche Seereederei

242

30. Malabar Coast–U.K. & Eire Conference

Area: From Malabar Coast ports (i.e. from Colachel in the south up to but excluding Karwar), to the United Kingdom of Great Britain and Northern Ireland and Eire.

Terms: Contract: Tariff rates less 9½% immediate
Non–Contract: Tariff rates less 10% 3 months deferred
(Rebate periods: 1 Jan.–31 Mar., 1 Apl.–30 June, 1 July–30 Sept., 1 Oct.–31 Dec.).

Members (January 1972):

The Clan Line Steamers
Hall Line
India Steamship Company
National Shipping Corporation
Pakistan Shipping Line
Scindia Steam Navigation Company
The Shipping Corporation of India

31. Malabar Coast–Continental Conference

Area: From Malabar Coast ports (i.e. from Colachel in the south, up to but excluding Karwar) to all ports on the Atlantic and Channel Coasts of France and in Belgium, Holland, Germany, Denmark, Norway, Sweden and Finland.

Terms: Contract: Tariff rates less 9½% immediate
Non–Contract: Tariff rates less 3 months deferred
(Rebate periods: 1 Jan.–31 Mar., 1 Apl.–30 June, 1 July–30 Sept., 1 Oct.–31 Dec.).

Members (February 1972):

The Clan Line Steamers
Deutsche Dampfschiffahrts-Gesellschaft 'HANSA'
East Asiatic Co.
Hall Line
India Steamship Company
Koninklijke Nedlloyd N.V.
Compagnie des Messageries Maritimes
National Shipping Corporation
Pakistan Shipping Line
Scindia Steam Navigation Company
The Shipping Corporation of India
Swedish East Asia Co.
VEB Deutsche Seereederei
Wilh. Wilhelmsen

32. Tuticorin–U.K. & Eire Conference

Area: From Tuticorin to the United Kingdom and Eire

Terms: Contract: Tariff rates less 9½% immediate
Non–Contract: Tariff rates less 10% 3 months deferred

(Rebate periods: 1 Jan.–31 Mar., 1 Apl.–30 June, 1 July–30 Sept.,
1 Oct.–31 Dec).

Members (January 1972):
  The Clan Line Steamers
  India Steamship Company
  National Shipping Corporation
  Pakistan Shipping Line
  Scindia Steam Navigation Company
  The Shipping Corporation of India

33. Tuticorin–Continental Conference
Area: From Tuticorin to Atlantic and Channel Coasts of France and in Belgium,
  Holland and Germany
Terms: Contract: Tariff rates less 9½% immediate
  Non–Contract: Tariff rates less 10% 3 months deferred
  (Rebate periods: 1 Jan.–31 Mar., 1 Apl.–30 June, 1 July–30 Sept.,
  1 Oct.–31 Dec).

Members (February 1972):
  The Clan Line Steamers
  Deutsche Dampfshiffahrts-Gesellschaft 'HANSA'
  India Steamship Company
  Koninklijke Nedlloyd N.V.
  National Shipping Corporation
  Pakistan Shipping Line
  Scindia Steam Navigation Company
  The Shipping Corporation of India
  VEB Deutsche Seereederei

34. Visakhapatnam–U.K. & Eire Conference
Area: From Visakhapatnam to the United Kingdom of Great Britain, Northern
  Ireland, and Eire
Terms: Contract: Tariff rates less 9½% immediate
  Non–Contract: Tariff rates less 10% 3 months deferred
  (Rebate periods: 1 Jan.–31 Mar., 1 Apl.–30 June, 1 July–30 Sept.,
  1 Oct.–31 Dec).

Members (January 1972):
  British India Steam Navigation Company
  Thos. & Jno. Brocklebank
  The City Line
  The Clan Line Steamers
  India Steamship Co.
  National Shipping Corporation
  Pakistan Shipping Line
  Peninsular & Oriental Steam Navigation Company
  The Scindia Steam Navigation Co.
  The Shipping Corporation of India

244

35. Visakhapatnam—Continental Conference
Area: From Visakhapatnam to the ports of Le Havre, Dunkirk, Antwerp,
           Rotterdam, Amsterdam, Hamburg and Bremen
Terms: Contract: Tariff rates less 9½% immediate
           Non—Contract: Tariff rates less 10% 3 months deferred
           (Rebate periods: 1 Jan.—31 Mar., 1 Apl.—30 June, 1 July.—30 Sept.,
           1 Oct.—31 Dec).
Members (September 1971):
           British India Steam Navigation Company
           Thos. & Jno. Brocklebank
           The City Line
           The Clan Line Steamers
           Deutsche Dampfschiffahrts-Gessellschaft 'HANSA'
           India Steamship Company
           Koninkijke Nedlloyd N.V.
           Compagnie des Messageries Maritimes
           National Shipping Corporation
           Pakistan Shipping Line
           Peninsular & Oriental Steam Navigation Company
           Scindia Steam Navigation Company
           The Shipping Corporation of India
           VEB Deutsche Seereederei

C. Cross Trade Conferences

Name of Conference and Area covered

(Conferences are given under the country of departure only)

I Australia
    36. Australia Northbound Shipping Conference
            From Australia and Papua/New Guinea to Philippines, Hong
            Kong, China, Taiwan, Japan, Korea and other eastern ports.
    37. Australia—West Pakistan Outward Shipping Conference
            From Australia to West Pakistan.
    38. Australia—East India Outward Shipping Conference
            From Australia to East India
    39. Australia—West India Outward Shipping Conference
            From Australia to West India
    40. Australia—Singapore and West Malaysia Outward Shipping Conference
            From ports in Australia to Singapore and ports in West Malaysia

II The Far East
    41. Australia and New Zealand—Eastern Shipping Conference
            Southbound trade from Japan, Korea, China, Taiwan, Hong
            Kong to Philippines, New Guinea (including Territory of New
            Guinea), Australia and New Zealand also the Northbound trade
            from New Zealand.

245

42. Hong Kong–Calcutta and East Pakistan Freight Conference
From Hong Kong to Calcutta and ports in East Pakistan.
43. Hong Kong–Japan Freight Agreement
From Hong Kong to ports in Japan
44. Hong Kong–Sabah, Brunei and Sarawak Freight Conference
From Hong Kong to Sabah, Brunei and Sarawak
45. Hong Kong–Straits Freight Agreement
From Hong Kong to Straits ports (Singapore and Malaya West Coast)
46. Hong Kong–Philippines Islands Freight Conference
From Hong Kong to Manila and Philippine Customs Outports
47. Japan–Hong Kong and Japan–Straits Freight Agreements
From ports in Japan to Hong Kong and Straits ports
48. Japan–Arabian and Persian Gulf–Japan Conference
From Japan and Hong Kong to India extending from but including Kakinada Southwards on the East Coat (but excluding Ceylon) to, and including the whole of the West Coast, West Pakistan and Arabian and Persian Gulf Ports, and vice versa. The eastern limit of the Arabian and Persian Gulf as defined by the Conference is a line drawn between Ras-al-Hadd in the south to a point where the West Pakistan/Iran frontier touches the coast in the north.
49. Japan–Philippines Freight Conference
From ports in Japan to ports in the Philippines
50. Japan–Sabah Freight Agreement
From Japan ports to Sabah ports (Kata Kinabalu, Scandakan, Labuan, Tawau, etc).
51. Overseas Joint Shipping Office, China
From main ports in Japan to main ports in Taiwan
52. Straits–Australia Conference
From Singapore, Port Swettenham and Penang to West Australian Coastal ports, Fremantle and East Australian main ports.
53. Malaya–China–Japan Conference
From Singapore, Port Swettenham and Penang to Manila, Cebu, Hong Kong and Japanese ports.
54. Straits–Bombay–Karachi–Persian Gulf Conference
From Singapore, Port Swettenham and Penang to Bombay and all West Coast India Ports, Karachi and Persian Gulf ports.
55. Straits–Calcutta–East Pakistan Conference
From Singapore, Port Swettenham and Penang to Calcutta and East Pakistan ports.
56. Philippines–Asia Conference
From ports in the Republic of the Philippines to ports in Japan, Korea, Okinawa, Taiwan, Hong Kong, Vietnam, Cambodia, Thailand, Malaysia, Singapore, Indonesia, Ceylon, Burma, India and Pakistan.

57. Overseas Joint Shipping Office, China.
   From main ports in Taiwan to main ports in Japan.
58. Sabah—Shanghai and Japan Freight Agreement
   From ports in Sabah to Shanghai and ports in Japan
59. Japan—Ryukyus—Japan Conference
   From ports in Japan to and from ports in the Ryukyu Islands.

III India and Pakistan
60. Bay of Bengal—Philippines Agreement
   From ports in the Bay of Bengal, North and East of Madras
   and North and West of Rangoon, inclusive of both Madras and
   Rangoon to ports in the Philippines direct or with transhipment.
61. Bay of Bengal—Japan—Bay of Bengal Conference
   From Calcutta including the anchorage at Haldia and ports on
   the East Coast of India, north of but including Kakinada, East
   Pakistan and Burma ports to Malaysia (excluding Sabah),
   Singapore, Thailand, Cambodia, South Viet-Nam, Hong Kong,
   Taiwan, China Mainland and Japan and vice versa.
62. Bombay—Australia Rate Agreement
   From Bombay, Mangalore and Saurashtra ports to Fremantle,
   Adelaide, Melbourne, Sydney and Brisbane (direct).
63. Calcutta—Australia Conference
   From East Coast India ports to Australian Mainports and
   Outports either direct or with transhipment, Tasmanian,
   Queensland ports, Southsea ports, Fiji ports and New Zealand
   ports via Australian ports.
64. Malabar—Far East Rate Agreement
   From Malabar ports (Cannanore, Tellicherry, Badagara, Calicut
   (Kozhikode), Beypore, Ponnani, Cochin, Alleppey, Quilon,
   Trivandrum and Colachel to Straits ports (Penang, Port Swetten-
   ham, Singapore), Hong Kong, Japan Main ports, Bangkok,
   Belawan Deli, Cebu, Cheribou, Djakarta, Haipong, Iloilo, Manila,
   Padang, Palembang, Pnompenh, Probolingo, Sabang, Saigon,
   Samarang, Pusan, Inchon and Sourabaya.
65. Malabar—Australia Rate Agreement
   From Malabar ports to main ports in Australia including
   on-carrying rates to New Zealand, Tasmania, minor Australian
   and South Seas ports.
66. Gulf/Arabian Sea—Orient Rate Agreement
   From Gulf ports, Karachi, Saurashtra, Bombay, Tuticorin and
   Mangalore to Straits, Indonesia, Bangkok, Saigon, Pnompenh,
   Sarawak, North Borneo, Formosa, Korea and Manila.
67. India Coastal Conference
   All Indian coastal ports ranging between Kandla and Calcutta.

Sources: The largest single source of data for this Appendix is Croner's World Directory of Freight Conferences. Croner's Publications Ltd. New Malden, Surrey. Other data set out have been collected from various conferences and from shipowners.

D. Inter-conference links of representative groups of shipowners

In Table Al which follows the membership of main and cross-trade conferences in the Australian and Eastern trades is traced in respect of the following representative groups of shipowners who are to some degree engaged in these trades.

I. Long-established conference members from developed, industrialised countries

Blue Funnel Line (Br.)

British India (Br.)

Federal Steam Navigation (Br.)

Peninsular and Oriental Steam Navigation (Br.)

Hapag—Lloyd Aktiengesellschaft (West Germany)

Koninklijke Nedlloyd. N.V. (Dutch)

Cie des Messageries Maritimes (France)

Nippon Yusen Kaisha (Japanese)

II. Conference members admitted in recent years from developed, industrialised countries

American President Line (U.S.A.)

The Baltic Steamship Company (U.S.S.R.)

Polskie Linie Oceaniczne (Polish)

V.E.B. Deutsche Seereederi (East Germany)

Lauro Lines (Italian)

III. Conference members admitted in recent years from developing and largely unindustrialised countries.[1]

Pakistan Shipping Line

Neptune Orient Lines (Singapore)

The Shipping Corporation of India

Malaysian International Shipping Corporation Berhad

1 In many cases these lines are state owned or state subsidised.

Table A1 *The membership of certain area conferences of selected major shipping lines*

| Name of Line | AUSTRALIA | | |
	Nationality	Outward	Homeward	Cross Trade from Area
A. Long-established conference members from developed, industrialised countries.				
a. Blue Funnel Line	British	1,2	3	40
b. British India Steam Navigation	British	1		37,38,39,40
c. Federal Steam Navigation	British	1,2	3	
d. Peninsular and Oriental Steam Navigation	British	1,2	3	39
e. Hapag–Lloyd	West	2	3	
f. Aktiengesellschaft	German			
g. Koninklijke Nedlloyd N.V.	Dutch	2	3	
h. Cie des Messageries	French	2	3	
i. Maritimes				
j. Nippon Yusen Kaisha	Japanese			36,40
B. Conference members admitted in recent years from developed, industrialised countries				
k. American President Line	United States			
l. The Baltic Steamship Company	U.S.S.R.	2	3	
m. Polish Ocean Lines	Polish			
n. V.E.B. Deutsche Seereederei	East German			
o. Lauro Lines	Italian			
C. Conference members admitted in recent years from developing and largely unindustrialised countries				
p. Pakistan Shipping Line	Pakistan			
q. Neptune Orient Lines	Singapore			40
r. The Shipping Corporation of India	Indian			38,39,40
s. Malaysian International Shipping Corporation Berhad	Malaysia			
(A)denotes Associate Membership				

250

	FAR EASTERN AREA			INDIA–PAKISTAN		
	Outward	Homeward	Cross Trade from and within area	Outward	Homeward	Cross Trade from area
a.	4,5,6,9,10	4,5,12,13,14,15	47,52,53			
b.	9		42,43,45,47,48, 52,53,55,56,61	16,17,18,19	20,21,22,23,24,25, 26,27,34,35	48,60,61,62, 63,64,65,66
c.						
d.	4,5,6,7,8,9, 10	4,5,12,13,14,15	43,45,46,47,48, 53,54,56	16,17,18,19	20,21,22,23,24,25, 26,27,34,35	48,62,63,66
e.	4,5,7,10	4,5,12,13,14,15	53,56			
f.						
g.	4,5,7,8,10	4,5,12,13,14,15	43,45,47,53,54, 56	17,19	21,23,25,27,29, 31,33,35	60,64,66
h.	4,5,6,8,9,	4,5,12,13,14,15	43,45,46,47,49, 53,56	17,19	21,25,27,31,35	64,65,66
i.	10,11					
j.	4,5,6,7,8,9, 10,11	4,5,12,13,14,15	41,42,43,45,46, 47,48,49,53,54, 55,56,59,61			48,61,66
k.	4,(A)5,(A)	4,(A)5,(A)12,(A) 14,(A)15,(A)	43,45,46,48,49, 53,54,56		25,	48
l.						
m.	4,10	4,12,14,(A)15,(A)	53			
n.				17	21,23,25,27,29, 31,33,35	
o.	4,(A)7	4,(A)12,(A)				
p.				16,17,18	20,21,22,23,24, 25,26,27,28,29, 30,31,32,33,34, 35	
q.	4,6,10	4,12	52			
r.	9,		42,43,45,47,48, 52,53,54,55,61	16,17,18,19	20,21,22,23,24, 25,26,27,28,29, 30,31,32,33,34, 35	48,61,62,63, 64,65,66,
s.	4,6,10	4,12,13				

251

Appendix B
Conference Freight Rate Changes and Surcharges 1948–1970

In this appendix are set out data which have been gathered on the general 'across-the-board' changes in the freight rates of the three conference groups which have been included in this study. Surcharges of various types are also noted and their origin and incidence explained. On the basis of these rate changes and of the surcharges indexes have been constructed and are set out here in respect of the trends in gross freight rates in both directions of trade and in respect of surcharged and unsurcharged rates of freight. An analysis of these data is given in Chapters 4 and 5 of the main text.

Table B.1 *United Kingdom – Australia Conference Group. General, across-the-board freight rate changes and surcharges, 1948–1970*

	Percentages Outwards		Homewards	
	Basic Rates	Surcharges	Basic Rates	Surcharges
1948	–	–	–	–
1949 Sept.	8	–	–	–
Oct.	–	–	10	–
1950	–	–	–	–
1951 Mar.	15	–	15	–
1952 Sept.	10	–	–	–
1953 Oct.	–	–	7½	–
1954	–	–	–	–
1955 July.	10	–	–	–
Sept.	–	–	7½	–
1956	–	–	–	–
1957 Feb.	–	–	14	–
Mar.	14	–	–	–
1958	–	–	–	–
1959	–	–	–	–
1960 Oct.	7½	–	7½	–
1961	–	–	–	–
1962 Oct.	5	–	5	–
1963	–	–	–	–
1964 Mar.	7½	–	–	–
1965 Oct.	–	–	6.6	–
Nov.	5	–	–	–
1966 Oct.	–	–	10	–
1967 Mar.	4	–	–	–
June.	–	5[a]	–	–
July.	–	–	–	3¾[a]
Nov.	–	12½[b]	–	12½[b]
1968 Apr.	–	–	–	2¼[c]
Oct.	–	–	1½[e]	–6[e]
1969 June.	5[d]	–5[d]	–	–
Dec.	–	10[f]	–	–
1970 July	–	–10[f]	–	–
Sept.	12½	–	–	–
Oct.	–	–	10	–

Notes:

(a) Suez surcharges.

(b) Devaluation surcharge. Rates of freight were quoted in sterling before devaluation and in U.S. dollars afterwards. The conversion between currencies was such as to increase rates by 12½ per cent to U.K. buyers.

(c) An increase of 2¼ *percentage points* in the Suez surcharge, thus raising it from 3¾ per cent to 6 per cent.

(d) The 5 per cent Suez surcharge, applied in June 1967, is here incorporated in the basic rates of freight.

(e) The 6 per cent Suez surcharge applied in two stages (3¾ per cent in July 1967 and 2¼ per cent in April 1968) is here incorporated in the basic rates. At the same time basic rates were reduced by 4½ per cent in accordance with the 'formula results for the previous year.

(f) A surcharge to cover the expenses involved in loading container ships at Antwerp while Tilbury was closed by a dockers' strike.

Table B.2 *United Kingdom – Australia Conference Group Outwards. Indexes of basic and surcharged liner freight rate movements, 1948–1970*

	1 Index of Liner Freight Rates	2 Surcharges	3 Index of Surcharged Liner Freight rates
1948	100.0	(None until	100.0
1949 Sept.	108.0	June 1967)	(as for col. 1
1950	108.0		until June 1967)
1951 Mar.	124.2		
1952 Sept.	136.6		
1953	136.6		
1954	136.6		
1955 July.	150.3		
1956	150.3		
1957 Mar.	171.3		
1958	171.3		
1959	171.3		
1960 Oct.	184.2		
1961	184.2		
1962 Oct.	193.4		
1963	193.4		
1964 Mar.	207.9		
1965	218.3		
1966	218.3		
1967 Mar.	227.0		
1967 June.	227.0	+ 5[a]	238.4
1967 Nov.	255.4	+ 12½[b]	268.1
1968	255.4		268.1
1969 June.	268.1[c]		268.1
1969 Dec.	268.1	+ 10[d]	294.9
1970 July.	268.1	− 10	268.1
1970 Sept.	301.7		301.7

Notes:
(a) Suez surcharge.
(b) Devaluation surcharge.
(c) Suez surcharge incorporated in basic rates.
(d) Surcharge due to loading UK cargo at Antwerp while Tilbury closed by a strike.

Table B.3 *United Kingdom – Australia Conference Group Homewards. Indexes of basic and surcharged liner freight rate movements, 1948–1970*

	1 Index of Liner Freight Rates	2 Surcharges %	3 Index of Surcharged Liner Freight Rates
1948	100.0	(None until	100.0
1949 Oct.	110.0	July 1967)	(As for col. 1
1950	110.0		until July 1967)
1951 Mar.	126.5		
1952	126.5		
1953 Oct.	136.0		
1954	136.0		
1955 Sept.	146.2		
1956	146.2		
1957 Feb.	166.7		
1958	166.7		
1959	166.7		
1960 Oct.	179.2		
1961	179.2		
1962 Oct.	188.2		
1963	188.2		
1964	188.2		
1965 Oct.	200.8		
1966 Oct.	220.9		
1967 July.	220.9	+ 3¾[a]	229.2
1967 Nov.	248.5	+ 12½[b]	257.9
1968 Apr.	248.5	+ 2¼[c]	262.9
1968 Oct.	252.2[d]		252.2[d]
1969	252.2		252.2[d]
1970 Oct.	277.4		277.4

Notes:
(a) Suez surcharge
(b) Devaluation surcharge, immediately incorporated in basic rates.
(c) An increase of 2¼ *percentage points* in the Suez surcharge applied in July 1967.
(d) The 6 per cent Suez surcharge applied in two stages (3¾ per cent in July 1967 and 2¼ per cent in April 1968) is here incorporated in the basic rates. At the same time basic rates were reduced by 4½ per cent in accordance with the 'formula' results for the previous year.

Table B.4 *Far Eastern Freight Conference. General, across-the-board freight rate changes, and surcharges, 1948–1970.*

	Outwards Basic Rates	Surcharges	Homewards Basic Rates	Percentages Surcharges
1948 Nov.	5	–	–	–
1949	–	–	–	–
1950	–	–	–	–
1951 Jan.	12½	–	15	–
1952	–	–	–	–
1953	–	–	–	–
1954	–	–	–	–
1955	–	–	–	–
1956 June.	15	–	–	–
Sept.	–	–	15	–
Nov.	–	15[a]	–	15
1957 May.	10	–10[a]	10	–10
June.	–	–5[a]	–	–5
1958	–	–	–	–
1959	–	–	–	–
1960 Feb.	5	–	–	–
1961 Sept.	10	–	10	–
1962	–	–	–	–
1963	–	–	–	–
1964 Mar.	10	–	10	–
1965 Dec.	5	–	5	–
1966	–	–	–	–
1967 June	–	10[a]	–	10[a]
Nov.	–	12½[b]	–	12½[b]
1968	–	–	–	–
1969 Dec.	9	–2½[c]	9	–2½[c]
1970	–	–	–	–

Notes:

(a) Suez surcharge.

(b) Devaluation surcharge. Before the devaluation of sterling, rates of freight were quoted in terms of that currency. After devaluation rates were quoted in U.S. dollars, and were converted so as to leave rates 12½ per cent higher to U.K. shippers, but slightly lower than previously to shippers in countries which did not devalue their currencies.

(c) The Suez surcharge of 10 per cent applied in June 1967 is here reduced by 2½ *percentage points.*

Table B.5 *Far Eastern Freight Conference Outwards. Indexes of basic and surcharged liner freight rate movements, 1948–1970*

	Index of Liner Freight Rates	Surcharges (%)	Index of Surcharged Liner Freight Rates
1948	100.0		100.0
1949	100.0		100.0
1950	100.0		100.0
1951 Jan.	112.5		112.5
1952	112.5		112.5
1953	112.5		112.5
1954	112.5		112.5
1955	112.5		112.5
1956 June.	129.4		129.4
Nov.	129.4	15[a]	148.8
1957 May.	142.3	−10[a]	148.8
June.	142.3	−5[a]	142.3
1958	142.3		142.3
1959	142.3		142.3
1960 Feb.	149.4		149.4
1961 Sept.	164.3		164.3
1962	164.3		164.3
1963	164.3		164.3
1964 Mar.	180.7		180.7
1965 Dec.	189.7		189.7
1966	189.7		189.7
1967 June.	189.7	10[a]	208.7
Nov.	213.4	12½[b]	234.7
1968	213.4		234.7
1969 Dec.	232.6	−2½[a]	250.0
1970	232.6		250.0

Notes:
(a) Suez surcharges.
(b) Devaluation surcharge.

Table B.6 *Far Eastern Freight Conference Homewards. Indexes of basic and surcharged liner freight rate movements, 1948–1970*

	Index of Liner Freight Rates	Surcharges (%)	Index of Surcharged Liner Freight Rates
1948	100.0		100.0
1949	100.0		100.0
1950	100.0		100.0
1951 Jan.	115.0		115.0
1952	115.0		115.0
1953	115.0		115.0
1954	115.0		115.0
1955	115.0		115.0
1956 Sept.	132.3		132.3
Nov.	132.3	15[a]	152.1
1957 May.	145.5	−10[a]	152.1
June.	145.5	−5[a]	145.5
1958	145.5		145.5
1959	145.5		145.5
1960	145.5		145.5
1961 Sept.	160.1		160.1
1962	160.1		160.1
1963	160.1		160.1
1964 Mar.	176.1		176.1
1965 Dec.	184.9		184.9
1966	184.9		184.9
1967 June.	184.9	10[a]	203.4
Nov.	208.0	12½[b]	228.8
1968	208.0		228.8
1969 Dec.	226.7	−2½[a]	243.7
1970	226.7		243.7

Notes:
(a) Suez surcharges.
(b) Devaluation surcharge.

Table B.7 *United Kingdom – India/Pakistan Conference Group. General, across-the-board freight rate changes, and surcharges, 1948–1970*

	Percentages Eastbound Basic Rates	Surcharges	Percentages Westbound Basic Rates	Surcharges
1948	–	–	–	–
1949	–	–	–	–
1950	–	–	–	–
1951 Jan.	25	–	25	–
Sept.	15	–	15	–
1952	–	–	–	–
1953	–	–	–	–
1954	–	–	–	–
1955 Feb.	10	–	10	–
1956 Mar.	10	–	10	–
Nov.	–	15[(b)]	–	15[(b)]
1957 Mar.	10	–	10	–
June.	–	−15[(b)]	–	−15[(b)]
1958 June.	–	–	−7½[(a)]	–
1959	–	–	–	–
1960	–	–	–	–
1961 Oct.	15	–	–	–
1962	–	–	–	–
1963 Oct.	–	–	10	–
1964	–	–	–	–
1965	–	–	–	–
1966 June.	7½	–	–	–
Sept.	–	–	7½	–
1967 June.	–	15[(b)]	–	15[(b)]
Nov.	–	12½[(c)]	–	12½[(c)]
1968	–	–	–	–
1969	–	–	–	–
1970 July.	15	−1½[(d)]	12½	−1½[(d)]

Notes:
(a) A result of increasing the loyalty rebate from 5/- per B/L ton, maximum, to 10 per cent in full.
(b) Suez surcharge.
(c) Devaluation surcharge. Before the devaluation of sterling, rates of freight were quoted in terms of that currency. Afterwards rates were quoted in U.S. dollars, and were converted so as to leave rates 12½ per cent higher to U.K. buyers.
(d) The Suez surcharge of 15 per cent, applied in June 1967, is here reduced by 1½ *percentage points*.

Table B.8 *United Kingdom – India/Pakistan Conference Group Outwards. Indexes of basic and surcharged freight rate movements, 1948–1970*

	Index of Liner Freight Rates	Surcharges (%)	Index of Surcharged Liner Freight Rates
1948	100.0		100.0
1949	100.0		100.0
1950	100.0		100.0
1951 Jan.	125.0		125.0
Sept.	143.8		143.8
1952	143.8		143.8
1953	143.8		143.8
1954	143.8		143.8
1955 Feb.	158.2		158.2
1956 Mar.	174.0		174.0
Nov.	174.0	15[a]	200.1
1957 Mar.	191.4		217.5
June.	191.4	−15[a]	191.4
1958	191.4		191.4
1959	191.4		191.4
1960	191.4		191.4
1961 Oct.	220.1		220.1
1962	220.1		220.1
1963	220.1		220.1
1964	220.1		220.1
1965	220.1		220.1
1966 June.	236.6		236.6
1967 June.	236.6	15[a]	272.1
Nov.	266.2	12½[b]	306.1
1968	266.2		306.1
1969	266.2		306.1
1970 July	306.1	−1½[a]	347.4

Notes:
(a) Suez surcharges
(b) Devaluation surcharge.

Table B.9 *United Kingdom – India/Pakistan Conference Group Homewards. Indexes of basic and surcharged freight rate movements, 1948–1970*

	Index of Liner Freight Rates	Surcharges (%)	Index of Surcharged Liner Freight Rates
1948	100.0		100.0
1949	100.0		100.0
1950	100.0		100.0
1951 Jan.	125.0		125.0
Sept.	143.8		143.8
1952	143.8		143.8
1953	143.8		143.8
1954	143.8		143.8
1955 Feb.	158.2		158.2
1956 Mar.	174.0		174.0
Nov.	174.0	15[b]	200.1
1957 Mar.	191.4		215.9
June.	191.4	−15[b]	191.4
1958 June.	177.0[a]		177.0
1959	177.0		177.0
1960	177.0		177.0
1961	177.0		177.0
1962	177.0		177.0
1963 Oct.	194.7		194.7
1964	194.7		194.7
1965	194.7		194.7
1966 Sept.	209.3		209.3
1967 June.	209.3	15[b]	240.7
Nov.	235.5	12½[c]	270.8
1968	235.5		270.8
1969	235.5		270.8
1970 July.	264.9	−1½[b]	300.7

Notes:

(a) A rate decrease due to a change in rebate policy.

(b) Suez surcharges.

(c) Devaluation surcharge.